Nietzsche, Psychohistory, and the Birth of Christianity

Nietzsche, Psychohistory, and the Birth of Christianity

MORGAN REMPEL

Contributions in Philosophy, Number 85

GREENWOOD PRESS
Westport, Connecticut • London

Library of Congress Cataloging-in-Publication Data

Rempel, Morgan, 1964–
     Nietzsche, psychohistory, and the birth of Christianity / Morgan Rempel.
          p.   cm.—(Contributions in philosophy, ISSN 0084–926X ; no. 85)
Includes bibliographical references and index.
     ISBN 0–313–32322–4 (alk. paper)
     1. Nietzsche, Friedrich Wilhelm, 1844–1900.   2. Christianity—Origin.   3. Jesus
Christ—Psychology. 4. Paul, the Apostle, Saint—Psychology.   I. Title.   II. Series.
B3318.C35.R46   2002
230'.092—dc21   2002276828

British Library Cataloguing in Publication Data is available.

Library of Congress Catalog Card Number: 2002276828
ISBN: 0–313–32322–4
ISSN: 0084–926X

First published in 2002

Greenwood Press, 88 Post Road West, Westport, CT 06881
An imprint of Greenwood Publishing Group, Inc.
www.greenwood.com

Printed in the United States of America

The paper used in this book complies with the
Permanent Paper Standard issued by the National
Information Standards Organization (Z39.48–1984).

10 9 8 7 6 5 4 3 2 1

Dedicated with love, gratitude, and admiration to

Joan Maxwell Rempel

Contents

Abbreviations

Nietzsche, Psychohistory, and the Birth of Christianity

Introduction

The nineteenth century was a period characterized by an exceptional amount of scholarly interest in the figure of Jesus of Nazareth. Indeed, when we consider that more than 60,000 studies of the life of Jesus appeared in that century alone,[1] and that at least one—Ernest Renan's *Life of Jesus*—proved to be one of the best-selling books in Europe in the 1860s, it is reasonable to characterize the *Life of Jesus* genre as a significant nineteenth-century phenomenon. Tellingly, a considerable number of these works were written by nontheologians. Endeavoring to strip away and, where possible, to look behind innumerable layers of tradition, to separate ecclesiastical teachings concerning Jesus from the individual who inspired them, countless historians, philologists, archaeologists, and philosophers of the period undertook secular, critical investigations into the life of the most written-about figure in history. Two of the more famous contributors to this nineteenth-century genre were, like Friedrich Nietzsche, philologists: David Friedrich Strauss (1808–74), representative of the Hegelian school[2] and much maligned subject of the first of Nietzsche's *Untimely Meditations*,[3] and Ernest Renan (1823–92), French historian, rationalist and best-selling writer.

In many ways, Strauss' 1,400-page *Life of Jesus* (1835) embodies the spirit of much of the critical Jesus scholarship of the period. Meticulous and dispassionate, Strauss' research compares and contrasts sources of information concerning the life of Jesus, unabashedly scrutinizes the inconsistencies found therein, and calmly challenges the historical evidence concerning, among other things, the supernatural in Jesus' life and ministry. Considering nothing beyond criticism and unwilling to fall back to the idea of the "miracle," much of the significance of Strauss' secular treatment of Jesus lies in its introduction of such concepts as "myth" or pious folk legend, long applied to profane history, to the modern study of the Gospels.

Renan's *Life of Jesus* (1863) on the other hand, despite the fact that its author was also a philologist, has the realistic flow and skilled plot development of a popular nineteenth-century narrative novel. Indeed, *it was* a popular nineteenth-century narrative novel. Through numerous printings and multiple translations, Renan's pleasant little volume proved to be an immensely popular book throughout Europe in the mid-1860s. While still skeptical of the many miracles there reported, and purporting to separate Jesus the man from the myths surrounding him, Renan, in marked contrast to Strauss' project, conceived it as his principal task to overcome New Testament discontinuities, to smooth over apparent inconsistencies in the Gospel's rendering of Jesus in the name of both "art" and "history" (p. 64). We may note that despite the popular appeal of his poetic entry into the *Life of Jesus* genre, Renan's academic career, like that of Strauss—whose study of Jesus not only resulted in his dismissal from Tubingen University but elicited threats of violence—never recovered from the controversy surrounding his secularized treatment of the Nazarene.

Considering how much the mature Nietzsche wrote about Christianity in general and its principal protagonists in particular, and how notoriously unrestrained he was with respect to voicing his opinions about other thinkers, it should come as no surprise that he found occasion to comment on both these famous nineteenth-century portraits of Jesus of Nazareth. At once admitting to the profound impact Strauss' *Life of Jesus* had on him while a theology student,[4] and harshly criticizing its author's very methodology, Nietzsche says the following in his *Antichrist*:

And here for the first time I touch on the problem of the *psychology of the redeemer*. I confess there are few books which present me with so many difficulties as the Gospels do. These difficulties are quite other than those which the learned curiosity of the German mind celebrated one of its most unforgettable triumphs in pointing out. The time is far distant when I too, like every young scholar and with the clever dullness of a refined philologist, savored the work of the incomparable Strauss. I was then twenty years old: now I am too serious for that. What do I care for the contradictions of "tradition"? How can legends of saints be called "tradition" at all! The stories of saints are the most ambiguous literature in existence: to apply to them scientific procedures *when no other records are extant* seems to me wrong in principle—mere learned idling . . . (*A* 28).

Likewise, the very next section of the *Antichrist* alludes, with equal candor, to Renan's recent bestseller:

What *I* am concerned with is the psychological type of the redeemer. For it *could* be contained in the Gospels in spite of the Gospels, however much mutilated and overloaded with foreign traits: as that of Francis of Assisi is contained in the legends about him in spite of the legends. *Not* the truth about what he did, what he said, how he really died: but the question *whether* his type is still conceivable at all, whether it has been "handed down" by tradition.—The attempts I know of to extract even the *history* of a "soul" from the Gospels seem to me proofs of an execrable psychological frivolity. Monsieur Renan, that buffoon *in psychologicis*, has appropriated for his explication of the type Jesus the two *most inapplicable concepts* . . . (*A* 29).

While many of the themes touched on in these characteristic excerpts from the *Antichrist* will only gradually come into proper focus in the following pages, one or two require prompt clarification if we are to properly situate Nietzsche's own efforts within the larger context of the nineteenth-century phenomenon of scholarly investigations of the life of Jesus. In one sense, despite its author's protestations to the contrary, Nietzsche's *Antichrist* (and to a lesser extent, his entire career-long catalogue of ruminations on the Nazarene) has much in common with Renan and Strauss' respective *Life of Jesus*. Each was written by a philologist—in the case of Nietzsche, a *brilliant* philologist[5]— endeavoring to treat the life of Jesus critically; to separate fact from fantasy; to look behind traditions surrounding the Nazarene in an effort to move closer to the real Jesus. Each comes to consider some Gospel stories more likely to be authentic than others, each looks suspiciously at the accounts of miracles involving Jesus, and the reputation of each author was significantly tarnished by his endeavor.[6]

But in another, more fundamental sense, Nietzsche's treatment of the life of Jesus of Nazareth is as far removed from the celebrated efforts of Strauss and Renan—indeed from the vast majority of his century's 60,000 analogous endeavors—as the philosopher himself repeatedly boasts. The essence of this fundamental distinction is alluded to in both of the above *Antichrist* excerpts, but particularly aphorism 28's contrasting of Strauss' philological emphasis on the "contradictions of 'tradition' "—his already noted focus on apparent inconsistencies within the Gospel tradition— with what Nietzsche refers to as "the problem of the *psychology of the redeemer*." Well aware of the lack of corroborative historical sources for the life of Jesus and firmly convinced that the historical Jesus' message was subject to alteration *prior* to the composition of the Gospels, Nietzsche considers Strauss' rigorous comparison of one Gospel with another to be an essentially wasted effort, "mere learned idling."

Indeed, given that virtually "no other records are extant" pertaining to the details of the life of Jesus (*A* 28), and that those few sources we do possess appear to be "mutilated and overloaded with foreign traits"

(*A* 29), some critical Jesus scholarship of the day, including that of Bruno Bauer, another Hegelian, went so far as to maintain that the life of Jesus was *solely* a matter of legend, that there was no historical substance of any kind behind the life presented in the Gospels. This is not Nietzsche's position. The fundamental issue for Nietzsche is not whether or not Jesus of Nazareth ever lived, but by what means he might be best apprehended some nineteen centuries later. Indeed, given the significant limitations with respect to our sources of information about his life, is it even possible that any researcher might succeed in stripping away these overlays and mutilations in such a manner as to get, if not a truly undistorted glimpse of Jesus, at least a less obviously corrupted picture than that advanced by both the actual sources of the Gospel tradition themselves, and by the countless philologists scrutinizing their every word? Such a picture "*could* be contained in the Gospels in spite of the Gospels . . . as that of Francis of Assisi is contained in the legends about him in spite of the legends" (*A* 29). The question for Nietzsche is how to get at it.

Like so many of his remarks, Nietzsche's unusual suggestion of who might conceivably be in a position to discern the *real Jesus*, of what type of researcher is best equipped to succeed where so many others have failed, is likely to raise as many questions as it answers. At *Antichrist* 31, not long after his summary dismissal of the much-touted efforts of Strauss and Renan as exercises in "learned idling" and "execrable psychological frivolity" respectively, Nietzsche suggests one possible candidate for this difficult task: "One has to regret that no Dostoyevsky lived in the neighborhood of this most interesting *decadent* [Jesus]—I mean somebody who would have known how to sense the very stirring charm of such a mixture of the sublime, the sick, and the childish" (*A* 31). A notebook entry from this period goes even further and suggests that Dostoyevsky had indeed "fathomed Christ."[7] Obviously, our treatment of the matters of Nietzsche's interest in particular themes in Dostoyevsky's writing, and his often-shocking choice of words to characterize Jesus, will have to wait. What needs clarification at this juncture, something merely alluded to in the *Antichrist*, is the matter of why Dostoyevsky is offered as one in a position to truly understand Jesus, to "fathom Christ." For as we shall see, Nietzsche is adamant that even the "first Christians," those who actually came into contact with the historical Jesus of Nazareth and significantly influenced the composition of the Gospels, had no more insight into this extraordinary figure than "Monsieur Renan, that buffoon *in psychologicis*." Accordingly, the type of researcher Nietzsche suspects is required by the task at hand is someone capable of distinguishing the first Christians' *misunderstandings* about Jesus—which itself depends upon an understanding of how such souls likely viewed the world, of how *they thought*—from the figure or "type" of the Nazarene himself. The *Twilight of the Idols*, whose composition precedes the *Antichrist* by a matter of days, provides a significant clue with respect to the later volume's high estimate of Dostoyevsky's abilities qua solver of the problem of Jesus. There Nietzsche sings the praises of "Dostoyevsky, the only psychologist, by the way, from whom I had anything to learn: he is one of the happiest accidents of my life" (9, 45). As we shall see, it is Dostoyevsky's psychological acumen, his penetrating insights concerning human behavior and motivation, that particularly impresses Nietzsche, that allows the philosopher to suggest Dostoyevsky was in a position to understand Jesus, and just as important, underlies Nietzsche's recognition in the Russian of a "kindred spirit."[8]

Accordingly, it should come as no surprise that Nietzsche includes himself on this rather short list of individuals capable of understanding Jesus, capable of separating "the psychological type of the redeemer" from the very different thinking, the very different "psychological type" of those early Christians one meets and reads about in the New Testament. Nietzsche's high regard for his own psychological acumen is well known. His unusual literary autobiography, *Ecce Homo*, unabashedly boasts of its author's "hitherto altogether unheard of psychological depth and profundity" (4,6) and "psychological antennae" of such "perfectly uncanny sensitivity" that "the inmost parts, the 'entrails' of every soul are physiologically perceived by me—*smelled*" (2,8). A similar sentiment is expressed in the foreword to his *Twilight*. There Nietzsche characterizes himself as "one who has ears behind his ears," "an old psychologist" in the "presence of whom that which would like to stay silent *has to become audible* . . . ." Typically then, the later Nietzsche, whose field of interest was increasingly Christianity, comes to characterize himself as "the foremost psychologist of Christianity."[9] The extent to which Nietzsche's writing lives up to such braggadocio is of course a matter of opinion. What is indisputable is that behind this boasting, underlying his often-confrontational remarks concerning the birth of Christianity, are any number of powerful insights that considered en masse, constitute a sizable portion of a profoundly original, profoundly psychological, philosophy of religion.

Nietzsche sees at least three dominant images of Jesus in the pages of the New Testament:

1. The gentle, peace-promoting embodiment of nonresistance, nonjudgment, and radically unalloyed love. The extraordinary soul who not only does not resist those doing evil to him, but loves them.
2. The angry, vengeful judge and preacher of frightening retribution. The aggressive enemy of the Jewish priestly establishment.

3. The atoning sacrifice. The lamb of God whose blood mysteriously expunges
   the guilt and sins of believers. While this third characterization of Jesus appears largely in the letters of St. Paul—a characterization the later Nietzsche
   comes to treat with outright contempt rather than mere suspicion—the first
   two are encountered throughout the Gospels. It is there that Nietzsche confronts what he considers a most extraordinary, though (for him) all too deci-
   pherable psychological contradiction: "a contradiction between the mountain,
   lake, and field preacher, whose appearance strikes one as that of a Buddha
   on a soil very little like that of India, and the aggressive fanatic, the mortal
   enemy of theologian and priest, which Renan has wickedly glorified as 'le
   grand maitre en ironie' " (A 31).

Nietzsche admits that though the possibility that such "multiplicity
and contradictoriness" are facets of a single personality "cannot be entirely excluded" (A 31), such an extraordinary union seems highly un-
likely. What is infinitely more likely, indeed what is to Nietzsche
palpably and painfully obvious, is that at least one of these polar opposite personalities is a corruption, and that a sizable portion of the
apparently contradictory figure depicted in the Gospels owes not to the
historical Jesus of Nazareth, but the "first Christians" one encounters in,
and who influenced the composition of, the Gospels. These figures, this
milieu, constitute the all-important "soil" to which Nietzsche repeatedly
refers in the *Antichrist* ("a soil very little like that of India"). Again, because this highly suspicious "multiplicity and contradictoriness" are
thoroughly woven into the entire Gospel tradition—essentially the sole
source for details concerning the life of Jesus—Nietzsche's methodology
for separating material he suspects actually derives from Jesus from that
he considers more likely to have originated in the earliest Christian community, is necessarily *not* philological. Rarely does Nietzsche cite and
question the authenticity of particular New Testament passages. In those
few places where he does—*Will To Power* 164 and *Antichrist* 45 for example—his primary interest lies not with suspicious words or references,
with how one particular verse seemingly conflicts with another, but the
very *spirit*, the way of thinking, the manner of viewing the world, he
discerns *behind* the words.

Accordingly, it is the psychologist, someone capable of distinguishing
the psychospiritual "soil" in which a message is planted from the communication itself, that is in the best position to at least catch a glimpse
of the Jesus behind the words of the Gospels. Essentially, what Nietzsche
considers necessary is someone skilled at asking psychohistorical questions and formulating hypotheses concerning underlying motivation. For
example: If the world-view of the "first Christians"—recruited generally
from Israel's powerless underclass (in the words of St. Jerome: "*de vila
plebecula*")[10]—*were* to color their understanding and resulting portrait of

Jesus, what form might this 'translation' take? Who were *their* enemies? What was *their* relationship to, and how did they likely view, the Jewish priestly establishment? Supernatural explanations aside,[11] what might account for St. Paul's phenomenal sudden transformation from zealous Pharisee, defender and upholder of the Judaic Law and fanatical persecutor of the early Christians, to equally zealous globe-trotting Christian leader, transformer of the early church and proclaimer of the Law's *abolition*? Supernatural notions of a necessary and atoning death aside, what conclusions might a psychologist draw from Jesus' posture of such radical nonopposition and nonenmity that he is said to have gone to an agonizing death without resistance, resentment, or anger, all the while blessing, indeed *loving* those doing evil to him? These are some of the extraordinary questions Nietzsche asks in his career-long engagement with Christianity's principal protagonists. What we soon discover is that despite the comparative lack of attention Nietzsche's reflections on these matters has received, both the type of question he asks of the birth of Christianity, and the remarkable hypotheses and conclusions he advances in reply, are entirely worth our consideration.

While the disembodied psychological analysis of individuals living centuries ago may strike the uninitiated as something of a precarious enterprise, two points bear emphasizing. First, such psychohistorical analyses have been part of psychoanalysis—a science well aware of its indebtedness to Nietzsche's philosophy[12]—since its inception. Freud of course undertook several famous psychohistories himself, on figures as diverse as Leonardo da Vinci and Woodrow Wilson, while Erik Erikson, following Nietzsche's lead, found considerable fodder for psychohistorical analysis in the life, writing, and history-altering "conversion" of Martin Luther.[13] This psychohistorical manner of encountering the past— with the researcher focusing on events, statements, or experiences of primarily psychological significance—continues to this day and is the subject of considerable multidisciplinary scholarship in publications such as the *Journal of Psychohistory*. We may note that while Freud's psychohistories have rightly been criticized for their tendency to ignore or downplay cultural influences, Nietzsche brings to his analogous treatments of Jesus, St. Paul, and the first Christians both a masterful understanding of and keen focus upon the cultural, religious, political, and moral factors at play in their lives. As we see, it is this profound interest in the sociopolitico-ethical milieu in which these ancient figures moved, the very "soil" from which Christianity emerges, that not only distinguishes Nietzsche's efforts from Freud's, but makes them of considerable interest to philosophers.

Second, in a very real sense, Nietzsche's entire philosophical enterprise cannot be properly understood *apart* from this psychological orientation.

For underlying his ruminations on Jesus, St. Paul, and the first Christians is the same career-defining conviction that informs his more famous "Problem of Socrates"[14] and "Case of Wagner."[15] Nietzsche is convinced that the *idea* itself—be it contained in Greek tragedy, Platonic dialogue, Schopenhauer's philosophy, Wagnerian opera, or Pauline epistle—is only *part* of the equation. Ideas, carefully considered, *psychologically* considered, can reveal much about a thinker, his manner of thinking, and world-view. For Nietzsche the *teaching* and the *teacher*, the *idea* and its *originator*, while theoretically separable, are fully understood only in the context of one another. As surely as art is an extension of personality, so too Nietzsche insists, are morality, philosophy, and religion.

Nietzsche's seemingly simple question at *Beyond Good and Evil* 187— "What does such an assertion say of the man who asserts it?"—turns out to be the psycho-historical starting point for a great deal of his philosophical activity. His career-long fascination with the *"problem of Socrates"* for example, while focused on the mind and possible motivation of the Greek philosopher, is in many ways an investigation of the "problems" of reason, theory, virtue, and morality. As Nietzsche confesses: "I seek to understand out of what idiosyncrasy that Socratic equation reason = virtue = happiness derives."[16] Nietzsche's ongoing psychological reflections on Wagner and Schopenhauer similarly serve as starting points for ruminations on such topics as art, decadence and Germany; and culture, pessimism, and the "will" respectively. Nietzsche's unorthodox discussion of Jesus, St. Paul, and the first Christians turns out to be a variation of rather than an exception to this notable tendency. As we shall see, the topics of love, pity, and suffering prove as inseparable from Nietzsche's remarkable "psychology of the redeemer" as the themes of power, faith, and fanaticism are from his psychology of Paul. Nietzsche's confrontational treatment of Judaism and earliest Christianity serves, meanwhile, as the launch pad for a series of aggressively original discussions of such subjects as the psychological origin of morality, the centrality of resentment to human behavior and belief, and the highly problematic character of communication.

Revealingly, while Nietzsche's literary autobiography—using Plato's manipulation of the figure of Socrates as a prototype—freely admits that his *Untimely Meditations* on Wagner and Schopenhauer reveal far more about their author than about their formal subjects,[17] no such confession was forthcoming with respect to his handling of Jesus and Paul. What one quickly discovers however, is that his ruminations on Christianity's principal protagonists *do* reveal a great deal about Nietzsche. In fact, rarely is the veracity of Nietzsche's famous protopsychoanalytical assertion—that "every great philosophy has hitherto been: a confession on the part of its author and a kind of involuntary and unconscious memoir" (*BGE* 6)—more evident than in his own idiosyncratic investigation of the birth of Christianity.

Rarely is one afforded as clear a glimpse of how Nietzsche viewed his own philosophical project, of how lofty a position he envisioned his own "good news" as emanating from, as that found in his critical evaluation of Jesus' and Paul's respective gospels. As is the case with his ruminations on Socrates and Schopenhauer, by examining what it is that Nietzsche celebrates, criticizes, and obviously identifies with in the life, teachings, and death of Jesus, and so passionately assails in the very different teachings of Paul of Tarsus, one is afforded new insight not only into these extraordinary figures (and ideas) themselves, but into the mind and philosophy of one of the nineteenth century's most original thinkers.

The aim of the present study is essentially twofold. Our first objective is simply to bring some order to Nietzsche's far-flung ruminations on Jesus, St. Paul, and the birth of Christianity. Nietzsche is notorious for his tendency to treat numerous topics concurrently not only in the same volume, but very often in the same paragraph or aphorism. Moreover, in his early and middle period writings especially, Nietzsche's isolated ruminations on Jesus for example, are often separated by years and hundreds of pages. What one discovers when these well-scattered reflections are brought together and considered alongside one another is by no means a seamless whole. Few, if any, aspects of his philosophizing meet this criterion. However, considered en masse, an indubitable sense of direction and purpose emerges from these isolated and often frustrating musings on such matters as the likely character of the "bringer of glad tidings" himself, the possible origin of his "good news," the dangers of love and pity, and the still unappreciated influence of Paul on the development of nascent Christianity.

Even within the *Antichrist*, where Nietzsche's psychologically informed discussion of Jesus and Paul is sustained in comparison to what one finds in the earlier works, Nietzsche's train of thought is not always easy to follow. This is largely attributable to two factors.

The first is Nietzsche's often frustrating tendency to treat several topics simultaneously and very often nonlinearly. In the *Antichrist*, Buddhism, Christian morality, Zarathustra, Luther, and Pascal are all treated *before* the topic turns to the actual figure of Jesus. As for "the bringer of glad tidings" himself, Jesus' birth narrative is glossed over entirely while his crucifixion is treated before, and in more detail than his actual ministry. In this sense very much like a Freudian case history, the reader is compelled to follow Nietzsche as he repeatedly moves back and forth over two or three aspects of Jesus' life—aspects of obvious *psychological* significance—with often disarming rapidity and little concern for chronology. And all the while, words and phrases as foreign to conventional treatments of the life of Jesus as they are to more traditional philosophies—"psychological type," "physiological reality," "conceptual epilepsy," and so forth—appear with astonishing frequency.

The second factor for the newcomer to the *Antichrist* in following Nietzsche's train of thought is the density of his prose. This trend toward shorter, ever more dense sentences had begun to emerge as early as the mid-1880s in such works as *Beyond Good and Evil*. In the *Antichrist* and other works from 1888 however, Nietzsche has, for better or for worse, achieved his stated objective to "say in ten sentences what everyone else says in a book—what everyone else *does not* say in a book."[18] By the time of the *Antichrist*—a mere seventy pages—Nietzsche's use of language has become so focused and economical that he is obliged to leave a great deal *unsaid*. Often it is what is alluded to that is especially fascinating. Behind many of the *Antichrist*'s unusual remarks—its characterization of Jesus as an "idiot," Paul as an "apostle of revenge," the first Christians as Judaism's "chandala"—lies a fully formed and very often astonishingly original intellectual reality (an intellectual reality, it bears emphasizing, often far less bizarre than Nietzsche's unorthodox and deliberately confrontational language seemingly suggests). One of the primary tasks of our project, therefore, is to bring a number of these underlying constellations of ideas out from behind Nietzsche's highly distilled and confrontational prose.

Our second major objective is simply to take seriously Nietzsche's repeated claims that his primary interest is in *the psychology of Christianity*. We shall take seriously his fundamental position that in order to understand Christianity in general, and its origins in particular, one needs to examine the New Testament with the probing eye of a psychologist. Whether or not he lives up to his self-conception as "the foremost psychologist of Christianity" the fact remains that Nietzsche conceived of his own investigation of Christianity and its key players as psychological case histories. To view it otherwise is not only unfair to Nietzsche, but is to invite frustration. Calling "each and every nihilistic religion: a systematized case-history of sickness employing religious-moralistic nomenclature" (*Will To Power* 152), Nietzsche's treatment of Christianity as a whole and its principal players in particular needs to be understood as precisely that: psychological *case-histories of sickness*. While his case histories of Jesus, Paul and the first Christians do indeed serve as entrees to any number of larger intellectual concerns, it is as psychohistorical hypotheses rather than philological discoveries or rigorous philosophical arguments that they are most impressive.

It is entirely possible that Nietzsche's unorthodox methodology is one of the reasons why so many commentators have failed to explore the specifics of what is, even by Nietzschean standards, a most extraordinary analysis of Christianity. It is likely that many philosophers simply do not know what to make of Nietzsche's repeated claims that what he is advancing is in fact the first *psychology* of Christianity, that he himself is "the foremost psychologist of Christianity," and that his study of the troubled minds and hidden motivations of "epileptics" like St. Paul (*Daybreak* 68) are written "in the light of the experience of psychiatry" (*D* 549). Even those not uncomfortable with his psychological posturing may find it difficult to look beyond Nietzsche's deliberately confrontational language. Jesus is characterized as a case of "retarded puberty" (*Antichrist* 32), St. Paul a "dysangelist" (*A* 42), and the first Christians "the refuse of the antique world" (*WP* 153). Nietzsche's calculatedly inflammatory choice of words has likely resulted in investigators failing to treat his insights into Christianity's principal players with the seriousness only closer investigation reveals is entirely warranted. What we soon discover however, is that the outcome befitting such lost opportunities to engage this unorthodox material on its own terms is a less than accurate representation of the essential character of the ideas themselves, and accordingly, a less than apt assessment of the merit and originality of Nietzsche's extraordinary philosophy of religion.

This study is divided into six broad sections. Chapter 1 endeavors to bring some order to Nietzsche's numerous pre-*Antichrist* ruminations on the figure of Jesus of Nazareth. As already noted, prior to the *Antichrist*, Nietzsche's reflections on the Nazarene are thoroughly scattered throughout his essays and books and typically come in the form of either parenthetical remarks or brief, isolated aphorisms. Again, while these early isolated remarks do not coalesce into a seamless whole, we soon discover that they tend to be organized around several distinct but functionally inseparable themes (themes that endure in Nietzsche's work until the very close of his career).

In chapter 2 we turn to the *Antichrist*'s extension and radicalization of a number of these organizing themes (Jesus' gentleness and overflowing love and pity, his apparent puerility, the character of his suffering, etc.). We discover that while Nietzsche at the close of his career at last offers a comparatively sustained treatment of Christianity in general and the figure of Jesus in particular, his reflections remain organized around the same psychohistorical themes one discovers in his early and middle period works. What has changed by the time of the *Antichrist* (1888) is *how far* Nietzsche extends these now familiar hypotheses, and the increasingly clinical, quasi-medical manner in which he explores them. If Nietzsche's early and middle period thoughts on Jesus may be characterized as tentative psychohistorical hypothesis, in the *Antichrist* and numerous notes from the period, he at last tenders his psychophysiological diagnosis.

Chapter 3 is devoted to Nietzsche's analysis of the meaning and significance of Jesus' martyrdom and death. From the early *Daybreak* and *Human, All Too Human*, to notebook entries written at the very close of his career, the event in the life of Jesus of unrivaled (psychological) significance, the event at the very center of Nietzsche's extraordinary "psychology of the redeemer," is the Nazarene's martyrdom. It is at Calvary, insists Nietzsche, that both the real Jesus and his singular message are utterly manifest.

In chapter 4 we analyze Nietzsche's remarkable account of St. Paul's famous conversion to Christianity on the road to Damascus. While Nietzsche's treatment of Jesus of Nazareth has received some scholarly attention, his reflections on the figure of Paul of Tarsus, the individual he considers most responsible for the development of Christianity, have largely been ignored. This chapter, focusing largely on the protopsychoanalytical rendering of Paul's history-altering metamorphosis found in *Daybreak*, endeavors to redress this unfortunate trend.

In chapter 5 we turn to the all-important matter of the fate of the suddenly absent Jesus' message. Nietzsche places great emphasis on the fact that Jesus' message was communicated not directly, but altogether symbolically (via metaphor, parable, allusion, etc.), and asks a number of thought-provoking questions concerning those first-century Jews fated to interpret or "translate" Jesus' symbolic communiqués.

Finally, chapter 6 examines Nietzsche's return to the figure of Paul in the *Antichrist*. At the close of his career, Nietzsche was particularly interested in how *and why* the teachings of Paul, qua celebrated globetrotting Apostle to the Gentiles, seem to differ from those of Jesus. What we discover is that nowhere does a more rounded representation of the Nietzschean Jesus emerge than when the philosopher endeavors to demonstrate how *and why* both the first Jewish-Christians and St. Paul have misconstrued the meaning and symbolic message of this radically misunderstood redeemer.

NOTES

1. Grant, p. 197.
2. The young Hegel of course made his own contribution to the *Life of Jesus* genre in 1795.
3. The actual target of Nietzsche's 1873 polemic—"David Strauss, the Confessor and the Writer"—was not Strauss' *Life of Jesus*, which appeared in 1835, but the just published *The Old Faith and the New* (1872), a celebration of quasi–Darwinian scientific materialism as a proposed replacement for Christianity. In the 1886 preface to Vol. 2 of his *Human, All Too Human* Nietzsche suggests that the ultimate topic of the meditation on Strauss was less the man than what he had come to represent to the philosopher: "German culture and cultural philistinism."

4. Speaking of the impact of Strauss' *Life of Jesus* on the 20-year-old Nietzsche, J.P. Stern writes: "The young Nietzsche's reading of it as a student of theology at Bonn (1864–65) completed a process begun during his last year at Schulpforta; it led to his rejection of the Christian faith and his refusal, at Easter 1865, to take Communion" (*Untimely Med.*, Intro.).

5. So impressed with Nietzsche's genius as philologist was Friedrich Ritschl, celebrated professor of philology at Bonn and Leipzig, that when the chair of classical philology at Basel became vacant Ritschl immediately and successfully recommended Nietzsche, who was appointed to the post at the age of 24 before having obtained his doctorate. His first book, *The Birth of Tragedy*, is still regarded by many classicists as ranking, with Aristotle's *Poetics* and Hegel's lectures on the subject, among the most important studies of Greek tragedy ever written.

6. *The Antichrist* was first published in 1895, seven years after its composition and six after its author's collapse. Much of Nietzsche's infamy derives from any number of shocking remarks found in its mere seventy pages.

7. Cited in O'Flaherty, p. 107.

8. "A few weeks ago I did not even know the name of Dostoyevsky," writes Nietzsche in a letter of Feb. 23, 1887 (cited on p. 202 of the *Antichrist*). "A chance reach in a bookshop brought to my notice a work just translated into French, *L'esprit souterain*. . . . The instinct of kinship (or what shall I call it?) spoke immediately, my joy was extraordinary."

9. Letter to Brandes, Nov. 20, 1888 (in O'Flaherty, p. 89).

10. "The lowest rabble," cited in Friedlander (III, p. 207).

11. Unlike the efforts of Renan or Strauss for example, Nietzsche nowhere formally lays out the ground rules for his investigation of Jesus, Paul, and the birth of Christianity. What soon becomes apparent to the reader, however, is that the entire question of the supernatural in the life of Jesus, a matter that receives considerable attention in many of the nineteenth-century's analogous efforts is—not surprisingly—a nonissue for the philosopher.

12. Freud self-servingly characterizes Nietzsche as the "philosopher whose guesses and intuitions often agree in the most astonishing way with the laborious findings of psychoanalysis" (*An Autobiographical Study*, p. 60).

13. As we shall see, Nietzsche's "psychological antenna" lead him to ask a number of probing questions concerning possible underlying contributors to Luther's own history-altering metamorphosis. Erikson returns to these same questions in *The Young Man Luther: A Study in Psychoanalysis and History*.

14. While much of Nietzsche's ongoing investigation into the figure of Socrates is concerned with the Greek's likely psychological experience, several passages are of particular relevance. In addition to the *Twilight*'s "Problem of Socrates," see especially the *Birth of Tragedy*'s treatment of Socrates' "divine sign" (sect. 13 and 14), and its rendering of his experiment with poetry in prison (sect. 14). See also *Gay Science* 340 and *Will To Power* 429–33 and 441–43.

15. Nietzsche's protopsychoanalytical analysis of Wagner—who by the time of the *Case of Wagner* and *Nietzsche Contra Wagner* in 1888, is characterized as the very embodiment of a thoroughly modern "decadence"—emerges not just in the several works formally dealing with the genius but in notes and reflections scattered liberally throughout the entirety of the Nietzschean corpus. See the *Birth of Tragedy*'s "Preface to Wagner," the "Attempt at Self-Criticism" added in 1886,

and its final nine sections (heralding Wagner's operas as the last hope for the rebirth of the spirit of tragedy). See also the 1876 essay "Richard Wagner in Bayreuth" (#3 of the *Untimely Meditations*); *The Case Of Wagner* (1888); and *Nietzsche Contra Wagner* (1895).

16. *Twilight of the Idols*, "Problem of Socrates," 4.

17. "Now that I am looking back from a certain distance upon the conditions of which these essays bear witness, I do not wish to deny that at bottom they speak only of me. The essay *Wagner in Bayreuth* is a vision of my future, while in *Schopenhauer as Educator* my innermost history, my *becoming* is inscribed . . . at bottom it is admittedly not 'Schopenhauer as Educator' that speaks here, but its opposite, 'Nietzsche as Educator' " (*Ecce Homo* 3, 2).

18. *Antichrist*, Introduction, p. 11.

1

Early Psychological Observations

Pre-*Antichrist* Reflections on Jesus

Buried in aphorism 235 of Volume I of *Human, All Too Human* (1878), as little more than an aside in a larger discussion of why the "highest intelligence and the warmest heart cannot coexist in the same person," lies a revealing characterization of Jesus as one "possessing the warmest heart." Elsewhere in that early volume are brief but similarly telling references to Jesus as "the noblest human being" (1,475),[1] yet clearly "not without the gravest shortcomings and prejudices in his knowledge of the human soul, and as a physician of the soul devoted to that infamous and untutored faith in universal medicine" (*HH-WS* 83). Also to be found in *Human, All Too Human*,[2] as part of a sustained and challenging treatment of the mind, motivation and significance of the "holy man," is the following observation:

Single exceptions stand out from the species, whether by virtue of great mildness and humanitarianism or by the magic of unusual energy; others are attractive in the highest degree because certain delusions inundate their whole nature with light—as is the case, for example, with the celebrated founder of Christianity[3] who considered himself the inborn son of God and therefore felt he was without sin; thus, by virtue of an illusion—which should not be judged too harshly, for the whole of antiquity was full of sons of gods—he attained the same goal, the feeling of complete freedom from sin . . . (*HH* 1,144).[4]

This theme of the Nietzschean Jesus' perceived "freedom from sin" informs another fleeting but similarly revealing pre-*Antichrist* reflection on the Nazarene, aphorism 138 of 1882's *Gay Science*.[5]

Christ's error—The founder of Christianity thought that there was nothing of which men suffered more than their sins. That was his error—the error of one who felt that he was without sin and who lacked firsthand experience. Thus his soul grew full of that wonderful and fantastic compassion for a misery that even among his people, who had invented sin, was rarely a very great misery.

We will treat the interesting matter of the Nietzschean Jesus' experience of utter sinlessness later in some detail within the context of the philosopher's frequently astounding depiction of what he takes to be the larger constellation of Jesus, Judaism, and the problem of sin. What needs to be noted at this juncture is (1) that Nietzsche's interest here lies with what he takes to be Jesus' own feeling of sinlessness; the Nazarene's subjective experience or psychological reality, and (2) that this characterization of Jesus as one who *felt* himself to be without sin persists in Nietzsche's writings and will prove to be an important theme in the more fully articulated *psychology of the redeemer* found in the *Antichrist* and notes of the period.

INEXPERIENCE AND IMMATURITY

Also worth noting at this juncture is the early appearance of one of the more significant leitmotifs of Nietzsche's steadily unfolding psychology of the redeemer: Jesus as one lacking experience or maturity. This proposed deficiency—already hinted at with *Human, All Too Human*'s reference to the Nazarene's "shortcomings" and "untutored faith" (II, 2,83), and said explicitly at *Gay Science* 138 to underlie what Nietzsche considers an apparent overestimation of the human suffering generated by sin (discussed below)—will prove to be one of the governing hypotheses employed by the mature philosopher both to explain Jesus' teachings and behavior, and to help interpret his psychic reality. As we shall see, by the close of his career Nietzsche will boldly (and explicitly psychologically) come to characterize this implied insufficiency with such nomenclature as "childish," a case of "retarded puberty" and "arrested adolescence";[6] but in terms of charting the philosopher's intellectual development it is important to make note of the appearance of this general theme in some of Nietzsche's earliest reflections on the figure of Jesus.

The most developed expression of this early/middle period emphasis on Jesus' apparent puerility is found within a remarkable sermon by Nietzsche's Zarathustra on the unfortunate timing of the death of "the Hebrew Jesus."[7] Zarathustra tells his disciples:

Many die too late and some die too early. Still the doctrine sounds strange: "Die at the right time." Die at the right time: thus Zarathustra teaches. Truly, too early died that Hebrew whom the preachers of slow death honor: and that he died too early has since been a fatality for many. As yet he knew only tears and the melancholy of the Hebrews, together with the hatred of the good and the just—the Hebrew Jesus: then the longing for death seized him. Had he only remained in the desert and far from the good and the just! Perhaps he would have learned to live and learned to love the earth—and laughter as well!

Believe it, my brothers! He died too early; he himself would have recanted his teaching had he lived to my age! He was noble enough to recant! But he was still immature. The youth loves immaturely and immaturely too he hates man and the earth.

While we turn to the topic of Nietzsche's general understanding of, and notable emphasis upon Jesus' death is treated carefully in chapter 3, here we provisionally note that unlike his Socrates, whom Kaufmann suggests[8] Nietzsche offers as an example of one who managed the deceptively difficult task of "going at the right time," Nietzsche's Jesus is here explicitly said to have "died too early."[9]

It is well to point out that this 1883 address also aptly reflects two more soon-to-emerge patterns in the philosopher's ever more frequent reflections on Jesus, St. Paul, and the birth of Christianity. First, it serves as an example of Nietzsche's marked tendency to challenge his reader to look beyond and behind the calculated affront of such passages—in this case insisting that had he lived to maturity, Jesus surely would have "recanted his teaching"—in search of his challenging and often partially concealed suggestions regarding the minds of Christianity's chief protagonists. The second (disconcerting) pattern clearly manifest in this excerpt from *Zarathustra* is Nietzsche's proclivity to mingle—in the same work, the same aphorism, and very often the same sentence—criticisms or reservations about the figure of Jesus, with the most unabashed and glowing praise. Indeed, as we shall soon see, in the majority of cases where Nietzsche expresses reservations or suggests some limitation with respect to Jesus in general and his psychophysiological constitution in particular, such sentiments are mitigated by and firmly rooted within a generally generous, often accommodating, and invariably sympathetic presentation of Jesus' condition *as a whole*. As already noted, Jesus'—possessor of "the warmest heart" (*HH* 235)—conviction that he was the Son of God (*HH* 144), though for Nietzsche an "illusion," not only "should not be judged too harshly," but made him "attractive in the highest degree," caused his "whole nature" to be "inundated" with "light," and most importantly enabled him to attain the admirable and thoroughly Nietzschean posture of complete freedom from all feelings of sin (discussed below). *Gay Science* 138 analogously, while depicting what Nietzsche considers Jesus' erroneous estimation of the degree to which men suffer from their sins, is tempered by mention of the Nazarene's "wonderful and fantastic compassion" while this "error" itself is nonjudgmentally explained in terms of his lack of so-called "firsthand experience."

As we shall see in his often virulent handling of Paul, though it is utterly devoid of the magnanimousness that characterizes the bulk of his reflections on Jesus, at times Nietzsche seems willing to extend to the figure of the pre-Damascus Pharisee a small measure of the even-handed diagnostic posture that also characterizes his scattered musings on the Nazarene. No such courtesy is extended to Paul's post-Damascus incarnation, however. "Even handed" is the last term one would use to describe Nietzsche's increasing bitter struggle with the Apostle to the Gentiles. As will become increasingly clear, while the language of Nietzsche's steadily emerging psychology of the redeemer is undeniably provocative, his struggle to understand the Nazarene is waged with kidgloves compared to his out-and-out attack on the "dysangelist" (*A* 42); the post-Damascus Paul. Typically then, in the same address Zarathustra brazenly suggests that had he "lived to my age" Jesus assuredly would have "recanted his teaching," the Nazarene is once again presented as an explicitly "noble" figure.[10]

THE JEWISH LANDSCAPE

Signaling yet another persistent theme in his extraordinary philosophy of religion, we may note Zarathustra's deliberate juxtapositioning of the noble yet immature Nazarene with the "tears," "melancholy," and "hatred" of the Hebrew milieu around him. Also characteristic of Nietzsche's larger image of the birth of Christianity is his generous and gentle depiction of the former at the obvious expense of the latter. As we shall explore, this ongoing vision of an utterly loving and peaceful Jesus tragically immersed in the seething and hate-filled world of first-century Palestine will also inform the later Nietzsche's passionate rendering of the unfortunate fate of both this "innocent from the country" himself (*WP* 383), *and* his singular message. Put simply, Nietzsche will come to blame precisely this "tear"- and "hate"-filled Hebrew milieu for both driving Jesus to his ultimate decision to die, and the rapid transmutation of the suddenly absent redeemer's gospel of love, peace, and reconciliation into a movement characterized by animosity and revenge (discussed in chapter 5).[11] While this defining juxtaposition of the subjectively sinless Jesus with what Nietzsche takes to be the tearful, sin-permeated culture of the Hebrews (a people "who had invented sin"— *GS* 138,135) is most fully and forcefully articulated in 1888's *Antichrist* and a handful of notes from the period, it is by no means restricted to those late-period reflections. Even more revealing than either *Gay Science* 138's positioning of an inexperienced and overly compassionate Jesus amidst the very inventors of sin, or *Thus Spoke Zarathustra*'s contrasting of the tears, melancholy and hatred of the Hebrews with the noble and innocent Nazarene, is aphorism 137 of *Gay Science*, titled *Speaking in parable*. Writes Nietzsche:

A Jesus Christ was possible only in a Jewish landscape—I mean one over which the gloomy and sublime thunder cloud of the wrathful Jehovah was brooding continually. Only here was the rare and sudden piercing of the gruesome and perpetual general day-night by a single ray of the sun experienced as if it were a miracle of "love" and the ray of unmerited "grace" . . . Everywhere else good weather and sunshine were considered the rule and everyday occurrences.

Again, while one must look to his writings of 1887-88 (the *Antichrist*, notes from the period, and to a lesser extent the *Genealogy of Morals*) for anything resembling a sustained exploration[12] of the far reaching and (for Nietzsche) "tragic" (*WP* 167) effect this "gloomy" "Jewish landscape" had both on Jesus himself and his singular message, one readily discerns in these brief, tantalizing, and scattered earlier vignettes, nascent conceptions which will come to define his mature psychology of the redeemer. Particularly interesting about *Gay Science* 137's representation of this doleful milieu is Nietzsche's effective image of the "brooding" "thunder cloud of the wrathful Jehovah['s] . . . sudden piercing by a single ray of the sun." Though meteorology in general does indeed figure prominently in both the philosophy and biography of Friedrich Nietzsche,[13] *Gay Science* 137's references to thunderclouds, sunbeams, "good weather" and so forth, is indicative of quite another tendency. While the rationale underlying his deliberate depiction of the "Jewish landscape [as] . . . gloomy . . . brooding . . . gruesome" and so forth, is fully explored in chapter 5, at this juncture it is telling to note the philosopher's marked proclivity for painting his Jesus with images of *light* and *warmth*. This motif—culminating in *Antichrist* 32's favorable treatment of Jesus' *inmost* illumination, his "inner 'lights' "—is already manifest in several of Nietzsche's already cited early-period asseverations on the Nazarene. Again, in addition to its fleeting but revealing characterization of Jesus as one "possessing the warmest heart" (235), 1878's *Human, All Too Human* insists not only that Jesus' "illusion" that he was the sinless son of God "should not be judged too harshly," but that this very belief made him "attractive in the highest degree" and caused his "whole nature" to be inundated "with light" (144). The extent to which Nietzsche's employment of these radiant images, like *Gay Science* 137's picturesque comparison of the Nazarene to "a single ray of the sun," is rooted in—or intended to bring to mind—recurring New Testament characterizations of Jesus as "the light of the world"[14] is unclear. What is certain is that Nietzsche's obvious situating of this luminiferous soul against a tear- and hate-filled gloomy Jewish background not only places both in strikingly sharp relief, but by the time of the writings of 1887 and 1888, serves as the very basis for understanding not only the Nietzschean Jesus, but the philosopher's strikingly original and thoroughly psychological account of the birth of Christianity.

JESUS' LOVE

Returning briefly to the general theme of a Jesus lacking in maturity or experience, and in particular Zarathustra's somber depiction of a noble innocent largely defined in terms of his immaturity:

Had he only remained in the desert and far from the good and the just! Perhaps he would have learned to live and learned to love the earth—and laughter as well! Believe it my brothers! He died too early; he himself would have recanted his teaching had he lived to my age! He was noble enough to recant! But he was still immature. The youth loves immaturely and immaturely too he hates man and the earth.

We note that here Jesus' immaturity is specifically and significantly manifest as one who had much to learn about love, who loves (and hates) immaturely. As we see below, this theme of the Nazarene's naive love is something to which Nietzsche will repeatedly refer in his ever more frequent reflections on Christianity and its principal protagonists. Pertinent to this motif is a characteristically Nietzschean sentiment—that even love needs to be understood in terms of effort and exertion—expressed beautifully the year before, at *Gay Science* 334:

One must Learn to Love. This is what happens to us in music: First one has to *learn to hear* a figure and melody at all, to detect and distinguish it, to isolate and delimit it as a separate life. Then it requires some exertion and good-will to *tolerate* it in spite of its strangeness, to be patient with its appearance and expression, and kindhearted about its oddity. Finally there comes a moment when we are used to it, when we wait for it, when it dawns upon us that we should miss it if it were missing; and then it goes on to exercise its spell and charm more and more, and does not cease until we have become its humble and enraptured lovers, who want it, and want it again, and ask for nothing better from the world. But that is what happens to us not only in music: it is precisely thus that we have learned to love everything that we love . . . there is no other way. Love also has to be learned.

Love as here defined by Nietzsche is not the easy, essentially effortless emotive experience so many people think of. Real love, *mature* love, unromantically presented by Nietzsche, is a serious and active endeavor

requiring significant effort and discipline. There "is no other way. Love
... has to be learned."

Though Nietzsche ruefully speculates that had this unseasoned soul
"only remained in the desert and far from the good and the just" he
might "have *learned* to live and *learned* to love," the sad fact of the matter
is that this youthful redeemer "knew *only* tears and the melancholy of
the Hebrews" and accordingly was afforded no such learning opportunities (Z 1, 21). "The youth," instructs Zarathustra, "loves immaturely."
Suggested in this sermon of Zarathustra, and more fully articulated in
the writings of the late 1880s,[15] is the notion that Jesus' very love for the
oppressive "Hebrew milieu" around him not only yielded a tragic personal outcome, but evidenced a disastrous lack of discretion (a failure
the philosopher consistently and forgivingly attributes to immaturity).

In our youthful years we respect and despise without that art of nuance which
constitutes the best thing we gain from life, and, as is only fair, we have to pay
dearly for having assailed men and things with Yes and No in such a fashion.
... the worst of all tastes, the taste for the unconditional, is cruelly misused and
made fool of until a man learns to introduce a little art into his feelings. ... youth
as such is something that falsifies and deceives (*BGE* 31).

That Nietzsche's youthful "founder of Christianity" was denied the opportunity to introduce "a little art into his feelings," to "learn" *how* to
love, to learn *who* to love—quite simply, to *mature*—is a persistent theme
in the philosopher's steadily emerging "psychology of the redeemer."
How and why this deficiency proved fatal for the Nazarene is clear. The
less obvious significance of Zarathustra's somber remark—"and that he
died too early has since been a fatality for many"—will fully emerge
only in the writings of 1888.

The topic of love and Jesus of Nazareth is picked up once again at
Beyond Good and Evil 269, a fascinating and seemingly autobiographical
passage that might well have been titled "the vulnerability of the super-
sensitive." This extraordinary aphorism begins with the suggestion that
the "born, unavoidable psychologist and reader of souls" must necessarily live with "the danger of his suffocating from pity: he needs hardness and cheerfulness more than other men," and goes on to suggest this
natural proclivity for "suffocating from pity" can too easily "make him
turn against his whole lot and drive him to attempt self-destruction—to
his own ruination." The philosopher then reflects upon pity's relation to
love, women, and Jesus of Nazareth. Continues Nietzsche: "woman—
who is clairvoyant in the world of suffering and unfortunately also eager
to help and save far beyond her powers to do so—those outbursts of
boundless, most devoted *pity*. ... This pity habitually deceives itself

about its strength; woman would like to believe that love can do *every-thing*—it is her characteristic faith."

Nietzsche's thoughts then turn to the faith in love of another:

Alas, he who knows the heart divines how poor, stupid, helpless, arrogant, blundering, more prone to destroy than save is even the best and deepest love! It is possible that within the holy disguise and fable of Jesus' life there lies concealed one of the most painful cases of the martyrdom of *knowledge about love*: the martyrdom of the most innocent and longing heart which never had sufficient of human love, which *demanded* love, to be loved and nothing else. . . .

He whose feelings are like this, he who knows about love to this extent—*seeks* death.[16]

Something that immediately differentiates *Beyond Good and Evil* 269's remarks on the character of Jesus' love from other pre-*Antichrist* reflections on the matter is Nietzsche's reference to the Nazarene as one "having become knowledgeable about love." Again:

It is possible that within the holy disguise and fable of Jesus' life there lies concealed one of the most painful cases of the martyrdom of *knowledge about love*: the martyrdom of the most innocent and longing heart which never had sufficient of human love, which *demanded* love, to be loved and nothing else. . . .

He whose feelings are like this, he who knows about love to this extent—*seeks* death.

While *Beyond Good and Evil*'s mention of Jesus' "innocent and longing heart" finds resonance with a number of early and middle-period depictions of the Nazarene's essential inexperience and immaturity, its repeated reference to his "knowledge about love" does not. On the contrary, we have seen that Zarathustra characterizes "the Hebrew Jesus" not merely as "immature" but quite explicitly as one who "*loves* immaturely," who had much to "learn" about love. Yet three years later at *Beyond Good and Evil* 269, Nietzsche presents Jesus as one who not only "knows about love," but seems to have indeed attained a special insight into love.

ON THE KNOWLEDGE ACQUIRED THROUGH SUFFERING

While Nietzsche was quite capable of reversing his position on such a matter, I suspect the explanation here has more to do with a change of focus than an outright change of mind. The key to understanding the Nietzschean Jesus' apparent transformation from one who, like *Beyond Good and Evil* 269's "woman," is deliberately characterized both by overflowing pity and a naïve understanding of love,[17] into one possessing noteworthy "knowledge about love" seems to be this challenging passages' particular focus on the Nazarene's "suffering" and "painful . . . martyrdom." *Beyond Good and Evil*'s Jesus apparently is one who ultimately comes to an all too penetrating understanding, not of love in general, but quite specifically of love's all too real limitations, risks, and dangers ("how poor, stupid, helpless, arrogant, blundering, more prone to destroy than save is even the best and deepest love") precisely *through* his tremendous suffering and eventual martyrdom. *Beyond Good and Evil*'s Jesus presumably, is one who not only has *learned* from suffering, but is seemingly *transformed* by it. Certainly, Nietzsche suggests precisely this, and does so quite unabashedly, in Book 2 of his *Daybreak* (written in 1880, published 1881). There, in an extraordinary aphorism entitled *On The Knowledge Acquired Through Suffering*, the 35-year-old Nietzsche (who months earlier resigned his professorship due to illness), writes:

The condition of sick people who suffer dreadful and protracted torment from their suffering and whose minds nonetheless remain undisturbed is not without value for the acquisition of knowledge—quite apart from the intellectual benefit which accompanies any profound solitude, any unexpected and permitted liberation from duties. He who suffers intensely looks out at things with a terrible coldness: all those little lying charms with which things are usually surrounded when the eye of the healthy regards them do not exist for him; indeed, he himself lies there before himself stripped of all color and plumage. If until then he has been living in some perilous world of fantasy, this supreme sobering-up through pain is the means of extricating him from it: and perhaps the only means. (It is possible that this is what happened to the founder of Christianity on the cross; for the bitterest of all exclamations 'my God, why hast thou forsaken me!' contains, in its ultimate significance, evidence of a general disappointment and enlightenment over the delusion of his life; at the moment of supreme agony he acquired an insight into himself of the kind told by the poet of the poor dying Don Quixote.) The tremendous tension imparted to the intellect by its desire to oppose and counter pain makes him see everything he now beholds in a new light (*D* 114).

The two outcomes that Nietzsche suggests are ultimately brought about by Jesus' proposed "supreme sobering-up through pain," and cruelly evidenced in "the bitterest of all exclamations"—"a general disappointment" and "enlightenment over the delusion of his life"—clearly warrant our closer inspection. But before turning to these interwoven themes a word or two seems appropriate concerning this passage's clearly autobiographical character. Surely one of the more telling facets of this fascinating reflection upon the psychointellectual ramifications of suffering is Nietzsche's obvious allusion to his *own* psychophysiological anguish alongside his moving treatment of the tremendous torment endured by "the founder of Christianity." Certainly, one of Nietzsche's professed objectives is the *contrasting* of Jesus' "dreadful and protracted" agony, with his own. Hence his distinguishing the psychological condition of "people who suffer dreadful and protracted torment . . . *from* the intellectual benefit which accompanies any profound solitude, any unexpected and permitted liberation from duties" [my italics]. But while on the surface it seems intent on underscoring *differences*, the thrust of this passage as a whole is suggestive of Nietzsche's identification with, or at the very least *comparison* of, Jesus' pain with his own.[18]

To those familiar with the unhappy circumstances surrounding Nietzsche's lifelong struggle with pressing health problems, their tragic effect on his brief but particularly promising professorship,[19] and his ongoing efforts to cast in a positive light both his great physical suffering,[20] and long-standing loneliness,[21] *Daybreak* 114's quiet yet unmistakable allusion to the "intellectual benefit which accompanies any profound solitude, any unexpected and permitted liberation from duties" within an aphorism on the psychological ramifications of great suffering in general, and Jesus' agony at Calvary in particular, is both sorrowful and revealing. The autobiographical character of these perceptive remarks on suffering is further evidenced by their easily unnoticed movement from *third* person objectivity to painful revelations in the *first* person that fill the reader with feelings of both empathy and voyeurism. So it is that *Daybreak* 114's musings "on the knowledge acquired through suffering," while initially examining "the condition of sick people" in general—"*he* who suffers intensively"—soon seamlessly (and likely unconsciously) becomes the forum for the all too telling, and altogether pitiful references such as "*our* condition . . . *we* experience . . . [and] *we* cry."

Considering how prominently the precise manner of Jesus' death and dying will figure in the writings of 1887 and 1888, another interesting feature of the early treatment of Jesus' crucifixion and death found in *Daybreak* has to do with Nietzsche's extraordinary hypothesis that by way of this "supreme sobering-up through pain" at Calvary, the "founder of Christianity" for the first time achieves "enlightenment over the delusion of his life . . . [and] insight into himself" (the latter, a quintessentially Nietzschean attainment). Prior to this "moment of supreme agony," suggests Nietzsche, Jesus—elsewhere represented as an "immature" "innocent from the country," one characterized by an "untutored faith in universal medicine" and an evident excess of the most "fantastic compassion"[22]—lives and loves not merely "without that art of nuance" (*BGE* 31) which bespeaks experience and education, but very likely on the basis of "delusion." He may well have "been living in some perilous world of fantasy."

While *Daybreak* is alone, at least among Nietzsche's early and middle period works, in its bold proposal that the naïve pre-Calvary Jesus may be viewed as "living in some perilous world of fantasy,"[23] the general tendency of these works to appeal to notions of "immaturity," "error," "illusion," and "delusion" in their interpretations of both the Nazarene's behavior and conceivable subjective experience, has already been discussed (Z 1,21; GS 138; HH 144). So has Nietzsche's linkage of this cluster of possible psychological constraints to Jesus' (limited) understanding and exercise of love and pity. Considered together, Daybreak's charting of Jesus' rapid pain-induced movement at Calvary from (1) "fantasy" and "delusion" to (2) "disappointment" to (3) "enlightenment," and Beyond Good and Evil's subsequent simultaneous themes of (1) boundless pity and naïve love and (2) Jesus' death as "one of the most painful cases of the martyrdom of knowledge about love" point to the emergence of a different person than the "untutored" soul treated in Zarathustra, Human, All Too Human, and The Gay Science. This is someone who, by means of a "supreme sobering-up through pain" (as evidenced by "the bitterest of all exclamations") comes, with frightening swiftness, to a more seasoned, more mature understanding of love, of love's limitations and dangers, of how "blundering, more prone to destroy than save is even the best and deepest love."[24]

NIETZSCHE'S GENERAL PSYCHOLOGY OF SUFFERING

What does not kill me makes me stronger.
Twilight of the Idols, Maxims and Arrows, 8

It is entirely conceivable that Nietzsche's Daybreak is correct in its unusual hypothesis that Jesus' "dreadful and protracted torment" was "not without value for the acquisition of knowledge." Insofar as it served to "extricate" the naïve Nazarene from "the delusion of his life" and afford him both a belated "enlightenment" and "insight into himself," his "supreme sobering-up through pain" at Calvary may indeed be said to have ultimately been of value, or "intellectual benefit." But if we are to come to understand the larger import of this curious psychohistorical hypothesis it is necessary that we briefly step back from the philosopher's thoughts on this very specific case of suffering, and examine his unusual (and once again clearly autobiographical) ideas concerning the psychointellectual ramifications of suffering in general. In particular, it is essential that we examine the extraordinary and recurring Nietzschean theme of the ultimate psychological desirability of disappointment, frustration, pain, and even great suffering.

One such provocative treatment of the potential psychointellectual benefit of pain and suffering comes in the preface to second edition of The Gay Science, added in 1887, five years after the book's original publication, and not long before the author's complete collapse. Indeed, one could readily come to the erroneous conclusion from reading this new and highly unusual preface that the topic of the book it supposedly heralds, the work Nietzsche considered "the most personal of all my books"[25] is in fact what consequences ill-health and suffering have on one's mind and manner of thinking. Section 1 of this unusual preface speaks emotionally of the "conclusions of pain" and the "unexpected" and "intoxicating convalescence" of its "resurrected author." Section 2 declares that "for a psychologist there are few questions that are as attractive as that concerning the relation of health and philosophy," and raises the intriguing question, "what will become of the thought itself when it is subjected to the pressure of sickness?" But it is a remark found in Section 3 that is most relevant to our present investigation of Nietzsche's reflections on the apparent psychointellectual ramifications of pain and suffering. There Nietzsche writes:

Only great pain, the long, slow pain that takes its time—on which we are burned, as it were, with green wood—compels us philosophers to descend to our ultimate depths and to put aside all trust, everything good-natured, everything that would impose a veil. . . . I doubt that such pain makes us "better"; but I know that it makes us more *profound*.

Whether we learn to pit our pride, our scorn, our will power against it, equaling the American Indian who, however tortured, repays his torturer with the malice of his tongue . . . out of such long and dangerous exercises of self-mastery one emerges as a different person, with a few more question marks—above all with the will henceforth to question further, more deeply, severely, harshly, evilly and quietly than one had questioned heretofore. The trust in life is gone: life itself has become a *problem*. Yet one should not jump to the conclusion that this necessarily makes one gloomy. Even love of life is still possible, only one loves differently.

This theme of the newfound depth and profundity afforded the sufferer of "great pain . . . long, slow pain" also figures prominently in the roughly contemporary *Beyond Good and Evil*.[26] Insisting "how deeply human beings can suffer almost determines their order of rank," *Beyond Good and Evil* 270 for example, goes on to speak of "the harrowing certainty, with which he [the sufferer] is wholly permeated and colored, that by virtue of his suffering he *knows more*." Apparently speaking from experience of "this spiritual, silent haughtiness of the sufferer, this pride of the elect of knowledge, of the 'initiated,' of the almost sacrificed," Nietzsche here concludes: "Profound suffering ennobles; it separates."

Contrasting the "naiveté" of those who would wish "*to abolish suffering*" with the routinely ignored but potentially very real *advantages* of "increased" suffering, *Beyond Good and Evil* 225, for its part, dares to go even farther in its celebration of human suffering:

The discipline of suffering, of *great* suffering—do you not know that it is *this* discipline alone which has created every elevation of mankind hitherto? That tension of the soul in misfortune which cultivates its strength, its terror at the sight of great destruction, its inventiveness and bravery in undergoing, enduring, interpreting, exploiting misfortune, and whatever of depth, mystery, mask, spirit, cunning and greatness has been bestowed upon it—has it not been bestowed through suffering, through the discipline of great suffering?

Admittedly, insofar as the formal topic of the *Gay Science* preface is the psychological implication of "great pain," not overall, but for "us philosophers," there may be some limitations built in to our paralleling this 1887 musing with *Daybreak* 114's earlier discourse on "dreadful and protected torment" in general, and Jesus' "supreme agony" in particular.[27] Nonetheless, as we soon see in our discussion of *Daybreak*'s cynical vision of the mind and possible motivation of St. Paul, Nietzsche's keen and often prophetic observations concerning the ideas and thinking of "philosophers" routinely lend themselves to application well beyond academic "philosophy" per se.[28] With respect to the ramifications of suffering in the particular case of Nietzsche's Jesus—his "sobering up," rapid deliverance from "delusion" and "fantasy," his belated "enlightenment" and insight into himself, a more mature understanding of love—we note that the pain and suffering experienced by Nietzsche's Nazarene in many ways exemplifies what we may regard as the Nietzschean autobiographical model of how one may benefit from pain. As the "great pain" of the quintessential Nietzschean sufferer quickly does away with all forms of deception (self or otherwise)—of "everything that would impose a veil" (*Gay Science*, preface)—so the "dreadful and protracted torment" of *Daybreak*'s Jesus is presented as doing away with "all those little lying charms" that characterize the vantage of the innocent pre-sufferer, and instantly "extricating" him from his "perilous world of fantasy . . . the delusion of his life." Likewise, as the *Gay Science*'s model sufferer both "loves differently" and "emerges as a different person" in the wake of his misery, so too, evidently, does Nietzsche's Jesus at Calvary. For as we have just explored, it is there that the untutored naïf, one who "loves immaturely," is transformed *through pain* into a belatedly *enlightened* figure characterized above all by an all too penetrating knowledge of love's dangers and limitations.

In a very real sense then, Nietzsche's Jesus may be understood to undergo truly *Nietzschean suffering*. His agony at Calvary was "not without value for the acquisition of knowledge," he does indeed derive "intellectual benefit" and "enlightenment" from his suffering (*D* 114), and while his torment (like Nietzsche's own) may not make him "better", it does seem to make him "more profound" (*GS*, preface). However, in another, equally real sense, the suffering of the pre-*Antichrist* Jesus falls tragically short of living up to Nietzsche's autobiographical paradigm. One essential facet of Nietzsche's model of suffering, implied in the *Gay Science* preface and made explicit in *Beyond Good and Evil*, is that the sufferer survives long enough to put his painfully won profundity and insight to use and has opportunity to apply "the knowledge acquired through suffering" to a post-suffering existence. As *Beyond Good and Evil* 270 lauds the "knowledge, of the 'initiated', of the *almost sacrificed*," so aphorism 225 celebrates the sufferer's "bravery in undergoing, *enduring, interpreting, exploiting misfortune*"[29] (my italics). Put simply, the pain-induced enlightenment of Nietzsche's pre-*Antichrist* Jesus ultimately fails to qualify as genuine Nietzschean suffering because the very torment said to "sober up" this innocent soul also kills him. *Beyond Good and Evil's* champion is one who not only *undergoes* great suffering, but *endures* and even *exploits* it. At Calvary, Jesus is denied far more than an opportunity to *exploit* the lessons there learned. Insofar as his enlightening misery proved fatal, he was denied opportunity to *endure*. *Beyond Good and Evil*, it bears repeating, extols the benefits of pain for the "*almost* sacrificed."

A notebook entry from 1887 labeled "Type of my disciples" at once underscores just how far Nietzsche would go in his championing of pain and suffering (in this case wishing them upon friends and potential followers), and the value he assigns to the sufferer's endurance and survival. "To those human beings who are of any concern to me I wish suffering, desolation, sickness, ill-treatment, indignities . . . the wretchedness of the vanquished: I have no pity for them, because I wish them the only thing that can prove today whether one is worth anything or not—that one endures" (*WP* 910). Though Jesus ultimately experiences everything Nietzsche here wishes on his "disciples," "those human beings who are of any concern to me,"[30] the simple fact of the matter is that he does not *endure*. Accordingly, with the notable exception his last, painful cry at Calvary—"the bitterest of all exclamations"—we will never know what effect great suffering might have had on the mind and message of the Nazarene. As discussed, Nietzsche's Zarathustra insists that such a message would have been markedly different than the one advanced in his "immaturity."[31] But even this bold and irreverent figure does not propose what such a message might consist of. Nonetheless, for Nietzsche the fact there is no post-suffering, post-enlightenment, mature teaching of Jesus to reflect upon is a somber one indeed. The truly titanic implications of his potent declaration—that "too early died that Hebrew whom the preachers of slow death honor: and that he died too early has since been a fatality for many"—reveal themselves as we proceed.

NOTES

1. "I should like to know how much must, in total accounting, be forgiven a people who, not without us all being to blame, have had the most grief-laden history of any people and whom we have to thank for the noblest human being (Christ), the purest sage (Spinoza), the mightiest book and most efficacious moral code in the world" (*HH* 1,475).

2. *Human, All Too Human* was first published in the spring of 1878. In 1886 Nietzsche published a new edition, adding two already published books of aphorisms—"Assorted Opinions and Maxims" (1879), and "The Wanderer and His Shadow" (1880)—to form Volume 2 of this now two-volume work.

3. In the early works especially, for reasons that become clear as we proceed, the titles "first," "original," or "founding" Christian are bestowed variously upon Jesus (*D* 114; *HH* 144) and St. Paul (*D* 68).

4. Kaufmann translation, appended to his edition of the *Genealogy of Morals*.

5. Nietzsche first published *The Gay Science* in 1882. In 1887 he published a second edition, which agrees with the edition of 1882, but contains a ten-page preface, a Book V (sections 343–384), and an Appendix of Songs.

6. *Antichrist* 31, 32, and *Nachlass* (in O'Flaherty p. 187).

7. *Thus Spoke Zarathustra*, Book One, *On Voluntary Death*. Interestingly, apart from its radically refashioned protagonist, "the Hebrew Jesus" is the only historical figure named in *Zarathustra*.

8. Kaufmann, *Nietzsche*, p. 403.

9. As we will discuss in chapter 3, Nietzsche's Jesus is one who "died for *his* [own] guilt," emphatically *not* "for the guilt of *others*," "not to 'redeem mankind' " (*A* 27,35).

10. Significantly, we have just begun our survey of Nietzsche's early and middle period reflections on the figure of Jesus and here we encounter the philosopher's second deliberate use of the word "noble" to characterize the Nazarene. Further, for the record, *Human, All Too Human* 1,475 doesn't speak of Jesus as *simply* "noble," but indeed "the *noblest* human being (Christ)" (my italics). Those familiar with Nietzsche's extraordinary moral universe will immediately appreciate just how high a compliment the philosopher's depiction of an explicitly noble Jesus is. Looking ahead, we note that regardless of the deliberately shocking things the philosopher would ultimately say of his Jesus, he remains to the end, a noble figure. As will soon become apparent, Jesus' essential nobility serves as one of many points of contrast with the philosopher's vision of the Apostle Paul—for Nietzsche, the very embodiment of the ignoble soul.

11. "The founder of Christianity," insists Nietzsche in 1888, "had to pay for having directed himself to the lowest class of Jewish society and intelligence. They conceived of him in the spirit they understood" (*WP* 198).

12. As stated in our Introduction, in even these more narrowly focused works one looks in vain for a traditional measured, systematic philosophy of religion in general or Christianity in particular.

13. Nietzsche's writings are littered with allusions to how climate and weather play a role in a given people's religiosity, philosophy, and so forth. *Antichrist* 21 for example, insists that the "precondition for Buddhism is a very mild climate."

Those familiar with Nietzsche's biography will also recall the extent to which meteorological conditions played a significant role in how *and where* Nietzsche spent the last years of his creative life (treated in *Ecce Homo* 2,2).

14. In John's gospel alone one reads: "I am the light of the world," "I have come into the world as a light," "The true light that gives light to every man" (8:12, 12:46, 1:9). Unless otherwise noted, New Testament passages are taken from Kenneth Barker, ed., *The NIV Study Bible: New International Version* (Grand Rapids Mich.: Zondervan Publishing, 1985).

15. Once more anticipating a central theme of chapter 5, we again cite *Will To Power* 198: "The founder of Christianity had to pay for having directed himself to the lowest class of Jewish society and intelligence."

16. Interestingly, Nietzsche ends this unusual aphorism with the seemingly truncated editorial remark; "But why reflect on such painful things? As long as one does not have to." As our ongoing paralleling of Jesus' and Nietzsche's respective sufferings illuminates, Nietzsche was apparently not among those fortunate individuals who do not *have to* "reflect on such painful things."

17. Nietzsche's "woman," "eager to help and save far beyond her powers to do so," characterized in terms of "those outbursts of boundless, most devote *pity*," is said to naively "believe that love can do *everything*—it is her characteristic faith" (*BGE* 269). The "soul" of Nietzsche's Jesus—"a physician of the soul devoted to that infamous and untutored faith in universal medicine" (*HH-WS* 83)—is likewise depicted in terms of his "wonderful," "fantastic" *and utterly disproportionate* "compassion for misery" (*GS* 138).

18. While we can of course assign comparatively little weight to the communiqués of the post-collapse Nietzsche, when treating the topic of Nietzsche's possible identification with Jesus and his suffering one cannot ignore the pathos built in to the fact that while the epithet *"Dionysus versus the Crucified"* is appropriately the last remark of his philosophical autobiography, weeks after *Ecce Homo*'s completion a number of Nietzsche's last semi-lucid correspondences, written in January 1889, were tellingly signed "the Crucified" (see Kaufmann p. 67).

19. By the summer of 1879 Nietzsche's steadily deteriorating health—plagued by acute myopia, nausea and other stomach upsets, and agonizing headaches since childhood—contributed to the resignation of his professorship at age 34. The bulk of his *Daybreak* was written shortly thereafter, amidst the newly "liberated" Nietzsche's wanderings through Italy in 1880.

20. "I do not want to take leave ungratefully from that time of severe sickness whose profits I have not yet exhausted even today . . . we have to give birth to our thoughts out of our pain . . . as for sickness: are we not almost tempted to ask whether we could get along without it?" (*GS*, preface to 2nd edition, section 3).

21. "I am solitude become man," writes Nietzsche in a note that was part of an earlier draft of *Ecce Homo* (included in appendix 4d, p. 343, of Kaufmann's edition of that text).

22. *Zarathustra*, "Of Vol. Death," *WP* 383, *HH-WS* 83, and *GS* 138 respectively.

23. A variant of this calculatingly confrontational hypothesis figures prominently in the *Antichrist* and notes from the period. As we shall see in chapters 3 and 5, the defensive efforts of the Nietzschean Jesus to psychologically retreat to and engage a reality *other* than the gloomy tear-filled one in which he is im-

mersed is a pivotal theme in the writings of 1888. There, the "instinct of self-preservation" itself is said to verily propel Jesus into a wholly "inner world" of symbol and metaphor; a world "undisturbed by reality of any kind" (*A* 29).

24. As if do underscore just *how* radical Jesus' apparent Calvary transformation is (and sharply delineate the consistently "warm" and luminiferous pre-martyrdom redeemer from the *disappointed* and *enlightened* figure on the cross), the long-suffering author of *Daybreak* insists not only that the sufferer of "dreadful and protracted torment" comes to behold everything "in a new light," but indeed soon "looks out at things with a terrible coldness."

25. In a letter to friend Paul Ree from the summer of 1882 Nietzsche writes: "Is *The Gay Science* in your hands—the *most personal* of all my books? . . . There my private morality will be found together, as the sum of the conditions of *my* existence." Ernest Pfeiffer, ed., *Friedrich Nietzsche, Paul Ree, Lou von Salome: Die Dokumente ihrer Begegnung*, (Frankfurt am Main: Insel Verlag, 1970), p. 224.

26. First published in August 1886, not long prior to the addition of *The Gay Science*'s painfully autobiographical preface.

27. Strictly speaking, the purported topic of the preface to the new edition of *The Gay Science*, written during an all too brief renewal of health and vigor, is the implication of pain and illness for "us philosophers." Our linkage of this odd preface with *Daybreak* 114's meditations on Jesus' suffering-induced "enlightenment" at Calvary is not to suggest that Nietzsche would include Jesus among the ranks of "us philosophers," that the Nazarene is to be considered a "philosopher" or that his teachings advance an actual philosophy per se. While Nietzsche nowhere formally precludes his Jesus from qualifying as a "philosopher," our examination of his *Antichrist* will soon reveal its author's (1) pointed ridicule of those, like "Monsieur Renan, that buffoon *in psychologicis*" who endeavor to cast the naïf Jesus as a "genius" (*A* 29), and (2) increasingly immoderate image of a Jesus ultimately said to act only from "instinct" (*A* 29,30,33), with neither *interest in*, nor even awareness *of* "theory" of any kind.

[T]he *experience* "life" in the only form he knows it is opposed to any kind of word, formula, law, faith, dogma . . . [He] stands outside of all religion, all conceptions of divine worship, all history, all natural science, all experience of the world, all acquirements, all politics, all psychology, all books, all art—his "knowledge" is precisely the pure folly of the fact that anything of this kind exists. He has not so much heard of *culture*. . . . Dialectics are likewise lacking, the idea is lacking that a faith, "a truth," could be proved by reasons. . . . Neither *can* such a doctrine argue: it simply does not understand that other doctrines exist, *can* exist, it simply does not know how to imagine an opinion contrary to its own (*A* 32).

Even within the broad parameters of Nietzsche's unorthodox vision of "philosophy", there is little doubt concerning the inapplicability of the "philosopher" moniker to his Jesus.

28. Early in chapter 4 (in the context of Paul's harsh pre-Damascus persecutions of the first Christians), we observe that the insight at the heart of *BGE* 6's famous assertion—that "every great philosophy has hitherto been: a confession on the part of its author and a kind of involuntary and unconscious memoir"—clearly has application wider than philosophy, philosophers, and philosophical texts per se.

29. Sadly, this notion of *exploiting* misfortune figures all too prominently in

Nietzsche's unorthodox literary autobiography, *Ecce Homo*. There, in Section 2 of the chapter entitled "Why I Am So Wise," its author asks: "What is it, fundamentally, that allows us to recognize who has *turned out well?* . . . He has a taste only for what is good for him; . . . He guesses what remedies avail against what is harmful; he exploits bad accidents to his advantage; what does not kill him makes him stronger." What becomes increasingly clear in our ongoing paralleling of Nietzsche's self-image with his image of Jesus is that unlike the philosopher's vision of himself, the Nietzschean Jesus was gravely lacking any awareness of what was "good for him," of what "remedies" he himself was in such dire need.

30. Worth considering is the separate matter of whether we may place Jesus' name among (1) the "type of my disciples" or (2)"those human beings who are of any concern to me" (sometimes translated as "those human beings in which I have a stake"). At first hearing, such a notion sounds fantastic. Surely the human beings to whom Nietzsche is here referring are the "free spirits," "immoralists," "philosophers of the future" (*BGE* 42, 43) and "supermen" heralded in his mature writing. Upon closer examination, however, it may be said that Nietzsche's "stake" in Jesus is great indeed. First, because so much of his philosophy is rooted in, and his reputation built upon, his repudiation of Christianity (as we see below, his psychological differentiation of the person of Jesus of Nazareth from the miserable world-view that would be developed in his name is a crucial if sometimes overlooked aspect of his anti-Christian philosophizing). Further, as we see in chapter 5, judging from the increasing amounts of time and energy devoted to his largely psychological exploration of Christianity's origins and ongoing character, it is clear that Nietzsche did have a stake, a very serious stake, in *distinguishing* what he sometimes calls Jesus' "genuine, primitive Christianity" (*A* 39) from the potent clutches of the "false-coiner" Paul (*A* 42), and the thoroughly distorted story advanced in the Gospels (*A* 31).

31. Recall Zarathustra's bold suggestion at *Of Voluntary Death*:

> Had he only remained in the desert and far from the good and the just!
> Perhaps he would have learned to live and learned to love the earth—
> and laughter as well! Believe it my brothers! He died too early; he
> himself would have recanted his teaching had he lived to my age! He
> was noble enough to recant! But he was still immature. The youth
> loves immaturely. . . .

2

The Psychology of the Redeemer

The *Antichrist*'s Jesus

Returning briefly to Nietzsche's simultaneously autobiographical and Jesus-related suggestion at *Beyond Good and Evil* 269—that because the "born, unavoidable psychologist and reader of souls," the "clairvoyant in the world of suffering," must live with the ever-present "danger of his suffocating from pity: he needs hardness and cheerfulness more than other men"—one point in particular warrants our immediate attention. For upon consideration, what is both apparent and especially telling is that the Nietzschean Jesus is woefully deficient in both of that aphorism's two prescriptions for the survival of the super-sensitive "reader of souls" and 'clairvoyant' of suffering: An abundance of "hardness" and "cheerfulness." Indeed as we have seen, even in those far-flung early and middle-period anticipations of his eventual "psychology of the redeemer," Nietzsche seems intent on delineating a Jesus characterized precisely in terms of the obvious absence and acute need of these very attributes.

ON CHEERFULNESS

> My soul is overwhelmed with sorrow to the point of death.
>
> Matthew 26:38

> I should believe only in a God who understood how to dance.
>
> *Zarathustra* 1, 7

It is well to remind ourselves that the image of Jesus as a serious, sorrowful, sufferer is by no means unique to Nietzsche, but is funda-

mental to the entire Christian tradition. Not only does the reader of the
Gospels never witness Jesus smile or laugh, but the figure there depicted
is very often a man of tremendous sorrow. Regularly we see Jesus
"moved with compassion" (Mt. 9:36; Mk. 8:2; Lk. 15:20); "overwhelmed
with sorrow" (Mt. 26:38; Mk. 14:34); and weep openly (Lk. 19:41; Jn. 11:
35). Moreover, as Nietzsche was keenly aware, after relating Jesus' fear
and "anguish" at Gethsemane, the Gospel tradition conscientiously doc-
uments each of the progressively more painful experiences and indignities leading to his crucifixion and martyrdom. And certainly, from
innumerable medieval depictions of a broken, bleeding, suffering savior
to Kazantzakis's more recent but no less solemn *Last Temptation of Christ*,
"cheerful" remains a term rarely associated with Jesus of Nazareth.

We have already made careful note both of (1) the recurring image of
a gentle innocent veritably overwhelmed by the suffering, "tear"- and
"hate"- filled Hebrew milieu—a "gruesome" landscape "over which the
gloomy and sublime thunder cloud of the wrathful Jehovah was brooding continually"; and (2) Nietzsche's somber hypothesis that had the
"noble" Jesus, "only remained in the desert and far from the good and
the just! Perhaps he would have learned to live and learned to love the
earth—and *laughter as well!*" (*GS* 137; *Z* 1, 21, my italics). Interestingly,
this sad image of a kindly, gentle figure somehow denied, or incapable
of, laughter or other expressions of joy, informs another isolated reference to Jesus in the Nietzschean corpus: *Human, All Too Human*'s fleeting
but fascinating differentiation of the Nazarene from the ever visible, ever
pliant figure of the Nietzschean Socrates. Writes Nietzsche: "*Socrates.*—
If all goes well, the time will come when one will take up the memo-
rabilia of Socrates rather than the Bible as a guide to morals and reason . . ." Championing those "modes of life . . . directed towards joy in
living and in one's own self," this deliberately confrontational aphorism
goes on to boldly declare that: "Socrates excels the founder of Christianity in being able to be serious cheerfully and in possessing that *wisdom
full of roguishness* that constitutes the finest state of the human soul. And
he also possessed the finer intellect" (*HH-WS* 86). Also relevant to our
discussion is *Gay Science* 340's characterization of Socrates as one "who
had lived cheerfully and like a soldier in the sight of everyone." While
Nietzsche's comparing and contrasting of Socrates and Jesus is treated
carefully in chapter 5, here it is important to make note not only of his
championing of the former's *intellect* over the latter's, but his celebration
of the Greek's ability to *live* cheerfully, be "serious *cheerfully*," to lace his
wisdom with a sense of mischief and play. Indeed, from the early asides
on Jesus that pepper *Human, All Too Human* and *Daybreak*, to the comparatively sustained reflections found in *The Antichrist* and notebook entries from the period, Jesus' essential (and unfortunate) seriousness is a

defining leitmotif of Nietzsche's steadily emerging "psychology of the redeemer."

ON HARDNESS AND PITY

> ... learn from me, for I am gentle and humble in heart, and you will find rest for your souls.
>
> Matthew 11:29

Tellingly, *Beyond Good and Evil 269*, where cheerfulness and hardness are championed as prescriptions for the survival of the super-sensitive, characterizes the death of Jesus as "the martyrdom of the most innocent and longing heart." From the early characterization of Jesus as "still immature" (Z 1, 21) to 1888's image of an "innocent from the country" (*WP* 383), "a gentle field-preacher" (*A* 31) moved by "the fear of pain, even of the infinitely small in pain . . . [who] feels every contact too deeply" (*A* 30), if ever there was a figure utterly devoid of "hardness," it is Nietzsche's Jesus.

One would be hard pressed to cite two traits Nietzsche so consistently, so universally, and so passionately lauds as "cheerfulness and hardness." For a philosopher to speak at all, never mind so persistently of laughter, dance, playfulness, "mischievousness in spirit," the need of a "gay science," and so forth, is extraordinary, as is his emphasis on hardness. Indeed, it is Nietzsche's career-long and career-defining celebration of hardness, power, strength, endurance, resoluteness, and so forth, and corresponding and equally blunt derision of pity, commiseration, meekness, weakness, and so forth, that rightly or wrongly underlies much of his infamy among philosophers and laymen alike. While a full treatment of Nietzsche's larger psychophilosophical critique of pity lies well beyond the scope of our present investigation, we may note the following. In the same *Antichrist* aphorism (7) that coldly insists that "Pity on the whole thwarts the law of evolution, which is the law of *selection*. It preserves what is ripe for destruction; it defends life's disinherited and condemned," Nietzsche both alludes to pity's "mortally dangerous character" *in general*, and comes to speak of the fatal danger of pity in the life of one individual in particular.

Pity stands in antithesis to the tonic emotions which enhance the energy of the feeling of life: it has a depressive effect. One *loses force* when one pities. The loss of force which life has already sustained through suffering is increased and multiplied even further by pity. Suffering itself becomes contagious through pity; sometimes it can bring about a collective loss of life and life-energy which stands in absurd relation to the quantum of its cause (the case of the death of the Nazarene).

We note this notion that pity—qua *response* to suffering in general, and with respect to Jesus in particular—can both prove as dangerous as the suffering itself, and stand "in absurd relation to the quantum of its cause," is related to important themes in Nietzsche's scattered early and middle-period reflections on the Nazarene. As discussed, Jesus, Nietzsche's naïve "physician of the soul devoted to that infamous and untutored faith in universal medicine," is characterized, like the philosopher's vision of "woman," by a "boundless, most devote *pity*" that while truly "wonderful" and "fantastic," is *utterly disproportionate* to its cause (tear- and hate-filled first-century Jewry) (*HH-WS* 83; *BGE* 269; *GS* 138, Z 1, 21).

There is an important parallel to be drawn between (1) *Beyond Good and Evil* 269's prescription of "hardness" and "cheerfulness" if the supersensitive "reader of souls" and "clairvoyant" of suffering is not to succumb to the "danger of his suffocating from pity, and (2) *Antichrist* 7's characterization of pity—through which "suffering itself becomes contagious"—as the very antithesis to those "tonic emotions which enhance the energy of the feeling of life." Not coincidentally, in both passages, in both juxtapositions, we find the philosopher's Jesus clearly on the *losing end* of the Nietzschean equation. Devoid of the "tonic emotions" that enhance energy and life, characterized by "untutored" and overzealous love, compassion, and pity, quite literally surrounded and at times verily *engulfed* by the tears, hatred, and thoroughly contagious suffering of first-century Jewry's disinherited[1] yet utterly deficient in those attributes capable of protecting such a sensitive soul from being "suffocated," the Jesus one encounters in the pages of the *Antichrist* is more than a figure in a precarious psychophysiological predicament. His "condition" is one of such acutely "morbid susceptibility" (*A* 29) that in a word, he is "sick." "One has to regret that no Dostoyevsky lived in the neighborhood of this most interesting *decadent*—I mean somebody who would have known how to sense the very stirring charm of such a mixture of the sublime, the sick, and the childish" (*A* 31).

On the one hand, it is only when one has come to an understanding of what Nietzsche means by each component of this three-part characterization of "this most interesting *decadent*"—the sublime, the sick, and the childish—that one can claim to have apprehended either the import of the *Antichrist* itself, or the philosopher's ultimate conception of Jesus of Nazareth. On the other hand, the more one becomes aware of the subtleties underlying Nietzsche's employment of such seemingly coarse terminology, the more one comes to appreciate how functionally inseparable each facet of this extraordinary tripartite portrait really are; of how true *Antichrist* 31's summation of Jesus' condition as "a *mixture* of the sublime, the sick, and the childish" really is. The actual extent to which these theoretically distinct components of the mature Nietzsche's picture of Jesus are thoroughly interwoven and inseparable, emerges as we proceed.

CHILDLIKE IDIOCY

What it is about his final assessment of Jesus that allows Nietzsche to speak of this extraordinary soul as "sublime" is explored in chapter 3's treatment of Nietzsche's return in the *Antichrist* to the all important and ever-present matter of Jesus' suffering, martyrdom, and death. With respect to *Antichrist* 31's reference to Jesus as "childish," we may note the following. Nietzsche's already discussed early and middle-period emphasis on Jesus' lack of experience and maturity also figures prominently in the *Antichrist* and notes from the period. But while the philosopher's emphasis on this facet of the "psychology of the redeemer" continues unabated, what changes, in keeping with the changing trajectory of his philosophical enterprise as whole,[2] is the language he employs to describe this inexperience and immaturity, and the context in which this familiar cluster of characteristics increasingly comes to be situated. By 1888, explicitly clinical, quasi-medical terminology figures ever more prominently in an examination of the figure of Jesus that in places comes to resemble an out-and-out psychophysiological case history. For example, whereas *Zarathustra* (1, 21) suggests that the youthful Jesus "loves immaturely" and had much to learn about life, love, and laughter, *Antichrist* 32 will insist that such a "type" is clearly to be construed as a case of "retarded puberty." "The occurrence of retarded puberty undeveloped in the organism as a consequence of degeneration" observes Nietzsche, "is familiar at any rate to physiologists." Similarly, while the author of 1882's *Gay Science* is content to suggest that Jesus' loving lifestyle and compassionate posture toward others is perhaps indicative of one "who lacked firsthand experience" in the world (138), by 1888 Nietzsche not only tenders a diagnosis of "arrested adolescence,"[3] but comes to devote growing attention to the Nazarene's proposed "instincts" and "physiological realities" (see below).

It is within the context of this shifting, increasingly clinical orientation that Nietzsche's infamous reference to Jesus as an "idiot" must be understood. Immediately after deriding the "psychological frivolity" of those scholars who would cast this hyper-sensitive innocent as a "genius" or "hero," Nietzsche writes: "To speak with the precision of the physiologist a quite different word would rather be in place here: the word idiot" (*A* 29). The claim to be speaking "with the precision of the physiologist" proves crucial to understanding this astonishing remark. For while he was by no means beyond hurling derogatory epithets at Christianity's key players in general and St. Paul in particular,[4] Nietzsche's usage of the word "idiot" in the *Antichrist* seemingly has more to do with the philosopher's efforts to assume a clinical-investigatory posture toward the figure of Jesus. "Idiot" is almost certainly used here after the manner of Nietzsche's beloved Dostoyevsky to denote child-like innocence and extreme naïveté.[5] As we shall see, Nietzsche's interest in what he takes to be Jesus' innocence and immaturity endures until the very end of his career. What separates the *Antichrist* (and notes from the period) from his early and middle-period ruminations on this recurring theme is *how far* Nietzsche is willing to extend these familiar hypotheses, and his increasing tendency to cast them as outright psychophysiological case-histories.

A CASE HISTORY OF SICKNESS

On the one hand then, the mature Nietzsche's introduction of such terminology as "idiot," "sick," and "morbid" to his analysis of the Nazarene's apparent sensitivity and vulnerability represents a new and especially bellicose development in the philosopher's career-long interest in Jesus of Nazareth. It is, after all, one thing to suggest that Jesus was lacking in experience, that his behavior evidenced certain "shortcomings" and an "untutored faith," that his unrestrained love, compassion, pity, are perhaps "immature" and lacking in discretion and nuance (*GS* 138; *HH-WS* 83; *Z* 1, 21), and quite another to maintain that such a posture, such a figure, is to be characterized as somehow "sick" or "morbid." I would suggest however, that the introduction of such striking vocabulary to the matter of the Nietzschean Jesus' vulnerability is more fruitfully viewed as another example of the *Antichrist*'s radicalization of many of the ideas that inform the philosopher's reflections on the Nazarene from *Human, All Too Human* onward. We have already devoted considerable attention to Nietzsche's defining pre-*Antichrist* proposal that the world-historic *combination* of Jesus':

1. untutored, immature and unrestrained love, compassion, and pity
2. notable deficiency of the very self-protective attributes required if such a super-sensitive soul is not to be veritably *overwhelmed by pity*, and
3. unfortunate immersion in the gloomy, suffering, tear- and hatred-filled milieu of first-century Jewry results in an extraordinarily precarious psychophysiological predicament.

The *Antichrist*'s "psychology of the redeemer" is best understood as Nietzsche's unrestrained attempt to explore the possible implications of this predicament; to take a number of long held hypotheses about the Nazarene to often striking psychophysiological conclusions.

Beginning with the simple but defining declaration that "What *I* am concerned with is the psychological type of the redeemer," *Antichrist* 29 endeavors to "translate" the characteristic motif that suffering can prove "contagious"; that pity's "depressive effect" accounts for Jesus' decline in "force" and "life-energy" (*A* 7), to "its ultimate logic":

We recognize a condition of morbid susceptibility of the *sense of touch* which makes it shrink back in horror from every contact, every grasping of a firm object. Translate such a physiological *habitus* into its ultimate logic—as instinctive hatred of *every* reality, as flight into the "ungraspable," into the "inconceivable" . . . as being at home in a world undisturbed by reality of any kind, a merely "inner" world, a "real" world, an "eternal" world. . . . "The kingdom of God is *within you*."

We will explore the fascinating matter of Nietzsche's extraordinary vision of Jesus as one who instinctively comes to distance himself from contact with reality below, in chapter 5's treatment of Jesus' manner of communication. We note at this juncture that Nietzsche—like Kierkegaard, especially interested in Jesus' notable employment of symbol, parable, and metaphor—comes to explore in the *Antichrist* the hypothesis that such an unusual manner of engaging the world is suggestive of one who has defensively endeavored to psychologically extricate himself from an especially painful reality (every contact with which he feels too deeply) via a "flight into the 'ungraspable,' " into the realm of symbol.

Returning to the very *cause* of such a "flight"—the Nazarene's already familiar "condition of morbid susceptibility" (29)—*Antichrist* 30 endeavors to trace the very essence of "the type of the redeemer" back to "two physiological realities."

Instinctive hatred of reality: consequence of an extreme capacity for suffering and irritation which no longer wants to be "touched" at all because it feels every contact too deeply.

Instinctive exclusion of all aversion, all enmity, all feeling for limitation and distancing: consequences of an extreme capacity for suffering and irritation which already feels all resisting, all need for resistance, as an unbearable *displeasure* (that is to say as *harmful*, as *deprecated* by the instinct of self-preservation) and knows blessedness (pleasure) only in no longer resisting anyone or anything, neither the evil nor the evil-doer—love as the sole, as the last possibility of life. . . .

These are the two *physiological realities* upon which, out of which the doctrine of redemption has grown. I call it a sublime further evolution of hedonism on a thoroughly morbid basis. Closest related to it, even with a considerable addition of Greek vitality and nervous energy, is Epicureanism, the redemption doctrine of the pagan world. Epicurus a *typical decadent*: first recognized as such by me.— The fear of pain, even of the infinitely small in pain—*cannot* end otherwise than in a *religion of love* . . .

Stated simply, both Jesus' manner of engaging the world around him, and the "religion of love" he embodies and demonstrates to others, are here traced back to "two *physiological realities*" and depicted as products of an obviously morbid psychophysiological condition.

If Nietzsche's pre-*Antichrist* ruminations are concerned with the risks facing such a vulnerable and child-like soul, the *Antichrist*, in increasingly clinical terminology, endeavors to examine the aftermath of such an extraordinary conflation of factors. As we have seen, *Antichrist* 7 and 29 set the stage for this clinical examination (the former, by situating "the death of the Nazarene" against the backdrop of pity's mortal dangers;[6] the latter, in its career-culminating diagnosis of "a condition of morbid susceptibility"). *Antichrist* 30 and beyond endeavors to lay bare the consequences of such a "morbid" condition. There one meets a figure so drained of "force," so depleted of "life-energy," so wide open and overly exposed (via excess pity) to the contagion "suffering," that he simply can endure no more. In short, he is an open wound, the psychological equivalent of a third-degree burn victim, a *neurasthenic*.

For one so *morbidly susceptible*, who experiences even "the infinitely small in pain" as "an unbearable displeasure," who "no longer wants to be 'touched' at all because it feels every contact too deeply," conflict, opposition, or resistance of any kind can easily prove fatal. If such a soul is to survive, "the instinct of self-preservation" itself verily *demands* an existence, a radical way of life, utterly free of conflict, anger, opposition, and resistance. Viewed from the dispassionate vantage of "the physiologist," such an extraordinary condition "*cannot* end otherwise than in a *religion of love*." What becomes increasingly clear as we proceed is that for Nietzsche, to the extent that the Nazarene's gentle posture of unadulterated love and exemplary embodiment of a way of life wholly devoid of enmity, hatred, and opposition, are viewed religiously, moralistically, theologically, etc., they are misunderstood. The precise and ongoing character of this misunderstanding is examined below in chapter 5. What is imperative to note at this juncture is that the world-historic path embarked upon by the Nietzschean Jesus is one dictated by instinct; "the instinct of self-preservation." "Love," for such a pathologically vulnerable soul, is simply "the sole, . . . the *last* possibility of life" (*A* 30). Like Luther's famous dictum, Nietzsche's Jesus is one who "cannot do otherwise."

INSTINCT AND DECADENCE

Of course, the Nietzschean Jesus' "instinct of self-preservation" can be viewed from at least two different perspectives. On the one hand Nietzsche is adamant that it is this morbidly sensitive soul's "instinct of self-preservation" that lies behind both (1) his defensive psychological distancing from a painful reality (every contact with which he feels too deeply)—what *Antichrist* 29 calls his "flight" to a symbolic "world undisturbed by reality of any kind" (see chapter 5)—and (2) his adopting a psychophysiological posture and way of life—free of enmity, anger, opposition of any kind (see chapter 3)—that helps such a sensitive soul not only to withstand his dealings with others, with the world around him, but achieve a "condition of the heart," an inner condition of "blessedness" the philosopher unhesitatingly characterizes as "sublime" (*A* 30,31).

On the other hand, underlying many of Nietzsche's observations concerning Jesus is the suggestion that his "instincts" in general, and of "self-preservation" in particular, are notably flawed and that *healthier* instincts might have better safeguarded such a soul from finding himself in, from remaining in, such a pathologically precarious psychophysiological predicament (a predicament *so calamitous* that on at least *five occasions* Nietzsche will speak of Jesus as one *opting* to die).[7] We have already made note of the fact that Nietzsche's Jesus fails to qualify, or is not afforded the opportunity to qualify, as a paradigmatically *Nietzschean sufferer*. Compared to Nietzsche's overtly autobiographical model of the potential benefits of pain and suffering, Nietzsche's Jesus fares rather poorly. While he may, at Calvary, have been "sobered-up" with respect to the limitations and dangers of love, he nonetheless fails to meet *Ecce Homo*'s most basic criterion for what "allows us to recognize who has turned out well" (1, 2). Unlike Nietzsche's self-image, his Jesus is *not* "made stronger" by his pain and torment. Unlike one "who has *turned out well*," Nietzsche's Jesus fails to qualify as one who "has a taste *only* for what is good for him." Implied by Zarathustra's somber lament— "As yet he knew only tears and the melancholy of the Hebrews, together with the hatred of the good and the just. . . . Had he only remained in the desert and far from the good and the just! Perhaps he would have learned to live and learned to love the earth—and laughter as well! Believe it my brothers! He died too early."—and made explicit in *Will To Power* 198's blunt insistence that—"The founder of Christianity had to pay for having directed himself to the lowest class of Jewish society and intelligence" (discussed below)—is the sense that the gentle and vulnerable Jesus' own interests would have been better served *away* from the "tears," "melancholy," "hatred," and dangerously *contagious suffering* characterizing "the lowest class of Jewish society." By continuing to immerse himself in such an environment, by continuing to expose himself, to open his especially vulnerable heart to such suffering, such a sensitive and acutely susceptible soul neglected his own interests to such a degree that the resulting impoverishment is pathological.[8]

Interestingly, it is another remark from that section of Nietzsche's literary autobiography concerned with what "allows us to recognize who has *turned out well"* (*EH* 1, 2) that allows us to more fully appreciate the import of *Antichrist* 31's description of Jesus as not only "a mixture of the sublime, the sick, and the childish," but "this most interesting *decadent*." While a thoroughgoing treatment of the Nietzschean notion of decadence is beyond the scope of the present investigation, we may note the following. Generally speaking, *decadence*—a term Nietzsche applies to nations as well as individuals[9]—is employed to denote an absence or decline in strength, life-force, vitality, will to power,[10] and so forth. Contrasting *"decadence"* with so-called *"ascending* life," *Antichrist* 17 for example declares that: "Wherever the will to power declines in any form there is also a physiological regression, a *decadence*." Accordingly, endeavoring to explain how, though "I am a decadent, I am also the *opposite* of a decadent," *Ecce Homo* declares: "I have always instinctively chosen the *right* means against wretched states; while the decadent typically chooses means that are disadvantageous for him" (1,2). This passage then goes on to boast of its author's "energy to choose absolute solitude and leave the life to which I had become accustomed . . . that betrayed an absolute instinctive certainty about *what* was needed above all at that time. I took myself in hand, I made myself healthy again."[11] And a few pages later, at Section 6 of *Why I Am So Wise*, Nietzsche again extols "my own behavior, my *instinctive sureness* in practice. During periods of decadence I forbade myself such feelings as [were] harmful; as soon as my vitality was rich and proud enough again, I forbade myself such feelings as *beneath* me." Again, to his credit, Nietzsche's Jesus, acting according to the "instinct of self-preservation," does come to both (1) *psychologically* distance himself from this painful reality and occupy a symbolic "world undisturbed by reality of any kind" (see chapter 5), and (2) defensively adopts a posture and way of life free of such dangerous sentiments as enmity, anger, and opposition (see chapter 3). To the extent that he instinctively precludes feelings of anger or opposition, he is indeed acting in accord with the instinct of self-preservation. But as Nietzsche repeatedly makes clear, Jesus is not one who "has a taste only for what is good for him." Recall that for one devoid of both hardness and cheerfulness, "pity" ranks as the most harmful, the most self-destructive, the most lethal sentiment of all. Recall *Antichrist* 7's situating of "the death of the Nazarene" against precisely this backdrop: "Pity stands in antithesis to the tonic emotions which enhance the energy of the feeling of life: it has a depressive effect. One loses force when one pities."

Put simply, unlike Nietzsche's image of his own "recovery" from *decadence*, the vitality, the "feeling of life" characterizing the *Antichrist's* "morbidly susceptible" (29) redeemer is simply *too depressed*; he has lost too much "force" and been immersed in too much suffering to be made fully "healthy" by those defensive maneuvers he does take. We may speculate that had his hyper-sensitive soul's instincts led him to remain in, or return to, Zarathustra's "desert," with its prospect of life and laughter; had he, like Nietzsche, instinctively sought "solitude . . . the breath of a free, light, playful air," that he too might have found "recovery" (*EH* 1,8). But he does not.

Section 2 of *Why I Am So Wise* provides a clue as to why, unlike the philosopher's image of himself, the Nietzschean Jesus was ultimately unable to achieve "recovery." For immediately after that passage's insistence: "I took myself in hand, I made myself healthy again" Nietzsche adds: "the condition for this—every physiologist would admit that—is *that one be healthy at bottom*. A typically morbid being cannot become healthy, much less make itself healthy." Nietzsche's Jesus is many things: "The noblest human being" (*HH* 475); "attractive in the highest degree" (*HH* 144); "the incarnate gospel of love" (*GM* 1, 8); a case of "retarded puberty" (*A* 32), a "most interesting *decadent*" and "combination of the sublime, the sick, and the childish" (*A* 31). What he is *not*—and this is made clear from the early scattered remarks in *Human, All Too Human* and *Daybreak* to notebook entries written at the very close of Nietzsche's career—is fundamentally "healthy."

NOTES

1. Even a fleeting familiarity with the Gospel's presentation of Jesus' predicament can easily give rise to a sense of claustrophobia. Jesus is depicted as one forever approached, surrounded and quite literally pursued by a hurting, ever-growing multitude seeking his pity, compassion, and healing. While we turn to the matter of Jesus as "miracle-worker" in chapter 5, here we remind ourselves that the Gospel Jesus, despite his ongoing efforts to find quiet, solitude, and some distance from the ever-present assemblage of suffering humanity, is rarely left alone. Mark's gospel, for example, relates the following scenario (3:7):

Jesus withdrew with his disciples to the lake, and a large crowd from Galilee followed. When they heard all he was doing, many people came to him from Judea, Jerusalem, Idumea, and the regions across the Jordan and around Tyre and Sidon. Because of the crowd he told his disciples to have a small boat ready for him, to keep the people from crowding him. For he had healed many, so that those with diseases were pushing forward to touch him.

2. Nietzsche's increasing tendency in the writings of 1888—*Twilight of the Idols, The Antichrist, Nietzsche Contra Wagner, The Case of Wagner, Ecce Homo*, and scores of notes and outlines for books—to employ terminology such as "physiology," "physiological," and "psychiatry" is difficult to ignore. What first strikes the reader as odd is that Nietzsche finds reason to speak of "physiology" at all in his already unorthodox treatment of such matters as Jesus' "glad tidings," Paul's conversion, and the very character of religious belief itself. By way of example, we note that the topic treated at *Will To Power* 152 is purportedly the "Physiology of Nihilistic Religions." In the Epilogue to his *Case of Wagner*, Nietzsche suggests "the Gospels present us with precisely the same physiological

types that Dostoyevsky's novels describe." And as we shall see, *Antichrist* 30 insists that the Christian "doctrine of redemption" rests entirely upon "two physiological realities."

Upon closer examination however, a second curiosity strikes the reader of such passages. In the majority of cases where Nietzsche claims to be drawing conclusions about Christianity and its chief protagonists on the basis of "physiology," the actual locus of his concern remains what we today would consider matters of *psychology*, or at best, *psychophysiology*. Stated simply, even when Nietzsche appears to be varying his pioneering psychological approach to Christianity and introducing elements of the more physical sciences to the investigation, *psychology* remains his chief concern. For example, the "paralytic phenomena" said to underlie "the Christian cult" in *Will To Power* 152–53's discussion of the "*Physiology of Nihilistic Religions*" turn out to be "phenomena" characterizing "the morally-obsessed," the "anti-pagan," "the politically-weary and the indifferent," and "those who were tired of themselves." While Nietzsche does endeavor to provide some linkage of the religious matters at hand, and matters *vaguely* "physiological"—he characterizes Christianity as "the party of the weak and ill-constituted"—his ultimate focus, both in terms of such specific passages and the totality of his larger ongoing project vis-à-vis Jesus and the birth of Christianity, proves time and time again to be mental states, underlying motivation, and psychological realities.

The marked tendency of Nietzsche, during his final frenetic months of literary activity, to routinely speak of "physiology" alongside or sometimes in place of "psychology" may be regarded as another facet of a broader shift in interest toward the physical sciences in general during his post-Basle career. As Kaufmann (52, 53) recounts, after his retirement from teaching, Nietzsche toyed with the idea of abandoning philosophical writing altogether and devoting himself to the full time study of the physical sciences (purportedly as part of a search for a firmer, more scientific basis for what *Will To Power* 55 calls "the *most scientific* of all possible hypotheses"; the notion of the *eternal recurrence*). Moreover, as Hollingdale points out in his Appendix to the *Twilight of the Idols*, by 1888 Nietzsche had become increasingly wary of the metaphysical connotations often attached to such notions as "psyche," "psychology," and so forth. Nietzsche of course had long been suspicious of the encroachment of metaphysical overlays of meaning. 1878's *Human, All Too Human*, for example, defines metaphysics as "the science . . . which deals with the fundamental errors of mankind—but as if they were fundamental truths" (18). But it is during his final, more "materialistic" period that Nietzsche becomes especially determined to differentiate insights based upon what he considered his more scientific understanding of "psychology" from their illegitimate metaphysical cousins. Accordingly, while the "foremost psychologist of Christianity" continued to trade in what were largely *psychological* hypotheses concerning Christianity and its key players, these insights and observations were now routinely wrapped in increasingly physiological parlance.

3. *Nachlass*, in O'Flaherty, p. 187.

4. Among other epithets, Nietzsche calls Paul a "hate-obsessed false-coiner" and "genius of hatred" (*A* 42); a "frightful impostor" (*A* 45); and a "moral cretin" (*WP* 171).

5. A conclusion bolstered by *Antichrist* 31's subsequent characterization of "the first Christian community" as: "That strange and sick world to which the Gospels introduce us—a world like that of a Russian novel in which refuse of society, neurosis and childlike idiocy seem to make a rendezvous." While Jaspers, in his *Nietzsche and Christianity* (p. 22) concludes that it is "doubtful" that Nietzsche read Dostoyevsky's *The Idiot*, with its Christ-like central protagonist, the most thorough research on the matter of Nietzsche's familiarity with the Russian's ideas was conducted by C.A. Miller and published in a series of articles in *Nietzsche Studien* in 1973 and 1975. Miller concludes that we can be certain Nietzsche read Dostoyevsky's *Notes from the Underground, House of the Dead, Insulted and Injured, The Landlady*, and *The Devils* (from which he took extensive notes)—and have considerable reason to believe that he also read both *Crime and Punishment*, and *The Idiot*.

6. "Pity," observes Nietzsche, "stands in antithesis to the tonic emotions which enhance the energy of the feeling of life: it has a depressive effect. One loses force when one pities . . . Suffering itself becomes contagious through pity."

7. "The two greatest judicial murders in world history are, not to mince words, disguised and well-disguised suicides. In both cases the victim *wanted* to die" (*HH* 2,94). "As yet he knew only tears and the melancholy of the Hebrews, together with the hatred of the good and the just—the Hebrew Jesus: then he was seized by the longing for death" (*Z* 1, 21). "He whose feelings are like this, he who knows about love to this extent—seeks death" (*BGE* 269). "He does not defend his rights, he takes no steps to avert the worst that can happen to him— more, *he provokes it*" (*A* 35). "He forbids his disciples to defend him; he makes it clear that he could get help but *will* not" (*WP* 207).

8. There is a parallel to be drawn between the mature Nietzsche's ongoing differentiation of himself from all things German, and his Jesus from "the Hebrews" (discussed more in chapter 5). Of course, strictly speaking Nietzsche was as German as Jesus was Jewish. But in both cases the philosopher not only sharply distinguishes the individual from his people, but is adamant that for himself as well as his Jesus—both super-sensitive *readers of souls* (*BGE* 269)— association *with* those people is deleterious to their health and well-being. In a fascinating passage lamenting the "expenditure [of] . . . energy wasted on negative ends" Nietzsche offers us a glimpse at the very different "commandments" issued by his more "prudent" instinct of self-preservation.

Not to see many things, not to hear many things, not to permit many things to come close— first imperative of prudence. . . . The usual word for this instinct of self-defense is *taste*. It commands us not only to say No when Yes would be "selfless" but also to say *No as rarely as possible*. To detach oneself, to separate oneself from . . . superfluous impoverishment. . . .

Suppose I stepped out of my house and found, instead of quiet, aristocratic Turin, a small German town: my instinct would have to cast up a barrier to push back everything that would assail it. Or I found a German big city—this built up vice where nothing grows, where everything, good or bad, is imported. Wouldn't this compel me to become a *hedgehog*? (*EH* 2, 8).

9. In addition to both himself and his Jesus, the philosopher finds evidence of *decadence* in such recurring Nietzschean personalities as Socrates, Plato (*Twi* 2, 2), Epicurus (*A* 30), Wagner, and Schopenhauer (*WP* 85). Among nations are

Greece in the time of Socrates, and the "German *Reich*" of Nietzsche's day (*Twi* 2, 2, 9, 39). Considering Nietzsche's emphasis on Jesus' apparent *decadence*, it is significant that ancient Israel is emphatically *not decadent*. While the larger matter of Nietzsche's emphasis on Jewry's position in the Roman world is treated carefully in chapter 5, we note the following with respect to the theme of *decadence*. Far from displaying an absence or decline in vitality (the hallmarks of Nietzschean *decadence*), *Antichrist* 24 insists "the Jewish nation is a nation of the toughest vital energy"; a nation not of *natural decedents*, but rather "compelled to *act* as *decedents*"—to define themselves in terms of *opposition* to Rome's "natural values"—in order to survive in a Roman world. For the Jews, "*decadence* is only a *means*." "The Jews are the most remarkable nation of world history because, faced with the question of being or not being, they preferred, with a perfectly uncanny conviction, being *at any price*."

10. The cardinal Nietzschean theme of the will to power is discussed in chapter 5.

11. The theme of solitude as salvation, of removing himself from contact with others that for Nietzsche was apparently quite debilitating, is writ large throughout his *Ecce Homo*. A remark in Section 8 of *Why I Am So Wise* leaves little doubt that *he too* is "a born, an unavoidable psychologist and reader of souls" (*BGE* 269).

May I still venture to sketch one final trait of my nature that causes me no little difficulties in my contacts with other men? My instinct for cleanliness is characterized by a perfectly uncanny sensitivity so that the proximity or—what am I saying?—the inmost parts, the "entrails" of every soul are physiologically perceived by me—*smelled*. This sensitivity furnishes me with psychological antennae with which I feel and get a hold of every secret: the abundant *hidden* dirt at the bottom of many a character. . . .

As has always been my wont—extreme cleanliness in relation to me is the presupposition of my existence; I perish under unclean conditions. . . . Hence association with people imposes no mean test on my patience: my humanity does not consist in feeling with men how they are, but in enduring that I feel with them. . . .

But I need solitude—which is to say, recovery, return to myself, the breath of a free, light, playful air.

3

The Death of Jesus

Zarathustra and the *Antichrist*

One may fruitfully contrast the essentially negative treatment of Jesus' final moments and death offered in *Thus Spoke Zarathustra* (1883) with Nietzsche's eminently more positive stance toward these very same events in the *Antichrist* and notes of the period five years later.[1] Without going into extraneous detail concerning many of the long-standing themes touched on in Zarathustra's strange discourse on death at *Thus Spoke Zarathustra's Of Voluntary Death*—one or two of which are discussed below—at the very least we may say the following. According to *Of Voluntary Death*, there are good ways to die and bad ways to die. Included among the latter are the death of one "who never lived at the right time";[2] "the grinning death, which comes creeping up like a thief"; the "yellow and shriveled" death of him that has stayed too long; and the "too early" death of the "still immature." Among the former Zarathustra includes such heroic scenarios as dying "in battle," and dying after handing one's torch to one's "heir." But Zarathustra's highest praise and most unabashed recommendation is certainly reserved for two forms of death in particular. What he terms the "voluntary death . . . death that comes to me because *I* wish it," and the so-called "consummating death," said to be "a spur and promise to the living [in which] . . . your spirit and your virtue should still glow like a sunset glow around the earth."

THE *ANTICHRIST* AND THE "REAL" MEANING OF JESUS' DEATH

What is particularly interesting is that while in *Of Voluntary Death* Jesus' death is clearly represented as falling on the unfavorable side of Zarathustra's thought provoking "ways to die" ledger—"he was still immature"; "as yet he knew only tears and the melancholy of the Hebrews"; "he himself would have recanted his teaching had he lived to my age!"—in the pages of the *Antichrist* in general, and sections 33 through 35 in particular, both Jesus' life and his death are celebrated in such a manner that even Nietzsche's self-generated apostle Zarathustra would be hard pressed not to characterize them as essentially "consummating" and "voluntary." Cleverly speaking simultaneously of the model of life (and death) offered by "the redeemer," and behavior bespeaking genuine Christianity,[3] Nietzsche writes:

It is not a "belief" which distinguishes the Christian: the Christian acts, he is distinguished by a *different* mode of acting. Neither by words nor in his heart does he resist the man who does him evil. He makes no distinction between foreigner and native, between Jew and non-Jew . . . He is not angry with anyone, does not disdain anyone . . . The life of the redeemer was nothing else than *this* practice—his death too was nothing else. (*A* 33)

At *Antichrist* 35 Nietzsche offers an even more precise rendering of the ultimate significance of Jesus' dying and death:

This "bringer of glad tidings" died as he lived, as he *taught*—*not* to "redeem mankind" but to demonstrate how one ought to live. What he bequeathed to mankind is his *practice*: his bearing before the judges, before the guards, before the accusers and every kind of calumny and mockery—his bearing on the *Cross*. He does not defend his rights, he takes no steps to avert the worst that can happen to him—more, he *provokes* it . . . And he entreats, he suffers, he loves *with* those, in those who are doing evil to him. His words to the *thief* on the cross next to him contain the whole Evangel. "That was verily a *divine* man, a child of God"—says the thief. "If thou feelest this"—answers the redeemer—*"thou art in Paradise,* thou art a child of God." *Not* to defend oneself, *not* to grow angry, *not* to make responsible . . . But not to resist even the evil man—to *love* him.

True to his intention to "say in ten sentences what everyone else says in a book—what everyone else *does not* say in a book,"[4] these excerpts from the *Antichrist*'s depiction of Jesus' martyrdom are bursting with clues that, when pursued, allow us to significantly sharpen our image of the Nietzschean Jesus. First of all, it bears emphasizing that what Nietzsche is here celebrating and what the thief on the cross next to Jesus is responding to, is not a doctrine or belief, but his behavior, his "practice," his "mode of acting." "What he bequeathed to mankind is his practice: his bearing before the judges, before the guards . . . his bearing on the *Cross* . . . he suffers, he loves *with* those, in those who are doing evil to him."

For Nietzsche, such a wholly nonoppositional, astonishingly loving practice is not only Jesus' embodied bequest to mankind, but is of course the hallmark of what he sometimes terms "genuine Christianity." This extraordinary posture, it bears repeating, is the direct consequence of what he consistently characterizes as the Nazarene's morbidly susceptible condition. "The consequence of such a condition," observes Nietzsche at *Antichrist* 33, "projects itself into a new practice . . . a different mode of acting." Devoid of life's "tonic emotions," dangerously depleted of life-energy through an excess of pity, such a neurasthenic comes to feel "all resisting, all need for resistance, as an unbearable displeasure (that is to say as harmful, as deprecated by the instinct of self-preservation) and knows blessedness (pleasure) only in no longer resisting anyone or anything, neither the evil nor the evil-doer." For such a vulnerable soul, a radical posture of unalloyed love and utter nonresistance is less a matter of religious or moral choice or deliberation, than a psychophysiological imperative; "love as the sole, as the last possibility of life" (30).

The fact that Jesus' extraordinary posture towards others, his radically loving way of living, is seemingly instinct-dictated, no more prevents Nietzsche from declaring it "sublime," than the thief next to Jesus from recognizing something extraordinary. Indeed, it is precisely Jesus' ability to extract a condition of "blessedness" from both a "tear"-, "suffering"-, and "hatred"-filled Hebrew milieu and a precarious psychophysiological condition that lies behind the philosopher's commendation of the Nazarene as explicitly "sublime" (30,31). So it is that *Antichrist* 33' closes by celebrating Jesus' "profound instinct for how one would have to *live* in order to feel oneself 'in Heaven,' to feel oneself 'eternal', while in every other condition one by *no* means feels oneself 'in Heaven': this alone is the psychological reality of 'redemption'.—A new way of living, *not* a new belief." Again, what is here being celebrated, what Nietzsche characterizes as "profound," is "*not* a new belief," but the Nazarene's instinctive awareness of what behavior, what way of life, what posture towards others might allow him to experience a condition of "blessedness"; to feel himself "in Heaven" in spite of overtly non-Heaven-like circumstances.[5] It is this all-important emphasis on Jesus' feeling of "Heaven," on the so-called "psychological reality of redemption," that allows us to better appreciate the import of Nietzsche's accentuation of the dying Jesus' conversation with the thief on the adjacent cross. "His words to the *thief* on the cross next to him contain the whole Evangel. 'That was verily a *divine* man, a child of God'—says the thief. 'If thou feelest this'—answers the redeemer—'*thou art in Paradise*, thou art a child of God' " (*A* 35).

Even more significant than his remarkable suggestion that "His words to the thief on the cross next to him contain the whole Evangel" is the fact that the all-important words here reported are *not* the words of the New Testament Jesus, but of Nietzsche himself! Neither are the words ascribed to the thief to be found anywhere in the Gospels. For the record, Luke, the only gospel writer to mention the conversation with the thief, reports one thief saying to the other (of Jesus); "We are punished justly, for we are getting what our deeds deserve. But this man has done nothing wrong." To Jesus the thief continues: "Jesus, remember me when you come into your kingdom." Finally, Luke's Jesus tells the thief; "I tell you the truth, today you will be with me in paradise" (23:41).

We may note that while he likewise takes the liberty of putting words into the mouth of the dying Socrates, in the case of the Greek, Nietzsche's additions do little to alter the underlying significance of the passage in question.[6] This is certainly not the case with Nietzsche's modification of Luke's gospel. First of all, by having Jesus tell the thief "If thou feelest this . . . *thou art in Paradise*, thou art a child of God," Nietzsche installs—as he does at *Gay Science* 138 with respect to "sinlessness"—the matter of *feeling*, subjective experience, or "psychological reality" at the very center of the proceedings.

Moreover, the philosopher's subtle tinkering with Luke's account of the crucifixion allows the central Nietzschean theme—that the "paradise," or "Kingdom of Heaven" achieved, embodied, and offered by Jesus is to be understood not as a literal state of affairs, but as a *feeling*, a subjective, psychological experience—to be articulated not only by Nietzsche, but the Nazarene himself. Also significant is the fact that Nietzsche's Jesus announces, "thou art in paradise." Even Luke's Jesus, who does on occasion speak of his "Kingdom" in the present tense, tells the thief; "today you will be with me in paradise." The difference between the two—the difference between "you *will*" and "you *are*"—is crucial to our understanding of Nietzsche's extraordinary psychology of the redeemer. One is a claim about a future, presumably after-death state of affairs. The other comments on an immediate, already existing "heavenly" reality: A psychological reality available *now*, available even to those, like the dying thief, in the midst of astonishingly non-heaven-like circumstances.

Though he does not offer access to a literal *other world*, Nietzsche's Jesus is in fact proposing something perhaps even more radical than Luke's. That even a man dying an especially agonizing death can experience, in the midst and in spite of his torment, "paradise," a condition of "blessedness," the "Kingdom of Heaven." Not that *he will* see paradise, not that he is *about to*, but that the "Kingdom of Heaven" is something that can be accessed, can be *experienced, now*! "It is not being promised," writes Nietzsche at *Antichrist* 29, "it is here." Accordingly, despite the fact that he boldly alters Luke's version of Jesus' conversation with the thief, Nietzsche is not wrong when he announces: "His words to the *thief* on the cross next to him contain the whole Evangel." What needs to be emphasized, however, is that the *words* in question, the *good news* in question, indeed the *Jesus* in question, are Nietzsche's.

Returning to the matter of Nietzsche's evolving understanding of Jesus' martyrdom and death we again note the striking manner in which these reflections from the *Antichrist* apparently represent a very different perspective on this pivotal event than that offered in the pages of *Zarathustra*. In marked contrast to Zarathustra's somber portrayal of the all "too early" and accordingly "fatal for many"[7] death of the "still immature" Jesus, the final moments in the life of the *Antichrist*'s Jesus are veritably celebrated. Not insignificantly, two of the more obvious attributes Nietzsche seems to associate with (and clearly respect about)[8] Jesus in the *Antichrist*'s depiction of his martyrdom and death, are:

1. That he makes no effort to *prevent* the horrible fate about to befall him. ("He does not defend his rights, he takes no steps to avert the worst that can happen to him—more, he provokes it . . . Not to defend oneself, not to grow angry, not to make responsible . . . not to resist even the evil man—to love him"). In a notebook entry titled *Christ's example* from this period that parallels this theme, Nietzsche adds: "he does not defend himself; he does more: he 'turns the other cheek' . . . He forbids his disciples to defend him; he makes it clear that he could get help but *will* not" (*WP* 207).

2. That the Nazarene's death is to be viewed as both a consequence and an extension of his life and his message. ("This 'bringer of glad tidings' " insists Nietzsche, "died as he lived, as he taught").

Two questions then present themselves to the researcher. First, whether the depiction of Jesus' martyrdom and death found in the *Antichrist* may not be said to exemplify what Nietzsche's Zarathustra so intently celebrates as the "voluntary" and "consummating" death. And second, if this is indeed the case, what might account for the later Nietzsche's apparent change of posture toward history's most famous death?

VOLUNTARY DEATH

> I commend to you my sort of death, voluntary death that comes to me because *I* wish it.
>
> *Zarathustra* 1, 21

Fortunately, compared to his imprecise and characteristically meta-phor-laden usage of the phrase "consummating death," Zarathustra's understanding of the "voluntary death" is manifest. "I commend to you my sort of death," he intones, "voluntary death that comes to me because I wish it." While Nietzsche's definition of this specific type of death is indeed comparatively clear, even clearer is his ongoing and long-standing conviction that the "bringer of glad tidings" is himself one who *opts* to die. In fact, as pointed out in the previous chapter, one of the more striking theoretical idiosyncrasies that soon confronts those at-tempting to gather together Nietzsche's early and middle-period rumi-nations on Jesus is the regular depiction of Jesus as one *wanting* (*HH* 2,94), *seeking* (*BGE* 269), and indeed *longing for* death (Z 1, 21) (a death which the philosopher goes so far to characterize as a "well disguised suicide") (*HH* 2,94). We may note that while these remarks appear in a number of contexts and over the course of many years (1) most are re-lated to the disappointment and disillusionment inevitably incurred by such a dangerously open, loving, pitying, and *morbidly susceptible* soul's dealings with others, and (2) this image of the Nazarene eventually *choos-ing* to die remains an important theme in Nietzsche's work to the end ("he takes no steps to avert the worst that can happen to him—more, *he provokes it*"—*Antichrist* 35).[9]

Of course the Christian tradition has long held, not that Jesus *wanted* to die, but that his death was *needed*; that he was *destined* to die in order to "redeem mankind" according to God's larger heavenly plan (a notion Nietzsche routinely—and quite justifiably—associates with St. Paul, and not surprisingly, repeatedly and summarily dismisses out of hand).[10] "This 'bringer of glad tidings' died as he lived, as he taught"—insists Nietzsche at *Antichrist* 35—"not to 'redeem mankind' but to demonstrate how one ought to live." "All ground is lacking for the assertion, however often it is made, that he died for the guilt of others" (*A* 27). We shall return to Nietzsche's understanding of this central Christian theme of the atoning death, that Jesus' death is somehow causally linked with mankind's redemption, in chapter 6. In particular, we explore Nie-tzsche's fascinating psychological suggestion that such a doctrine is more likely to be the product of Paul's psyche than Jesus'. What needs to be emphasized at this juncture is that Nietzsche's morbidly susceptible naïf, one explicitly and repeatedly said by the philosopher to have ultimately *chosen* to die, assuredly appears to meet the cardinal criterion offered for Zarathustra's highly recommended "voluntary death . . . death that comes to me because I wish it" (Z 1, 21).

CONSUMMATING DEATH

The man consummating his life dies his death triumphantly. . . .
Zarathustra 1, 21

Immediately prior to Zarathustra's doleful portrayal of the "too early" and "fatal for many" death of the "still immature . . . Hebrew Jesus," *Of Voluntary Death* offers the following poetic insights into the "consummating death":

I shall show you the consummating death, which shall be a spur and a promise to the living. The man consummating his life dies his death triumphantly, surrounded by men filled with hope and making solemn vows. Thus one should learn to die: and there should be no festivals at which such a dying man does not consecrate the oaths of the living! To die thus is the best death. . . .

Later on in the same passage, immediately after suggesting that the youthful Jesus had much to learn about both "laughter" and "love," Zarathustra picks up the theme of the "consummating death" once again:

I wish preachers of *speedy* death would come! They would be the fitting storm and shakers of the trees of life! But I hear preached only slow death and patience with all "earthly things." Ah, do you preach patience with earthly things? It is these earthly things that have too much patience with you, you blasphemers![11]
Truly, too early died that Hebrew whom the preachers of slow death honor: and that he died too early has since been a fatality for many . . . That your death may not be a blasphemy against man and the earth, my friends: that is what I beg from the honey of your soul. In your death, your spirit and your virtue should still glow like a sunset glow around the earth: otherwise yours is a bad death. Thus Spoke Zarathustra: I want to die myself, that you friends may love the earth more for my sake; and I want to become earth again, that I may have peace in her who bore me.

While the purpose of our comparison is not merely a sentence by sentence collating of the "consummating" death celebrated by Zarathustra with the indisputably exemplary death of Jesus depicted at *Antichrist* 33 and 35, we note that there is much about the overall tone and apparent intent of the *Antichrist*'s apparently admiring depiction of Jesus' crucifixion and death that seems to resonate with the type of death Nietzsche's prophet celebrates as *consummating*. For example:
1. Zarathustra extols the "consummating death . . . [as] a spur and a promise to the living." Significantly, the pivot upon which moves not only *Antichrist* 35 but *all* of that work's discussion of Jesus' death is that the sole meaning and purpose one can accurately assign to the death of the redeemer is that of an example or demonstration—obviously to "the living"—of how one might practice one's life. Again, the death of *Antichrist* 35's Jesus explicitly has nothing at all to do with an atoning sacrifice in the name of an en masse after-death "deliverance" (as Nietzsche's Paul will suggest—see chapter 6), and everything to do with an utterly lived, embodied, message *to the living*. The relevance of Jesus' death, as the philosopher reminds us time and time again, is not to the

fate of the dead, but the living: To show the *living* how they might live. *Antichrist* 35's Jesus dies "not to 'redeem mankind' but to demonstrate how *one ought to live* . . . not to grow angry, not to make responsible . . . not to resist even the evil man—to love him." Note too that Zarathustra's celebration of the *consummating* death focuses on how "the man consummating *his life* dies". . . . (my italics). As is the case with *Antichrist* 35, though the nominal topic of *Of Voluntary Death* is death, in both scenarios it is the protagonist's manner of *life* and the betterment of the lives of others that is of singular importance.

2. There is also a parallel to be drawn between Zarathustra's suggestion at *Of Voluntary Death* that "the man consummating his life dies his death triumphantly surrounded by men filled with hope and making solemn vows," and (1) the already touched-upon matter of *Antichrist* 35's deliberate emphasis upon the extraordinary experience of the thief dying on the adjacent cross, combined with (2) that aphorism's obvious admiration for "his bearing before the judges, before the guards . . . his bearing on the Cross." Again, that a dying thief could speak so warmly and reverently of a bleeding, broken, and dying Jesus, says much of the incredible (if not "triumphant") impression left by this extraordinary soul and his singular martyrdom on those around him. Indeed *Will To Power* 162's slightly different (from *Antichrist* 35) and once again modified version of the thief's verdict—"*The thief on the Cross*:—When even the criminal undergoing a painful death declares: 'the way this Jesus suffers and dies, without rebelling, without enmity, graciously, resignedly, is the only right way,' he has affirmed the gospel: and with that he is in Paradise."—with its emphasis on this very point ("When even the criminal undergoing a painful death declares . . ."), suggests Nietzsche was intent on underscoring just how incredible, judging from the thief's confident and tellingly reverent conclusion, was the impression left by the dying Jesus. Both in the solemn remarks he places in the mouth of the thief ("the way this Jesus suffers and dies, without rebelling, without enmity, graciously, resignedly, is the only right way"), and in his own awe at Jesus' truly extraordinary (if not indeed "triumphant") "bearing before the judges, before the guards . . . his bearing on the Cross," we again see Nietzsche laying tremendous stress upon and apparently assigning great significance to the manner in which one handles suffering (even if not afforded opportunity to "profit" from it).

3. And last, while the precise meaning of Zarathustra' poetic suggestion—"In your death, your spirit and your virtue should still glow like a sunset glow around the earth"—is not altogether transparent, a case could certainly be made that the entirely and deliberately life-consistent death celebrated in the pages of the *Antichrist* has much in common with the sentiment *Of Voluntary Death* here touches on. Clearly, if we identify Nietzsche's luminiferous Jesus' "spirit" and "virtue" with his ongoing

emphasis on *practice* rather than belief, on *love* rather than enmity or anger, and *peace* rather than struggle or opposition, then in his death— which *Antichrist* 33 insists "was nothing else than this practice"—his "spirit" unquestionably shines forth as a glowing beacon for all to see and all to learn from. To again quote *Antichrist* 33 and 35 on this extraordinary martyrdom:

Neither by words nor in his heart does he resist the man who does him evil . . . He is not angry with anyone, does not disdain anyone.
This "bringer of glad tidings" died as he lived, as he *taught*—not to "redeem mankind" but to demonstrate how one ought to live. What he bequeathed to mankind is his *practice* . . . he suffers, he loves with those, in those who are doing evil to him . . . *Not* to defend oneself, *not* to grow angry, *not* to make responsible . . . not to resist even the evil man—to *love* him.

Although the poetic language of Zarathustra makes it difficult to determine the precise components, to quantify the exact constituents of his much lauded *consummating death,* there is no doubt that it seems to have much in common with the tone and trajectory of the *Antichrist*'s treatment of Jesus' extraordinary martyrdom. Clearly, if ever there were a death that can be said to have fully consummated the *life* of an individual, it is the martyrdom and death depicted in the pages of the *Antichrist.* As surely as the life of Nietzsche's Jesus was characterized by the utter absence of anger, hatred, enmity, revenge, and opposition, so too was his most extraordinary death. If ever a death may be said to have ultimately been "a spur and a promise *to the living,*" it is the martyrdom and death respectfully depicted in the *Antichrist.* In marked and deliberate contrast to the meaning assigned to Jesus' death by St. Paul (see chapter 6), *Antichrist* 35's Jesus dies "not to 'redeem mankind' but to demonstrate how *one ought to live* . . . not to grow angry, not to make responsible . . . not to resist even the evil man—to love him." And if ever there was a death-scene "surrounded by men filled with hope and making solemn vows" it is the philosopher's unique version of Jesus' martyrdom at Calvary. As Nietzsche says so beautifully: "When even the criminal undergoing a painful death declares: 'the way this Jesus suffers and dies, without rebelling, without enmity, graciously, resignedly, is the only right way,' he has affirmed the gospel." Indeed.

What might account for the apparent difference between *Thus Spoke Zarathustra*'s sombre 1883 depiction of the naïve Jesus' unfortunate and altogether premature death, and the *Antichrist*'s veritable *celebration* of the redeemer's inspiring, voluntary, and clearly "consummating" martyrdom five years later? It is well to remind ourselves that a number of ideas one encounters in the works of the last two or three years of Nietzsche's career often vary significantly from, or are presented in a very different manner than, those found in his early and middle period writing. No one was more aware of this than Nietzsche himself, as anyone familiar with either his *Ecce Homo* or the new prefaces added in the late 1880s to a number of his earlier works can attest. "One is *fruitful*," writes Nietzsche in 1888's *Twilight of the Idols*, "only at the cost of being rich in contradictions" (5, 3). In the case of his apparent change of attitude with respect to how tragic, successful, or "consummating" the death of "the Hebrew Jesus" really was in the five years between *Of Voluntary Death* and the *Antichrist*, two things in particular need to be considered.

1. As we have seen, at the time of *Of Voluntary Death*'s appearance in 1883, the figure of Jesus, while of obvious concern to Nietzsche, had yet to be the subject of any sustained discourse. While not relegated to the margins of his writing, the figure of the early and middle-period Nietzschean Jesus still has to be patched together from the occasional parenthetical reference, brief aphorism, and so forth. By the time of the *Antichrist*, however—and this is especially evident from numerous notebook entries of the period (see *WP* 135–252)—Jesus of Nazareth has become one of several topics of seemingly burning concern to the increasingly isolated, increasingly agitated Nietzsche. At the very least we may say that the *Antichrist*'s more laudatory presentation of Jesus' message, martyrdom, and death emerges from a period where Christianity in general, and its principal protagonists in particular had become one of, if not *the* major concerns of Nietzsche's life. While isolated and half-developed ideas about these matters are still prevalent, they are at last joined by more fully developed and comparatively sustained reflections, such as those found at *Antichrist* 33 and 35.

2. Of course one facet of Christianity of increasing, and increasingly passionate, concern to Nietzsche in 1888 was what he took to be the yawning gulf separating so-called Christianity, and Jesus of Nazareth. As we explore in chapter 6, Nietzsche comes to place increasing blame for this divide on St. Paul, surely the most hated figure on the mature Nietzsche's not inconsiderable list of ideological opponents. By 1888, a great deal of Nietzsche's energy and vitriol has been devoted to how *and why* others have misunderstood or misrepresented Jesus' good news, and at the very centre of this issue lies the all-important matter of the Nazarene's martyrdom and death. The *Antichrist*'s insistence that the *sole* significance of Jesus' extraordinarily peaceful and loving death is as a demonstration of how one might live, is as much an attack on Pauline Christianity as it is a celebration of Jesus' singular way of living (and dying). "This 'bringer of glad tidings' died as he lived, as he taught—not to 'redeem mankind' but to demonstrate how one ought to live." Though Paul—Nietzsche's "dysangelist" (*A* 42)—is not actually mentioned in this pivotal remark from *Antichrist* 35, he is nonetheless as much its topic as the philosopher's bringer of "glad tidings."

NOTES

1. *Of Voluntary Death* appears toward the end of Part One of *Zarathustra*. Nietzsche originally published Parts One and Two as a separate volume in 1883, with Parts Three and Four emerging in 1884 and 1885, respectively.

2. Most of the ingredients Zarathustra seems to assign to the "good" death obviously have to do with effort, will, insight, and unselfishness. But evidently the options available to those simply born at the wrong time are severely limited through no fault of their own. "To be sure, he who never lived at the right time could hardly die at the right time! Better if he were never to be born!—Thus I advise the superfluous."

A related matter to Zarathustra's focus on the negative ramifications of being born (and therefore dying) "at the wrong time" is Nietzsche's obvious and ongoing conception of *himself* as one not belonging to his time. While his *Untimely Mediations* and the *Twilight*'s "Expeditions of an Untimely Man" spring to mind initially, it would be difficult even to *estimate* how many times Nietzsche characterizes himself as "untimely"; as one fundamentally out of sync with the world around him. Whether or not the philosopher would have accordingly precluded himself from falling on the favorable side of Zarathustra's ledger, if he would concede it were "better" if he had never been born, remains an open question.

3. Indeed, since the *Antichrist* is adamant that "In truth, there was only one Christian and he died on the cross" (*A* 39), the behavior of "the redeemer" and "the Christian" are necessarily one and the same for Nietzsche.

4. *Antichrist*, Introduction, p. 11.

5. Interestingly, Nietzsche touches on a very similar theme some sixteen years earlier in section 7 of the *Birth of Tragedy* (1872). There, in his famous treatment of art's ability to *redeem*, Nietzsche speaks of "the *sublime* as the artistic taming of the horrible."

6. In that section of the *Twilight of the Idols* titled *The Problem of Socrates*, Nietzsche twice compels Plato's Socrates to verbalise the unspoken sentiment traditionally ascribed to his life-culminating reference to owing an offering to Asclepius. Since the tradition was to give a cock to Asclepius upon recovering from an illness, Socrates' famous remark in the *Phaedo* has long been construed as suggesting either (1) that life is, or Socrates' life has been, an illness, or (2) that he was entering into life, rather than death.

> Even Socrates said as he died: "To live—that means to be a long time sick:
> I owe a cock to the saviour Asclepius." Even Socrates had had enough of it (1).
> "Socrates is no physician," he said softly to himself: "death alone is a
> physician here . . . Socrates himself has only been a long time sick" (12).

7. Fatal not only for the "still immature" Jesus, but for the "many" (presumably centuries of well meaning Christians misled by the thoroughly self serving meanings assigned to the figure of Jesus by the early Church—see chapter 5). Two implications of Zarathustra's suggestion that the "noble" Jesus' premature death proved "a fatality for many" seem to be (1) that "believers" and nonbelievers alike have been denied the opportunity of hearing the mature teachings of a *grown-up* Jesus. Again, one can imagine few claims more shocking to the

Christian than Nietzsche's deliberately provocative assertion that had he lived to maturity, the "noble" Jesus would surely have disavowed the naïve teachings of what was, after all, a protracted "adolescence." And (2) that this unfortunate and entirely premature death proved to be one of several key factors that came together to facilitate the eventual co-opting of his name and hijacking of his message by "the preachers of slow death."

8. It is entirely worth emphasizing that while many facets of Jesus' way of life and death clearly differ from Nietzsche's *own* ideal—he is not made "stronger" by his suffering (*EH* 1, 2); his boundless pity, insofar as it "defends life's disinherited and condemned" interferes with Nietzsche's championed "law of *selection*" (*A* 7), and so forth—his treatment of Jesus' martyrdom at *Antichrist* 33 and 35 (like *Daybreak* 117's personalized and markedly sympathetic rendering of Jesus' Calvary suffering) as fundamentally and obviously *respectful*.

9. Mark's gospel reports an obviously frustrated Pilate (Roman governor of Judea), upon hearing the many accusations levied at Jesus by the chief priests, asking the Nazarene: "Aren't you going to answer? See how many things they are accusing you of." When "Jesus still made no reply . . . Pilate was amazed" (15:3–5).

10. As we see in chapter 6, Nietzsche lays the blame for the "repulsive" doctrine that Jesus died for the "guilt of others" squarely at the feet of Paul's extraordinary will to power. "The guilt sacrifice, and that in its most repulsive, barbaric form, the sacrifice of the innocent man for the sins of the guilty! What atrocious paganism!" (*A* 41).

11. Zarathustra's contrasting of "the Hebrew Jesus" with those who preach "patience with all earthly things," the "Preachers of slow death" who supposedly honor him, is well worth noting. Written in 1883, its differentiation of Jesus from Paul anticipates a distinction that by the time of the *Antichrist* will become a chasm of immense proportion.

Of course, "patience with all earthly things" is a dominant theme in Paul's letters. That life, *this life*, is something to be endured en route to an immeasurably better other-worldly *after-death* existence (treated in detail in chapter 6). That *this* world is but a provisional dwelling. "Now we know that if the earthly tent we live in is destroyed, we have a building from God, an eternal house in heaven, not built by human hands," writes Paul at II Corinthians 5:1–4, "while we are in this tent, we groan and are burdened, because we do not wish to be unclothed but to be clothed with our heavenly dwelling." "Set you minds on things above, not on earthly things" Paul admonishes the Colossians (3: 1–5), "Put to death, therefore, whatever belongs to your earthly nature." "Their destiny is destruction, their god is their stomach" Paul tells the church at Philippi, "their mind is on earthly things. But our citizenship is in heaven" (3:19–20).

Considering Nietzsche's well-earned reputation not only as iconoclast, but indeed as tenacious *enemy* of Christianity—"the *one* immortal blemish of mankind" (*A* 62)—Zarathustra's cry of "you blasphemers" is fascinating and not a little ironic. It is by no means inconceivable that Nietzsche's charge of blasphemy is meant as a Jesus-like turning of the tables on the Pharisees who accuse the Nazarene of "blasphemy" with surprising regularity in the Gospels. As we see in chapter 6, it is what Paul—quintessential preacher of patience with earthly things, paradigmatic devaluer of *this world*—makes of Jesus' message, that for Nietzsche is the ultimate "blasphemy." "This is the humor of the situation, a tragic humor: Paul reerected on a grand scale precisely that which Christ had annulled through his way of living" (*WP* 167).

4

The Road to Damascus

As we have seen, Nietzsche's early, middle, and late period reflections on the figure of Jesus of Nazareth run the gamut from glowing praise and heartfelt respect to deliberately irreverent remarks to quasi-clinical psychophysiological hypotheses. While his controversial diagnosis of Jesus is certainly too multifaceted to be rendered in a single phrase, the *Antichrist*'s powerful characterization of Jesus as "a combination of the sublime, the sick, and the childish" (31) is certainly representative of the balance, the scope, and the tenor of Nietzsche's psychobiography of the Nazarene as a whole. Nietzsche's assessment, or diagnosis, of the psyche of St. Paul is another matter altogether. As will become increasingly apparent, if the diagnostic posture from which Nietzsche's psychological assessment of Jesus emerges may be characterized as sympathetic ambivalence, his attitude toward Paul appears to be one of openly hostile astonishment mixed with the occasional indication of a begrudging respect. Among other colorful epithets, Nietzsche characterizes St. Paul as a "hate-obsessed false-coiner"; a "frightful impostor"; a "moral cretin"; and "the greatest of apostles of revenge" (*A* 42,45; *WP* 171; *A* 45). He is also repeatedly characterized by Nietzsche as a "genius"—albeit a "genius of hatred" (*A* 42)—of truly world historic proportions (*A* 58; *WP* 175).

Though Nietzsche devotes a remarkable amount of attention to the character and importance of Paul (a figure he considers more important to the development of Christianity than even Jesus), compared to the moderate amount of attention his psychohistorical reflections on the

Nazarene has received, his fascinating hypotheses concerning Paul's mind, motivation, and significance have largely been ignored. This is unfortunate, for nowhere can one observe Nietzsche's abiding vision of religion as "systematised case-history of sickness employing religious-moralistic nomenclature" (*WP* 152) in action, than in his career-spanning ruminations on the figure of Paul. In the interest of clarity and in accord with the changing focus within Nietzsche's own writing, Nietzsche's psychohistory of St. Paul is here divided into two broad sections. This chapter is concerned with Nietzsche's extraordinary account of what "really" happened in the case of Paul's celebrated "vision" of Jesus and conversion to Christianity on the famous road to Damascus. Though he will return to this topic in passing in aphorism 42 of the *Antichrist*, written just months before his collapse, Nietzsche's most detailed and systematic treatment of Paul's conversion is to be found in 1881's *Daybreak*. Chapter 6, on the other hand, treats Nietzsche's psychohistorical rendering of the activities of the *later* Paul, the celebrated and powerful proselytising Apostle to the Gentiles. It is this Paul, "this dysangelist" (*A* 42) to whom Nietzsche devotes a remarkable amount of attention both in the *Antichrist* and notes from the time of its composition, that is the object of what is surely the most passionate attack of Nietzsche's by no means peaceful philosophical career.

DAYBREAK 68

As is the case with his thoughts on Jesus, Nietzsche's reflections on Paul are scattered throughout his writings. But the chief locus of his thoughts on the *pre-Damascus* Paul and the famous Damascus-road experience itself is certainly *Daybreak*'s lengthy aphorism 68, tellingly titled "The First Christian";[1] a bold, sustained, and in places ingenious series of hypotheses concerning the mind and motivation of Paul, both in his pre-Christian role as Saul, aggressive anti-Christian Pharisee,[2] and in his new-found status as Paul the Christian. Nietzsche's concern in this unusual passage is precisely what psychological determinants might conceivably lie *behind* (for example) Paul's fervid pre-Damascus persecution of the earliest believers and troublesome relationship with, and complex attitude toward, the Law. Announcing what will be the leitmotif of a decade-long engagement with this world historic figure, *Daybreak* 68 characterizes Paul as "one of the most ambitious and importunate souls," and goes on to insist:

But without this remarkable history, without the storms and confusions of such a mind, of such a soul, there would be no Christianity; we would hardly have heard of a little Jewish sect whose master died on the cross. To be sure: if this history had been understood at the right time, if the writing of Paul had been read, not as the revelations of the "Holy Spirit", but with a free and honest exercise of one's own spirit and without thinking all the time of our own personal needs—*really read*, that is to say (but for fifteen hundred years there were no such readers)—Christianity would long since have ceased to exist: for these pages of the Jewish Pascal expose the origin of Christianity as thoroughly as the pages of the French Pascal expose its destiny and that by which it will perish. That the ship of Christianity threw overboard a good part of the Jewish ballast, that it went and was able to go among the heathen—that is a consequence of the history of this one man, of a very tormented, very pitiable, very unpleasant man who also found himself unpleasant.

For Nietzsche the all-important key that ultimately unlocks the Pauline psyche (and accordingly, our understanding of the surprising direction taken so early on by the "ship of Christianity") is the Law, more specifically, Paul's troubled relationship with the Law. On the topic of that crucial dynamic, Nietzsche suggests that:

In his youth he had himself wanted to satisfy it, voracious for this highest distinction the Jews were able to conceive . . . Paul had become at once the fanatical defender and chaperone of this God and his law, and was constantly combating and on the march for transgressors and doubters, harsh and malicious toward them and with the extremest inclination for punishment. And then he discovered in himself that he himself—fiery, sensual, melancholy, malevolent in hatred as he was—*could* not fulfill the law . . . Many things lay on his conscience—he hints at enmity, murder, sorcery, idolatry, uncleanliness, drunkenness and pleasure in debauch—and however much he tried to relieve his conscience, and even more his lust for domination, through the extremest fanaticism in revering and defending the law, there were moments when he said to himself: "It is all in vain! The torture of the unfulfilled law cannot be overcome." Luther may have felt a similar thing when he wanted in his monastery to become the perfect man of the spiritual ideal: and similarly to Luther, who one day began to hate the spiritual ideal and the Pope and the saints and the whole clergy with a hatred the more deadly the less he dared to admit it to himself—a similar thing happened to Paul.

When his inner turmoil and frustration toward the demands of the law could no longer be assuaged through the targeting and persecution of "transgressors and doubters," Paul endeavors, perhaps unconsciously, to realize a more permanent solution; one that would have lasting and far-reaching ramifications for Christianity. *Daybreak* 68 continues:

at last the liberating idea came to him, together with a vision, as was bound to happen in the case of this epileptic: to him, the zealot of the law who was inwardly tired to death of it, there appeared on a lonely road Christ with the light of God shining in his countenance, and Paul heard the words; "Why persecutest thou *me*?" What essentially happened then is rather this: his mind suddenly became clear: "it is *unreasonable*", he says to himself, "to persecute precisely this Christ! For here is a way out, here is perfect revenge, here and nowhere else do I have and hold the *destroyer of the law!*" Sick with the most tormented pride, at a stroke he feels himself recovered, the moral despair is as blown away, destroyed—that is to say, *fulfilled*, there on the Cross! . . . The tremendous consequences of this notion, this solution of the riddle, whirl before his eyes, all at once he is the happiest of men—the destiny of the Jews—no, of all mankind seems to be tied to this notion, to this second of his sudden enlightenment, he possesses the idea of ideas, the key of keys, the light of lights; henceforth history revolves around him . . . This is the *first Christian*, the inventor of Christianness! Before him there were only a few Jewish sectarians.

Typically, this aphorism is so densely packed with meaning, that were one to allow oneself to be distracted by Nietzsche's deliberately confrontational language (referring to the Paul as "this epileptic" for example) one could easily lose sight of the challenging and original insights and hypotheses that reveal themselves upon unpacking. It is likely that few readers of Nietzsche would be surprised by his assertion that the best approach to Paul's writing is "not as the revelations of the 'Holy Spirit'." But what is the meaning and significance of Nietzsche's insistence that such an exposition of Christianity's origins depends upon Paul's letters being *"really read"* (and that "for fifteen hundred years there were no such readers")? Nietzsche himself provides the first clue, when he invites us to read Paul *honestly* and without thinking of our *"own* personal needs" (i.e., what interpretation of the Apostle, his authority, inspiration, etc., makes *our* lives easiest). To read Paul, to *"really read"* Paul, suggests the general thrust not only of *Daybreak* 68 but all Nietzsche's far flung musings on the matter, means to do so with an eye to *his* needs. To read Paul then, as Nietzsche reads him—with the eye of a psychologist. To have the courage to ask instead; what needs of *Paul* might conceivably be being met both by his behavior (pre- and post-Damascus) and his teaching? To again quote *Beyond Good and Evil* 187's deceptively simple question; "What does such an assertion say of the man who asserts it?" Note that in asking this type of question about the mind and motivation of Paul, Nietzsche, the self-professed "foremost psychologist of Christianity"[3] is:

1. Adopting the very same psychohistorical stance from which he approaches virtually all the pivotal figures of history that interest him (N.B. his "Case of Wagner," the "Problem of Socrates," the "Psychology of the Redeemer," etc.). Nietzsche's famous assertion that the teachings of philosophers need to be understood as, and ultimately amount to unconscious autobiographies,[4] clearly has application wider than philosophy per se.

2. Employing a psychohistorical strategy very similar to that utilized by Freud, who like Nietzsche, insists that "there is no one so great that it would be a

disgrace for him to be subject to the laws that govern normal and pathological activity with equal severity" (Gay, p. 269).[5] Indeed, the underlying starting point of so many of Freud's case histories and psychobiographies is the very same question Nietzsche repeatedly asks and boldly endeavors to answer. What need (either conscious or unconscious) might be being met by this individual's pattern of behavior, course of action, and thought processes?

According to Nietzsche, much of the troubled Pauline psyche (and by extension, because of Paul's extraordinary role in the development of post-Jesus Christianity, so much of Christianity itself) seems to revolve around the ever-present Law. In describing the early Paul as simultaneously (1) "voracious for this highest distinction the Jews were able to conceive," yet (2) unable to live up to the rigorous demands built in to such a distinction ("the perfect man of the spiritual ideal"), *Daybreak* 68 discreetly sets the stage for what Nietzsche takes to be the first of a two phase, uniformly defensive, relationship toward the Law on the part of Paul.

PHASE ONE—PAUL'S OBSESSION

In my obsession against them, I even went to foreign cities to persecute them.

Acts 26:9

At first seemingly not yet consciously aware of his inability to live up to this "highest distinction," the young Pharisee Paul, or Saul,[6] Nietzsche observes with great interest, initially plays the part of the "fanatical defender and chaperone of this God and his law . . . on the march for transgressors and doubters, harsh and malicious toward them and with the extremest inclination for punishment." We note that here, Nietzsche's characterization is thoroughly in accord with New Testament evidence; specifically with chapters 8 and 9 of the book of Acts, where the pre-Damascus Paul is said to have given his "approval" to the stoning of Stephen, and that "going from house to house, he dragged off men and women and put them in prison."

Of even greater interest is the extent to which Nietzsche's psychohistorical focus on the pre-Damascus Paul's fanatical, "harsh and malicious" persecutions, agrees with the Apostle's *own* rendering of his passionate pre-Christian excesses. Not only does Paul retrospectively describe his youthful posture toward the Jewish tradition as "extremely zealous" and speak of how "intensely," "violently," or "savagely"[7] "I persecuted the church of God" (Gal. 1:13–14), but in the presentation of his case before King Herod Agrippa II, the now-Christian Paul revealingly characterizes his early commitment to persecuting the first Christians as his "obsession" (Acts 26:9). There, in an apparently psychologically informed account of his own zealotry, Paul recounts the following:

I too was convinced that I ought to oppose the name of Jesus of Nazareth. And that is just what I did in Jerusalem. On the authority of the chief priests I put many of the saints in prison, and when they were put to death, I cast my vote against them. Many a time I went from one synagogue to another to have them punished, and I tried to force them to blaspheme. *In my obsession against them, I even went to foreign cities to persecute them* (my italics).

That Paul himself speaks, not of his *interest* in transgressors, nor his *concern* for doubters, but of "my *obsession* against them," is interesting in the extreme, and suggests that he too may have come to see something out of the ordinary at play in his initial posture toward these early "saints." Nietzsche certainly does, and like any good psychologist, quite justifiably endeavors to uncover what hidden determinants might conceivably lie behind this confessed "obsession."

To better appreciate just what the youthful Paul's fanatical pre-Damascus persecutions of the early believers, (exhibiting as they do "the extremest inclination for punishment"), suggest to Nietzsche about his psychological makeup, we again turn to the pages of *Thus Spoke Zarathustra*. In the section of *Zarathustra* entitled *"Of the Tarantulas"*—a sustained and poetic critique of (among other things) the psychology of Christian morality and the possible underlying motivation of priests—Zarathustra cautions:

Thus, however, I advise you, my friends: Mistrust all in whom the urge to punish is strong! They are people of a bad breed and a bad descent; the executioner and the bloodhound peer from out of their faces. Mistrust all those who talk much about their justice! Truly, it is not only honey that their souls lack. And when they call themselves "the good and the just", do not forget that nothing is lacking to make them into Pharisees except—power!

Of most obvious interest is the reappearance of the phrase: "the good and the just." Recall Zarathustra's earlier depiction of Jesus' unfortunate predicament (Z 1, 21): "As yet he knew only tears and the melancholy of the Hebrews, together with the hatred of the good and the just—the Hebrew Jesus: then he was seized by the longing for death. Had he only remained in the desert and far from the good and the just! Perhaps he would have learned to live and learned to love the earth—and laughter as well!" Significantly, the very class of person, the so-called "good and the just," that Zarathustra earlier contrasts with the gentle Jesus—who *hated* Jesus, who Zarathustra laments the naïve Nazarene hadn't stayed *away from*—also figure prominently in *"Of the Tarantulas."* Tellingly, they are here associated not only with a strong "urge to punish," with talking

too much about *"their* justice," but specifically with Pharisaic Judaism
and the quest for power (crucial themes, as we shall see, to Nietzsche's
unfolding psychohistory of Paul of Tarsus). Indeed, the resonance of Zarathustra's potent warning regarding the psychophysiological state of
those demonstrating a powerful predilection for punishment is extraordinarily far-reaching. It extends backward, to the psychological portrait
of Paul at *Daybreak* 68 (published in 1881, two years prior to the first
appearance of *Zarathustra* in 1883), and forward, both to Nietzsche's further reflections on the psychology of Paul at the end of the decade in
the *Antichrist* and numerous notes from the period, and to Freud's new
science of psychoanalysis in general, and his "discovery" of the celebrated defence mechanism of *projection* in 1895 in particular.

Certainly the two most salient factors said by Zarathustra to lie behind
the general proclivity to inflict harsh punishment—*power* and *lack* respectively—figure prominently in Nietzsche's remarkable psychohistory
of the unhappy Pharisee Paul, both pre- *and* post-Damascus. Indeed, it
is precisely the *convergence* of these very factors in the Pauline psyche
that allows Nietzsche to account for the Apostle's dramatic, epoch-
defining metamorphosis from ardent Jewish attacker of the first believers' failure to observe the Law, to ardent defender of these same believers
and tireless critic of both Judaism and its precious Law (in the name of
Christ)! *Daybreak* 68 makes several interesting points about the mind of
Nietzsche's pre-Damascus Paul, each related to the twin issues of *power*,
and a sense of *lack* in one's soul. First of all, the fanatical punishment he
inflicts upon the Law-transgressing first believers is related to, but *precedes*, his realization that he himself was incapable of fulfilling God's
Law. ("On the march for transgressors and doubters, harsh and malicious toward them and with the extremest inclination for punishment.
And then he discovered that he himself . . . could not fulfil the law")[my
italics].

Second, his fanatical persecution of the early Christians ultimately
stemmed from (1) something amiss in Paul's own conscience, and (2) his
own thirst for power. ("However much he tried to relieve his conscience,
and even more his lust for domination, through the extremest fanaticism
in revering and defending the law.")

And third, Nietzsche intimates that the very issues Paul *the Apostle*
would later rail so passionately against in his thoroughly dogmatic letters—improper sexual behavior, improper worship, the pleasures of
drink, and so forth—were not coincidentally, the same issues "torment-
ing" the young, troubled mind of the pre-Damascus Pharisee ("Many
things lay on his conscience—he hints at enmity, murder, sorcery, idolatry, uncleanliness, drunkenness, and pleasure in debauch"). Nietzsche
characteristically fails to make explicit the *precise* psychic connection between the passionate apostolic concerns of the mature crusading prose-

lytizer on the one hand, and the "very pitiable" state of young Paul's soul (tormented by enmity, uncleanliness, and matters of sexuality). Similarly, the matter of just how it is he is able to work backward from Paul's fanatical Pharisaic persecution of "transgressors and doubters" to his underlying, torturing doubt concerning his own ability to fulfil the Law, is in need of clarification. But such retroactive psychological puzzle solving, it seems apparent, is exactly what Nietzsche is engaged in at *Daybreak* 68.

PROJECTION

> Whoever is dissatisfied with himself is continually ready for revenge, and we others will be his victims, if only by having to endure his ugly sight.
>
>   *Beyond Good and Evil* 290

The more precise terminology developed by Freud and psychoanalysis to characterize the less obvious workings of the human mind is of considerable use to our effort to more fully comprehend Nietzsche's psychologizing in general, and his psychohistory of St. Paul in particular. This is certainly true of Nietzsche's protopsychoanalytical hypotheses concerning the psychic determinants of the pre-Damascus Paul's "extreme" and "malicious" treatment of the first Christians, and is especially the case with Nietzsche's "intuitive"[8] understanding (at *Daybreak* 68) that (1) the early Paul's fanatical struggle against "transgressors and doubters" was psychologically linked to his own (as yet non-conscious) doubt concerning his ability to fulfill the Law, and (2) that these persecutions are to be seen, not so much as the heartfelt, dutiful work of an offended Pharisee, but as the attempts "of a very tormented, very pitiable, very unpleasant man . . . to relieve his conscience, and even more, his lust for domination."

Nietzsche does not use the German term *Projektion* in his ingenious account of how this remarkable casting of Paul's own personal doubts and transgressions onto people around him constitutes a bid to relieve his own troubled soul. Yet one familiar with both his well-documented appreciation of the existence of not only the unconscious mind, but defensive, mental maneuvers,[9] and the notion of "projection" as employed by Freud and psychoanalysis, soon comes the conclusion that *projection* seems to be the very defense mechanism at work in the troubled mind of Nietzsche's pre-Damascus Paul.

We note that though Freud first formalized his influential conception of "projection" as a defense mechanism in the 1890s, the underlying sentiment had certainly been understood for centuries, and is plainly at play both in Shakespeare's portrayal of the central character in *Richard III*, and Ludwig Feuerbach's famous characterization of God as but an out-ward reflection of man's own inner nature in 1841. As the name suggests, *projection*, according to psychoanalysis, has to do with the "projection" of feelings one does not want oneself, onto another person, or occasion-ally some *thing* outside of the self. Projection involves the seeing in an-other what one refuses to see in oneself, and is often characterized in terms of a psychic expulsion, purging oneself of an unwanted idea, trait, or feeling by casting it upon someone else. In terms not unfamiliar from Nietzsche's treatment of both Paul's self image and his early fanatical persecution of transgressors of the Law, Freud ("Remarks on the Neuro-Psychosis of Defense," p. 184) casts projection as follows: "self-reproach is repressed in a manner which may be described as *projection*. It is re-pressed by erecting the defensive symptom of *distrust of other people*. In this way the subject withdraws his acknowledgment of the self-reproach." Note Freud's deliberate delineation of (1) self-reproach, (2) the defensive suspicion of others, and (3) the *connection* between this distrust of others and the failure to acknowledge this self reproach, as the three chief characteristics of the key psychoanalytic concept of pro-jection. Note too that each component of the Freudian mechanism of projection finds resonance with *Daybreak* 68's protopsychoanalytical anal-ysis of Paul and his troubled relationship to the Law. ([1a] "a very un-pleasant man who also found himself unpleasant"; [2a] "fanatical defender . . . on the march for transgressors and doubters"; [3a] "he tried to relieve his conscience, and even more his lust for domination, through the extremest fanaticism in revering and defending the law.")

EPILEPSY PART 1: FLIGHT FROM ONESELF

It is this protopsychoanalytic emphasis on the apparently related mat-ters of Paul's self-reproach, and his self-confessed "obsession" with, and fanatical persecution of so-called "transgressors" that allows us to better understand Nietzsche's seemingly flippant dismissal of Paul as "this ep-ileptic" at *Daybreak* 68. As is the case with his deliberately confrontational characterizations of Jesus as an "idiot" (*A* 29) and Socrates a "monstros-ity" (*BT* 13), Nietzsche's apparently flippant epithets very often carry with them fairly well defined clusters of ideas. While it is noteworthy that a number of New Testament scholars have suggested that the his-torical Paul of Tarsus was in fact epileptic,[10] to better understand the significance of this disease to Nietzsche, we look to *Daybreak*'s other ref-erences to the disease, at aphorism 549. There, Nietzsche queries whether epilepsy might indeed be the cause of the "intellectual spasms" of a fascinating handful of especially energetic and active epoch-defining world historic individuals (individuals, we may note, generally afforded some of Nietzsche's highest praise). But neither praise nor condemnation is the point here. Insisting that "four of the most active men of all time were epileptics (namely Alexander, Caesar, Mohammed, and Napoleon)," *Daybreak* 549 endeavors, "in the light of the experience of psychiatry," to relate the extraordinary "activity" of the members of this curious assemblage to not just the disease in question, but to the apparently allied matter of their profoundly negative feelings toward themselves. As *Daybreak* 68 deliberately paints Paul as one who "found himself unpleasant," so *Daybreak* 549 characterizes these four extraordinary souls as all "gloomily inclined towards themselves."

In this remarkable aphorism, tellingly titled "Flight from Oneself," Nietzsche suggests that such individuals, thoroughly dissatisfied with themselves, and in an (unconscious) bid to keep their unhappy consciousness from turning its attention upon itself, defensively endeavors to "dissolve into something *'outside.'* " This strange, avoidance-motivated shifting of energy and focus from the self to the world "out there" may take a variety of forms, but here Nietzsche is interested in one in particular. "[B]ecause *action* draws us away from ourself even more than do thoughts" (*D* 549), Nietzsche continues, it is precisely yet paradoxically those unhappy souls *most* dissatisfied with themselves and hence most reluctant to engage in reflection, that manage to effect extraordinary changes upon the world around them. Too psychologically weak to confront, let alone *master* themselves (an exceedingly Nietzschean virtue), gloomily inclined "epileptics" such as the Apostle Paul or Napoleon *defensively* manage to *master* much of the world around them via extraordinary activity. In other (more explicitly psychoanalytical) words, the repression of negative feelings about the self is bolstered through compulsive activity. While the precise connection between this compulsive action-inducing self-loathing and the disease of epilepsy is characteristically alluded to rather than formalized, Nietzsche is very clear as to its potential consequences. Asks Nietzsche: "could all impulse to action perhaps be at bottom flight from oneself?" (*D* 549).

Clearly, Nietzsche's unusual yet regular use of the label "epileptic" in general[11] and in his examination of the Pauline psyche in particular (*D* 68; *WP* 171), together with his calculated characterization of the Apostle as one who "found himself unpleasant" (*D* 68), not only aligns him with an unusual assemblage of other souls "gloomily inclined toward themselves" (*D* 549), but carries with it quite specific implications concerning the truly extraordinary, and not necessarily conscious, lengths such soul-sick individuals are wont to go in the name of avoiding the displeasure associated with reflection. The first half of *Daybreak* 68 then, is about one such maneuver. Nietzsche's specific concern here is how it is that the distinct vicissitudes of St. Paul's psyche—in particular his (apparently initially unconscious) doubts concerning his ability to fulfil the Law—are projected onto those around him. Such unconscious scapegoating[12] enables Paul to *simultaneously* avoid the painful acknowledgement of self-reproach, to placate his lust for dominance, and in so doing partially relieve his troubled conscience. The second half of *Daybreak* 68, on the other hand, is concerned with what Nietzsche sees as Paul's equally defensive but infinitely more significant *second* psychological maneuver to avoid truly confronting himself, his apparent limitations and shortcomings vis-à-vis the Law: his conversion to Christianity.

PHASE TWO: PAUL'S CONVERSION

What essentially happened then is rather this . . .

Daybreak 68

Acts 9 describes Paul's famous Damascus-road experience as follows:

Meanwhile, Saul was still breathing out murderous threats against the Lord's disciples. He went to the high priest and asked him for letters to the synagogues at Damascus, so that if he found any there who belonged to the Way, whether men or women, he might take them as prisoners to Jerusalem. As he neared Damascus on his journey, suddenly a light from heaven flashed around him. He fell to the ground and heard a voice say to him, "Saul, Saul, why do you persecute me?"

"Who are you, Lord?" Saul asked.

"I am Jesus, whom you are persecuting," he replied. "Now get up and go into the city, and you will be told what you must do."

The men traveling with Saul stood there speechless; they heard the sound but did not see anyone. Saul got up from the ground, but when he opened his eyes he could see nothing. So they led him by the hand to Damascus. For three days he was blind, and did not eat or drink anything.

Then Ananias went to the house and entered it. Placing his hands on Saul, he said, "Brother Saul, the Lord-Jesus, who appeared to you on the road as you were coming here—has sent me so that you may see again and be filled with the Holy Spirit." Immediately, something like scales fell from Saul's eyes, and he could see again. He got up and was baptized, and after taking some food, he regained his strength . . . Saul spent several days with the disciples in Damascus. At once he began to preach in the synagogues that Jesus is the Son of God. All those who heard him were astonished and asked, "Isn't he the man who raised havoc in Jerusalem among those who call on his name? And hasn't he come here to take them as prisoners to the chief priests?" Yet Saul grew more and more powerful and baffled the Jews living in Damascus by proving that Jesus is the Christ.

Nietzsche, while thoroughly conversant in the New Testament account of Paul's conversion, is true to his belief that if we are to "expose the origin of Christianity" (*D* 68) we must look to *Paul's* needs rather than our own, and accordingly chooses a more psychological reading of the

famous proceedings than the one offered by the author of Acts. Writes
Nietzsche:

The law was the cross to which he felt nailed: how he hated it! How he had to
drag it along! How he sought about for a means of destroying it—and no longer
to fulfill it! And at last the liberating idea came to him, together with a vision,
as was bound to happen in the case of this epileptic: to him, the zealot of the
law who was inwardly tired to death of it, there appeared on a lonely road Christ
with the light of God shining in his countenance, and Paul heard the words;
"Why persecutest thou *me*?" What essentially happened then is rather this: his
mind suddenly became clear: "it is *unreasonable*", he says to himself, "to persecute
precisely this Christ! For here is a way out, here is perfect revenge, here and
nowhere else do I have and hold the *destroyer of the law!*" Sick with the most
tormented pride, at a stroke he feels himself recovered, the moral despair is as
blown away, destroyed—that is to say, *fulfilled*, there on the Cross! Hitherto that
shameful *death* had counted with him as the principal argument against the
"Messiahdom" of which the followers of the new teaching spoke: but what if it
were *necessary* for the *abolition* of the law!—The tremendous consequences of this
notion, this solution of the riddle, whirl before his eyes, all at once he is the
happiest of men—the destiny of the Jews—no, of all mankind seems to be tied
to this notion, to this second of his sudden enlightenment, he possesses the idea
of ideas, the key of keys, the light of lights; henceforth history revolves around
him! For from now on he is the teacher of the *destruction of the law*! . . . Even if it
is still possible to sin, it is no longer possible to sin against the law: "I am outside
the law."

   Doubtless the first thing to strike many readers about this extraordinary passage is its audacity. On the basis of only his own distinctive
psychological investigation into Christianity, its origins, teachings, principal protagonists, and so forth, Nietzsche takes one of that tradition's
most familiar and cherished stories and after nonchalantly remarking—
"What essentially happened then is rather this"—proceeds to advance a
cynical, acutely accusatory alternate reading of the proceedings (a reading clearly with an eye to what dark psychopolitical realities may conceivably lie behind this famous history-altering "conversion"). But as
was the case in our treatment of his unique rendering of the obsessive
persecutions of the pre-Damascus Paul, I am convinced both that Nietzsche's unflattering psychohistorical portrayal of the Damascus experience itself, and more important, his thoughts on its truly fantastic,
far-reaching, and ongoing reverberations throughout all of Christendom,
are very much worth our attention.

   The above excerpt at once demonstrates the practical application of (1)
Nietzsche's tendency to conceive of the text as a "confession on the part
of its author and a kind of involuntary and unconscious memoir" (*BGE*
6), (2) his extraordinary understanding of religion as "systematised case-

histor[ies] of sickness employing religious-moralistic nomenclature" (*WP* 152), and (3) precisely what he means by his fascinating distinction between merely reading Paul, and *really* reading Paul (*D* 68). To *really* read Paul, we see once again, necessitates approaching these hallowed texts with the probing eye of the psychologist, with an eye to what these texts suggest about the *needs* of Paul. To *really* read Paul means to ask with Nietzsche, of Paul's account of his conversion experience: "What does such an assertion say of the man who asserts it?" (*BGE* 187).[13]

As we have seen with respect to his emphasis on the supposed subjective experience of Jesus and Socrates, it is imperative we note Nietzsche's remarkable focus on the supposed subjective experience of Paul. *Daybreak* 68 speaks of Paul being *inwardly* tired of the Law, of his mind suddenly becoming "clear," of Paul saying to himself[14] that "the Law is unreasonable," of being sick with tormented pride, and ultimately, that "at a stroke he feels himself recovered." Indeed, only the self-professed "foremost psychologist of Christianity" would dare to suggest such familiarity with the psychic experience of one living in the first century. But again, though such a psychobiographical approach is highly unorthodox in mainstream philosophy, it would soon become commonplace among practitioners of Freud's new science of psychoanalysis, a school of thought built upon belief in the value of endeavoring to make objective, insofar as is possible, the vicissitudes of the individual psyche.

We may provisionally note that while the psychological needs of Nietzsche's Paul remain relatively constant before and after the Damascus experience, the means by which he endeavours to meet those needs changes dramatically. The first half of *Daybreak* 68 calculatingly lays the seeds for this (ultimately world-historic) change in Paul's pre- and post-Damascus psychic strategies in its linkage of (1) Paul's own doubts and insecurities vis-à-vis the demands of the Law, and (2) his fanatical persecution of supposed "transgressors and doubters" of that Law. The combination of profound self-loathing, a great lust for power, and the fanatical projection of his soul's vicissitudes onto those around him is a volatile one indeed. The fact that this mechanism of projection seems to break down, or more likely is overwhelmed by the matters apparently weighing so heavily on the conscience of this "very tormented, very pitiable, very unpleasant man," is hardly surprising. Nietzsche hints at the looming breakdown of Paul's short-lived strategy for avoiding recognition of his self-reproach when he suggests that "however much he tried to relieve his conscience . . . through the extremest fanaticism in revering and defending the law, there were moments when he said to himself: "It is all in vain! The torture of the unfulfilled law cannot be overcome." Despite Paul's tireless efforts to see and punish in others what he is apparently so afraid of recognizing in himself, the torture fails to recede. Indeed, so far as Nietzsche is concerned, had Paul's original defensive method of avoiding the recognition of self-reproach been entirely successful, had he been able to keep his personal demons at bay through the fanatical persecution of Christians, his troubled journey would surely have ended with him as one more Jerusalem Pharisee. That it did not end there, says Nietzsche, would soon prove most lamentable.

Returning to *Daybreak* 68's rendering of Paul's history-altering personal metamorphosis, we see that according to Nietzsche, what "comes" to the tortured Paul[15] on the road to Damascus is of course *not* the risen Christ, but rather a "liberating idea . . . a way out." This liberation, according to Nietzsche, is not just from his immediate "moral despair," but indeed from the very *source* of that despair: The Law itself. While any "vision" Paul may or may not have experienced en route to Damascus is quickly and summarily dismissed as the product of an epileptic mind, what Nietzsche takes to be the psychohistorical reality behind the orthodox account of his metamorphosis is treated in considerable detail.

It is at this point in Nietzsche's portrait of Paul, that two fundamental shifts seem to occur.

1. The figure of Paul proceeds from a "tormented" soul driven unconsciously by a thoroughgoing fear of confronting the issues underlying the profound sense of lack and insufficiency at the core of his soul, to a "recovered," and indeed triumphant figure who has found the "solution of the riddle" that gave rise to both his despair and his fanatical behavior, and as a result become "the happiest of men."
2. Nietzsche's depiction of the "recovered" Paul, of Paul the Christian, also seems to change at this juncture. Indeed, his mood toward Paul seems to move inversely to the improved frame of mind he attributes to the Apostle.

As already noted, while his assessment of the pre-Damascus Paul is certainly not laudatory, Nietzsche is willing to extend to the Pharisee a small measure of the relatively even-handed diagnostic posture that characterizes his scattered musings on the Nazarene. The pre-Damascus Paul is portrayed as one who desperately longed to be a pious Jew, apparently lacked all that is required to meet that high distinction, struggled against conscious awareness of these insufficiencies by projecting them onto others, and emerges a "very pitiable, very unpleasant man."

This temporary air of at least some degree of the psychologist's customary neutrality is all but abandoned in Nietzsche's rendition of the post-Damascus "recovered" Paul. While we will return to the topic of Nietzsche's vision of the Apostle Paul's calculated manipulation of Jesus' original message in chapter 6, we may provisionally note that while his special focus on the mind and underlying motivation of his subject continues to dominate his investigation of Paul the "Christian," any vestige

of an even-handed or balanced diagnosis is lost as Nietzsche treats with
ever mounting suspicion and animosity what he takes to be Paul's self-
serving and wholly "ironic" (*A* 36) hijacking of the "ship of Christianity"
(*D* 68).

As a Pharisee, Paul is "pitiable" (*D* 68), as a Christian leader he is a
"moral cretin" (*WP* 171). Saul the Jew is "tormented" and "sick" (*D* 68),
Paul the Apostle is a "genius in hatred" (*A* 42). While *Daybreak* 68 examines "the storms and confusions of such a man," *Will To Power* 172
speaks of his "absolute lack of intellectual integrity." No one, not even
Wagner, is subjected to the kind of fierce and relentless condemnation
Nietzsche directs at the "recovered" or post-Damascus Paul. The question is *why*? No doubt, Nietzsche would argue, because only he has
dared to "really read" Paul, to read Paul with the eye of a psychologist.
Nietzsche is both convinced and disappointed that apparently only he,
"one who has ears behind his ears . . . [and in the] presence of whom
precisely that which would like to stay silent has to become audible"
(*Twilight*, Foreword), has apprehended (1) what factors really came together on that famous road to Damascus, and (2) what a tremendous
and sinister harvest this remarkable coming together has yielded, and
tragically continues to yield.

According to Nietzsche, it is precisely the convergence on the road to
Damascus of three distinct and heretofore ignored factors that accounts
for both Paul's remarkable transmutation from fanatical opponent to
equally fanatical proselytizer of Christianity, and the extraordinary and
unfortunate change of course taken by the "ship of Christianity." They
are:

1. Paul's troubling apparent inability to live up to the demands of the "spiritual
   ideal" before him.
2. His exceptional "lust for domination," which prior to his Damascus "recovery" exhibits itself in his tireless search for and "harsh and malicious" treatment of the first Christians (the supposed "transgressors and doubters" of the
   all-important Law).
3. The singular fact that the leader of this fledgling movement, Jesus of Nazareth,
   had met an early death on the cross, leaving his "shaken and disappointed"
   (*A* 40) followers not only without a leader but without a clear understanding
   of the meaning of his life, death, and message (what Nietzsche terms "the
   problem of the person of Jesus" [*WP* 177], explored in chapter 5).

That the coming together of three so volatile ingredients "at a stroke . . .
all at once" on the road to Damascus causes Paul's own "moral despair
. . . to be blown away, destroyed" (*D* 68), is almost secondary. For when
the conceptual dust from this world-historic eruption began to clear—
and Nietzsche argues that it is only *now* beginning to fully settle—what

emerged was "the *one* great curse, the *one* great intrinsic depravity, the *one* great instinct for revenge for which no expedient is sufficiently poisonous, secret, subterranean, petty—I call it the *one* immortal blemish of mankind" (*A* 62): Christianity.

A notebook entry from the spring of 1888 entitled "Toward a Psychology of Paul" (*WP* 171) sees Nietzsche return to the theme of Paul's explosive, history-altering idea, but this time paying more explicit attention to items two and three above. Here Nietzsche's interest in Paul's "idea of ideas" (*D* 68) is focused on both the Apostle's tremendous lust for power, and his keen appreciation of the extraordinary vacuum created by Jesus' early death.

The given fact is the death of Jesus. This has to be explained—That an explanation may be true or false has never entered the minds of such people as these: one day a sublime possibility comes into their heads: "this death *could* mean such and such"—and at once it *does* mean such and such! A hypothesis is proved true by the sublime impetus it imparts to its originator.

Here, the sudden feeling of power that an idea arouses in its originator is everywhere accounted proof of its value—and since one knows no way of honoring an idea other than calling it true, the first predicate with which it is honored is the predicate "true"—How otherwise could it be so effective? . . . The idea is understood to have been inspired: the effect that it exercises possesses something of the violence of a demonic influence.

An idea that such a decadent is unable to resist, to which he succumbs, is thus "proved" true!!!

None of these holy epileptics and seers of visions possessed a thousandth part of that integrity in self-criticism with which a philologist today reads a text or proves the truth of an historical event—Compared with us, they are moral cretins.

And at *Will To Power* 177, as part of an apparently sincere warning to "the faithful" to take care to distinguish their spiritual indebtedness to Jesus from any indebtedness to Paul, Nietzsche adds that:

at some time or other this founder was something very uncertain and insecure, in the beginning—Consider with what degree of freedom Paul treats, indeed almost juggles with, the problem of the person of Jesus: someone who died, who was seen again after his death, who was delivered over to death by the Jews— A mere "motif": *he* then wrote the music to it—A zero in the beginning.

While astonished that essentially *all* of Christendom remains ignorant of an ideological hijacking that for him is painfully apparent, the specific nature of Paul's "juggling," his explosive and "liberating . . . idea of ideas" (*D* 68), comes as no surprise to Nietzsche. *Of course* Paul, a "genius" (*A* 42,58; *WP* 175) and shrewdly political figure moving in "an absurdly unpolitical society" (*A* 27), comes to see that "it is *unreasonable* to persecute precisely this Christ! For here is a way out . . . here and no-where else do I have and hold the *destroyer of the law*." Paul (and Nie-tzsche) alone seem to recognize the "tremendous consequences" of his recasting of the life of this suddenly absent, and largely ambiguous Jesus of Nazareth, as signifying the "destruction of the law," and his death, as somehow "necessary for the abolition of the law!" (*D* 68). If indeed Jesus' death really was necessary for the abolition of the Law, if in fact his existence did herald the destruction of the Law, then it really would no longer be possible to transgress, sin against, fail to live up to, the Law. As Paul himself makes clear in his letter to the church at Rome: "And where there is no law there is no transgression" (Romans 4:14).

This idea, suggests Nietzsche, is simply too much for "a decadent [like Paul] to resist." Like Freud—who constantly is at pains to distinguish "psychic reality" from objective reality—Nietzsche is well aware that in many cases "truthfulness" is secondary to psychic efficacy. "This death *could* mean such and such—and at once it *does* mean such and such!" (*WP* 171). Once again, Nietzsche's focus is on the likely psychological *needs* of Paul. It is psychological *need* and not "the truth of an historical event" (*WP* 171), that ultimately determines the "music" Paul writes on the still pliable, "very uncertain . . . motif" of Jesus of Nazareth. So it is that *Will To Power* 172 makes it clear that for such a type, "it does not matter whether a thing is true, but what effect it produces." And the effects are indeed extraordinary. "At a stroke he feels himself recovered, the moral despair is as blown away, destroyed—that is to say, fulfilled, there on the Cross!" (*D* 68). In effect, the soul-wrenching sense of lack, of insufficiency, of self-reproach, that plagued and drove the tormented Paul to such (ultimately defensive) extremes in behaviour, is fulfilled, *without him having ever fulfilled the Law*! For Paul such a solution really does represent "the key of keys."

EPILEPSY PART 2: FANATICISM

Psychological weakness is again associated with epilepsy at *Antichrist* 54, one of Nietzsche's more interesting references to the disease. Used here in an even broader sense than was the case in the *Daybreak*, *Antichrist* 54 appeals to epilepsy—or more specifically "conceptual epi-lepsy"—as part of a larger psychological investigation of the "fanatic," the holder of absolute and unbending convictions. Unlike *Daybreak*'s consideration of the possible defensive role played by hyperactivity in the flight of the mentally weak from themselves, from self-reflection, this later mention of epilepsy finds Nietzsche pondering the flight of the mentally weak from intellectual and spiritual freedom.

More specifically, he turns to the matter of a possible psychic connec-

tion between the often distressing uncertainty and ambiguity that necessarily accompanies such freedom, and the absolute faith, conviction,
and undisturbed certainty of the "fanatic." Having defined "faith" as
"not wanting to know what is true" (52), and declaring absolute convictions to be "a requirement of weakness" (54), the *Antichrist* suggests that
for certain "sick spirits" and "conceptual epileptics"—unable to withstand the vicissitudes of intellectual freedom and uncertainty—the holding of an absolute conviction, *any* absolute conviction, may have more
to do with psychoconstitutional deficiencies than the particular cause
about which he is convicted. Indeed, speaking of the fanatic's "need for
belief, for some unconditional Yes and No," Nietzsche goes so far as to
suggest that:

Not to see many things, not to be impartial in anything, to be party through and
through, to view all values from a strict and necessary perspective—this alone
is the condition under which such a man exists at all.
    The pathological conditionality of his perspective makes of the convinced man
a fanatic—Savonarola, Luther, Rousseau, Robespierre, Saint-Simon—the antithetical type of the strong emancipated spirit (*A* 54).

The task of *Antichrist* 54 is precisely the psychological unmasking of
such men of extraordinary conviction, weak souls who resort to the
"slavery" of fanaticism and absolute beliefs less out of sincere conviction
than psychological self-interest. For such "sick spirits"—apparently unable to deal with the liberty and dissonance well known to the Nietzschean "free spirit"—firm conviction, *any* firm conviction, is not only less
demanding than the fundamental scepticism "of the truthful man," but
perhaps "the [very] condition under which such a man exists at all" (54).
Worth noting about *Antichrist* 54's roster of "conceptual epileptics"—
Savonarola, Luther, Rousseau, Robespierre, Saint-Simon—is that unlike
the *Daybreak*'s comparable references to Paul, Alexander, Caesar, Mohammed, and Napoleon (*D* 68,549) (historical figures traditionally linked
with the disease of epilepsy), *Antichrist* 54's inventory of men are seemingly united only by the strength with which they held their respective
convictions. By the time of the *Antichrist*'s composition, "epilepsy" for
Nietzsche appears no longer to be even tenuously linked to the so-named
neurological disorder. For the increasingly sceptical, violently iconoclas-
tic writer of 1888—for whom "the vigour of a mind, its freedom through
strength and superiority of strength, is proved by scepticism"—the
pressing "need for belief, for some unconditional Yes and No" is not just
"a requirement of weakness" in general (54), but sufficient cause to raise
the spectre of the specific underlying psychoconstitutional weakness he
terms "conceptual epilepsy."
    Recall *Daybreak*'s suggestion that far from restricting their effectiveness

in the world, the possible underlying psychological limitations of Paul, Caesar, Napoleon, et al., may indeed have been *responsible* for the extraordinary changes these figures effected upon the world around them. Interestingly, the *Antichrist* likewise maintains that despite their possible origins in psychological weakness, in the need for certitude, that absolute convictions and fanaticism by no means curtail the conceptual epileptic's impact and importance. Speaking of "Conviction as a means," Nietzsche is clear that "there is much one can achieve by means of a conviction." Far from being suspicious of the (for Nietzsche, and later for Freud) *too firmly* held convictions of the fanatic, the average man finds such absolutism compelling. "The larger-than-life attitudes of these sick spirits, these conceptual epileptics, impresses the great masses," Nietzsche readily concedes, "fanatics are picturesque, mankind would rather see gestures than listen to reasons" (*A* 54).

Also noteworthy about *Antichrist* 54's remarks is that though Paul is not cited among the aforementioned "sick spirits" and "conceptual epileptics":

1. Luther is, and as was made clear in *Daybreak* 68's effective paralleling of their respective means of, and possible motivations for, freeing themselves from the rigorous and anxiety-generating standard before them—"the perfect man of the spiritual ideal"[16]—Nietzsche considered these two shapers of Christianity to be kindred spirits.

2. Insofar as the topic of *Antichrist* 54 is the psychological weakness and defensive strategies of the "fanatic," the "convicted man," it bears repeating that Paul of course is Nietzsche's quintessential "fanatic." While we treat Nietzsche's attitude toward the tireless globe-trotting preaching of Paul *the Apostle* in considerable detail in chapter 5, we may note that some six years after *Daybreak* 68's characterization of the young Pharisee as a *"fanatical* defender and chaperone of this God and his law" and suspicion toward his "extremest *fanaticism* in revering and defending the law," Nietzsche was still endeavouring to expose what he terms "the Jewish *fanaticism* of a Paul" (*WP* 155, my italics).

The *Antichrist's* examination of the psychology of fanaticism, or "conceptual epilepsy," can help us to better understand Nietzsche's deep suspicion concerning Paul's dramatic and history-altering conversion on the road to Damascus (where Paul's "fanaticism" remarkably survives his 180 degree transposition from anti-Christian Jewish persecutor, to anti-Jewish Christian proselytizer).[17] Paul's extraordinary about-face—surely the most celebrated in history—is of tremendous significance for a variety of reasons. So radical is this transformation, so absolute this change of heart, that for millennia the pious have cited God's intervention as the only plausible explanation. Religious conviction aside, looked at purely conceptually, one cannot but be struck by the tremendous distance traversed by Paul's metamorphosis. He moves not just from one side of neutrality to the other (i.e., a moderate Jewish interest in transgressors of the Law gradually developing into a curiosity about the movement behind these transgressions), but from the *farthest* limits of one side of the equation ("extremely zealous for the traditions of my fathers" (Gal. 1:14), driven by an "obsession . . . to persecute" perceived transgressors of that tradition and its Law (Acts 26:9)) to the outermost limits of the *opposite* side (tireless supporter and globe-trotting leader of these same transgressors, herald of this Law's "end" and "abolition"(Rom. 10:4, Eph. 2:15).

Nietzsche of course does not look at the matter supernaturally, nor is he particularly impressed by the extraordinary conceptual distances involved in Paul's reversal. Though Paul's name does not appear in the following depiction of Christian rebirth from his *Daybreak*, it leaves little doubt concerning the philosopher's opinion on the matter of who, or what approach, is best suited to understanding such phenomena:

[W]hat such a sudden, irrational and irresistible reversal, such an exchange of the profoundest wretchedness for the profoundest well being, signifies psychologically (whether it is perhaps a masked epilepsy?)—that must be determined by psychiatrists, who have indeed plenty of occasion to observe similar "miracles" (in the form of homicidal mania, for example, or suicide mania). The relatively "more pleasant consequences" in the case of the Christian make no essential difference. (*D* 87)

Looked at with the suspicious and penetrating eye of the psychologist, there is nothing supernatural nor even particularly exceptional about Paul's Damascus-road "conversion." For Nietzsche—who at *Will To Power* 55 keenly observes that "extreme positions are not succeeded by moderate ones but by extreme positions of the opposite kind"—Paul's conversion is to be regarded simply as the trading of one fanaticism for another. What Nietzsche detects on the road to Damascus is simply the psychically defensive maneuver of a mind too weak, too "epileptic" to tolerate anything less than the certainty of fanatical faith. What would have been exceptional for such a sick spirit would be if he had found the fortitude—à la Nietzsche's image of himself and his apostle Zarathustra[18]—to live with skepticism and without "the unconditional Yes and No" (54). What would indeed have impressed Nietzsche qua psychologist would be Paul managing to endure anything less than absolute certainty with respect to himself, Judaism, or Christianity. Such an outcome, such a demonstration of strength—indeed, such a "miracle" psychologically speaking—was understandably not to be.

The temporarily effective mechanism of projection seeming to have broken down,[19] and lacking the psychological mettle to confront either himself (*D* 68, 549) or indeterminacy (*A* 54), Nietzsche's Paul makes the only leap left open to such a type. Unable to live up to the spiritual ideal before him, the "highest distinction the Jews were able to conceive," his nagging doubts no longer assuaged through projection, yet too weak to live with anything less than absolute conviction and certitude, the "cunning" Paul, by recognizing in the figure of Jesus "the destroyer of the law, . . . [that] I am outside the law" (*D* 68), instantaneously transfers the *object* of his conviction without sacrificing the (for him) necessary *fanaticism*. Simply put, "for an old psychologist and pied piper like me, in presence of whom precisely that which would like to stay silent *has to become audible*,"[20] what resonates loudly from the famed road to Damascus is not the voice of Jesus, but the world-historic yet all too human machinations of a very troubled soul.

NOTES

1. It is noteworthy that in *Daybreak* alone, depending on Nietzsche's target du jour, the titles "first," "original," or "founding" Christian are bestowed variously upon Jesus (*D* 114, *HH* 144), Paul (*D* 68), and Pascal (*D* 192).

2. One of the main Jewish parties at the time of Christianity's birth, the Pharisees were characterized by zealousness for the Law and a strong emphasis on regulations concerning purity. The Gospels portray the Pharisees principally as opponents to Jesus and the early Christian movement.

3. Letter to Brandes, Nov. 20, 1888 (in O'Flaherty, p. 89).

4. *Beyond Good and Evil* 6 reads: "It has gradually become clear to me what every great philosophy has hitherto been: a confession on the part of its author and a kind of involuntary and unconscious memoir."

5. It is noteworthy that though Freud's eclectic *Moses and Monotheism* covers some of the same ground well-traveled by the later Nietzsche—the nature of Christianity's indebtedness to Judaism, the problems inherent to the idea of a sinless Jesus sacrificing himself for the guilt of others, Paul's crucial role in the development of Christianity, and so forth—Freud does not attempt to psychoanalyze either Jesus or Paul. Perhaps Nietzsche had less to lose in launching such a loaded enterprise.

6. A member of a Hellenistic Jewish family and a Roman citizen, Saul of Tarsus was given the Hebrew name Saul as well as the Roman name Paul. After his conversion to Christianity, the book of Acts refers to him by his Roman name Paul (13:9ff). In the interest of clarity, I generally employ the name Paul, and where appropriate speak of the "pre-Damascus Paul," "the Apostle Paul," the "Apostle to the Gentiles," etc.

7. NIV, NRSV, and REB translations respectively. Again, unless otherwise noted, New Testament passages are taken from Kenneth Barker, ed., *The NIV Study Bible: New International Version* (Grand Rapids, Mich.: Zondervan Publishing, 1985).

8. Recall Freud's characterization of Nietzsche as the "philosopher whose guesses and intuitions often agree in the most astonishing way with the laborious findings of psychoanalysis" (*An Autobiographical Study*, p. 60).

9. Writes Nietzsche at *Beyond Good and Evil* 68: " 'I have done that,' says my memory. 'I cannot have done that' says my pride, and remains adamant. At last—memory yields." For more on Nietzsche's appreciation of the unconscious mind, and the mind's unconscious and defensive machinations, see Ellenberger (1970), Lavrin (1973), and Golomb et al. (1999).

10. Howard (1993, p. 191), for example, recounts the efforts of scholars to discern evidence of post-traumatic epilepsy in the apparent temporal relationship of Paul's self-described "thorn in the flesh" (2 Cor. 12:7) and an "out of the body" experience (2 Cor. 12:4–7) possibly induced by numerous beatings and stonings (2 Cor. 11:23–25).

11. See *Daybreak* 68, 87, and 549, *Will To Power* 171, *Antichrist* 54.

12. By projecting negative feelings and a negative self-image onto others, and reinforcing that projection by punishing them, individuals manage, at some level, to delude themselves with the idea that "I'm not the bad one, *they* are." In explicitly psychoanalytic terms, the hurting subject gets out from under the attack of his superego by directing its attack toward others who stand for the "bad" self.

13. Strictly speaking, we are not "reading Paul" in the book of Acts but an unnamed author, a self-described companion to Paul (historically Luke—see Acts 16:10–17; 20:5–15; 21:1–18). We may note, however, (1) that the author purports to be relating Paul's own words, (2) the portrait of the Apostle offered in Acts is especially rich in detail, and (3) the account of his conversion experience in Paul's own letters (1 Cor. 9:1 and 15:8) agrees *in its essentials* with Acts' rendering. While Paul's own depiction of his experience does not always concur entirely with that found in Acts—at times he seems to allude not to a sensory perception of Jesus (as in Acts 9), but a new-found *inner* awareness (Gal. 1:16)—what matters most to our present investigation is that Nietzsche apparently accepts the account offered in Acts as Paul's. Whether Nietzsche was unaware of the above differences, or more likely (given his familiarity with the NT) considered them of minor import, the fact is that *Daybreak* 68's account of Paul's Damascus road "vision"—complete with Jesus' words; "Why persecutest thou *me*?"—necessarily derives from Acts, the sole account of this communiqué. That Nietzsche recounts *this* version of Paul's conversion experience in an aphorism emphasizing the need to *"really read"* Paul suggests that the comparative veracity of the book of Acts and the Pauline epistles was a non-issue for the philosopher.

14. Recall Nietzsche's equally bold suggestion of familiarity at *Twilight* 2, 12: "Socrates is no physician," *he said softly to himself*: "death alone is a physician here . . . Socrates himself has only been a long time sick" (my italics).

15. Now "sick" in the full and *conscious* realization that "all is in vain! The torture of the unfulfilled law cannot be overcome."

16. Recall *Daybreak* 68's suggestion that:

there were moments when he [Paul] said to himself: "It is all in vain! The torture of the unfulfilled law cannot be overcome." Luther may have felt a similar thing when he wanted in his monastery to become the perfect man of the spiritual ideal: and similarly to Luther, who one day began to hate the spiritual ideal and the Pope and the saints and the whole clergy with a hatred the more deadly the less he dared to admit it to himself—a similar thing happened to Paul (*D* 68).

17. The relationship of the post-Damascus Paul to Judaism is highly complex

and the subject of considerable scholarship. Fredriksen, in *From Jesus to Christ* (pp. 160ff.) distills the many interpretations of the matter to three principal readings:

1. Paul rejects Judaism (the Law is dead).

2. Paul rejects Judaizing (the Law is not required for Gentile salvation).

3. Paul rejects everything other than Christ.

Fredriksen observes that interpretation #1—the "Torah abrogation view," that St. Paul understood Judaism as a religion of empty legalism—has traditionally been the dominant one, and was held by Augustine and Luther. In addition to Fredriksen, see Pfleiderer's *Christian Origins* and Hall's *Christian Anti-Semitism and Paul's Theology*.

18. "One should not let oneself be misled: great intellects are skeptics. Zarathustra is a skeptic . . . Freedom from convictions, of any kind, the *capacity* for an unconstrained view, *pertains* to strength" (*A* 54).

19. Again, Nietzsche hints at the looming breakdown of Paul's short-lived strategy of projecting his own limitations onto those around him when he suggests that "however much he tried to relieve his conscience . . . through the extremest fanaticism in revering and defending the law, there were moments when he said to himself: It is all in vain! The torture of the unfulfilled law cannot be overcome' " (*D* 68).

20. *Twilight*, Foreword.

5

Christian Misunderstandings

That mankind should fall on its knees before the opposite of what was the origin, the meaning, the right of the Gospel, that it should have sanctified in the concept 'Church' precisely what the 'bringer of glad tidings' regarded as *beneath* him, *behind* him—one seeks in vain a grander form of *world-historical irony*.

Antichrist 36

The type of the redeemer has been preserved to us only in a very distorted form. That this distortion should have occurred is in itself very probable: there are several reasons why such a type could not remain pure, whole, free of accretions.

Antichrist 31

According to Nietzsche, three factors above all combined to ensure that both the figure of Jesus himself, and the simple message he embodied— what the *Antichrist* terms "genuine, primitive Christianity" (39)—were significantly altered soon after his death at Calvary:

1. Jesus of Nazareth communicated his message not directly, but altogether symbolically.
2. The first Christian community consisted almost entirely of Jews. Upon Jesus' sudden death, it was this very particular community that had thrust upon it the daunting task of translating this message and this messenger into notions more in accord with their own reality and experience. Since the instincts, psychological needs, and psychological reality of the first Christians were so di-

ametrically different from those of Jesus (a hardly surprising fact given his extraordinary psychophysiological condition), the inevitable and all too apparent consequence of this world-historic exercise in "mistranslation" and "misunderstanding" was a post-Jesus Christianity bearing astonishingly little semblance to the "genuine" Christianity embodied by its founder.

3. In the figure of Paul of Tarsus Nietzsche recognizes a history-altering combination of tremendous "genius" (A 58; WP 175), extraordinary "ruthlessness" (A 58), and an "intractable lust for power" (D 68).

THE GREAT SYMBOLIST

he did not say anything to them without using a parable
Matthew 13:34

it is precisely on condition that nothing he says is taken literally that this antirealist can speak at all
Antichrist 32

It is important to underscore the emphasis Nietzsche consistently places on what he, very much like Kierkegaard, takes to be Jesus' method of indirect, or symbolic communication. According to both philosophers, the fact that Jesus' manner of teaching was almost invariably concerned with symbol, allusion, metaphor, and parable is of paramount importance not only to a proper understanding of the world-historic individual the Dane identifies as the "God-man" but to the eventual, unfortunate fate of that teaching. Unlike Kierkegaard, who insists that qua *God made flesh*, "direct" communication on the part of Jesus to those around him was an utter impossibility,[1] Nietzsche interprets Jesus' ongoing employment of metaphor and symbol as arising out of an apparent pressing psychophysiological *need*. Nietzsche's vision of a "redeemer" essentially *compelled* to communicate symbolically is at once an especially revealing window into the soul or "condition" of the Nietzschean Jesus, and the first of several unfortunate conditions the philosopher regards as ultimately combining to essentially guarantee that "mankind should fall on its knees before the opposite of what was the origin, the meaning, the right of the Gospel" (A 36).

Of the implications of Nietzsche's Jesus' hypersensitivity *not* explored in chapters 2 and 3, perhaps most significant to the subsequent development of Christianity is the effect of this psychophysiological "condition" on his method and manner of communication. For the very "two physiological realities upon which, out of which the doctrine of redemption has grown"—the "instinctive hatred of reality" and "instinctive exclusion of all aversion, all enmity" (A 30) respectively—turn out, according to Nietzsche, to have very specific (and ultimately unforeseen and unfortunate) consequences vis-à-vis the attempts of Jesus to communicate his "inner condition" to those around him. Recall that the combination of (1) a Jesus characterized in terms of a condition of psychophysiological "morbid susceptibility"—who experiences even "the infinitely small in pain" as "an unbearable displeasure" (*A* 30)—and (2) what Nietzsche refers to simply as the "instinct of self-preservation"—the organism's natural impulse to do what is necessary for it to survive—results in Jesus adopting, not a new *belief*, but an unusual and apparently instinct-dictated *way of life*. "The *consequence* of such a condition," observes Nietzsche at *Antichrist* 33, "projects itself into a new *practice* . . . a *different* mode of acting." Though the hyper-sensitive "condition" underlying this mode of action is routinely characterized as "sick" (*A* 31) or "morbid" (*A* 30), Nietzsche's Jesus—possessor of a "profound instinct for how one would have to *live* in order to feel oneself 'in Heaven' " (*A* 33) despite clearly non–heavenlike circumstances—ultimately attains both a "way of living," and a "psychological reality" (*A* 33) the philosopher consistently deems "sublime" (*A* 30, 31). Again, it is this extraordinary ability to find peace, blessedness, the "kingdom of heaven," and so forth in overtly *hellish* circumstances that allows Nietzsche to both compare Jesus' situation and message to "Epicureanism, the redemption doctrine of the pagan world" (*A* 30), and ultimately define this extraordinary soul as "a combination of the sublime, the sick, and the childish" (*A* 31).

To extract this sublime "condition of the heart" from a pained reality characterized by suffering, "tears and the melancholy of the Hebrews" (Z 1, 21)—every contact with which such a pathologically vulnerable soul feels "too deeply"—it is not enough to simply assume a posture of radical non-enmity and nonopposition. To achieve his extraordinary inner condition of "blessedness," this "Kingdom of Heaven," while fully immersed in a painful world of "hatred" and thoroughly *contagious* suffering, Nietzsche's Jesus also instinctively and defensively endeavors to reduce the role and importance of that reality to his own existence. The "instinctive hatred of reality: consequence of an extreme capacity for suffering and irritation which no longer wants to be 'touched' at all," suggests Nietzsche (*A* 30), results in an apparently defensive "flight into the 'ungraspable', into the 'inconceivable' . . . a world undisturbed by reality of any kind" (*A* 29). The world this super-sensitive soul retreats to, Nietzsche makes abundantly clear, is "purely inward" (*WP* 160). Instinctively reducing the import of all external realities—"all religion, all conceptions of divine worship, all history, all natural science, all experience of the world, all acquirements, all politics" (*A* 32)—Nietzsche's Jesus is one who nonreflectively comes to occupy, emphasize, and value *inner* reality. Again we note Nietzsche's ongoing characterization of Jesus in terms of his *inner condition* and subjective experience, his *"feeling* of perfection" (*A* 34); "psychological reality" (*A* 33); "inner feelings of pleasure" (*A* 32), and so forth. More specifically, Nietzsche conjectures that Jesus effectively reduces the role and import of the potentially painful outside world to a ready palette of metaphors to be employed in the description and communication of this remarkable inner condition, psychological reality, and so forth.

> He speaks only of the inmost thing . . . everything else, the whole of reality, the whole of nature, language itself, possesses for him merely the value of a sign, a metaphor . . . such a symbolist *par excellence* stands outside of all religion . . . all experience of the world . . . *his* proofs are inner "lights", inner feelings of pleasure and self-affirmations (*A* 32).
>
> If I understand anything of this great symbolist it is that he took for realities, for "truths," only inner realities—that he understood the rest, everything pertaining to nature, time, space, history, only as signs, as occasion for metaphor (*A* 34).

While the crucial matter of Jesus' relation to first-century Judaism is discussed in detail below, at this juncture we note that as one endeavoring to communicate to fellow Jews in an essentially poor, rural, and unsophisticated Jewish milieu, the palette of symbols and metaphors from which Jesus paints his "Kingdom of Heaven" is understandably firmly rooted in that milieu and geared towards its understanding. So it is that Jesus regularly speaks of such things as bread and wine, his "father," the "son" of the father, and repeatedly tells his audience that the "Kingdom of Heaven" *is like* a seed, growing grain, a wedding banquet, our father's house, a fisherman's net, and so forth. But while Nietzsche's Jesus considers such familiar points of reference as metaphors to help speak of a subjective psychic state, his listeners typically failed to grasp their symbolic character.

> Chance, to be sure, determines the environment, the language, the preparatory schooling of a particular configuration of concepts: primitive Christianity employs *only* Judeo-Semitic concepts (—eating and drinking at communion belong here . . .). But one must be careful not to see in this anything but a sign-language, a semiotic, an occasion for metaphors. It is precisely on condition that nothing he says is taken literally that this anti-realist can speak at all. Among Indians he would have made use of Sankhyam concepts, among Chinese those of Lao-tse— and would not have felt the difference.—One could, with some freedom of expression, call Jesus a "free spirit"—he cares nothing for what is fixed: the word *killeth*, everything fixed *killeth* . . . such a symbolist par excellence stands outside of all religion . . . all history . . . all experience of the world (*A* 32).

The concept "the Son of Man" is not a concrete person belonging to history, anything at all individual or unique, but an 'eternal' fact, a psychological symbol freed from the time concept. The same applies supremely to the *God* of this typical symbolist, to the "kingdom of God," to the "kingdom of Heaven," to

'God's children'. Nothing is more un-Christian than the *ecclesiastical crudities* of God as a *person*, of a "kingdom of God" which *comes*, of a "kingdom of Heaven" in the *Beyond*, of a "Son of God," the *second person* of the Trinity. All this is . . . world-historical cynicism in the mockery of symbolism . . . But it is patently obvious what is alluded to in the symbols "Father" and "Son"—not patently obvious to everyone, I grant: in the word "Son" is expressed the entry into the collective feeling[2] of the transfiguration of all things (blessedness), in the word "Father" *this feeling itself*, the feeling of perfection and eternity.—I am ashamed to recall what the Church has made of this symbolism (*A* 34).

While Jesus endeavors to communicate symbolically, wholly nonliterally, about a condition of the heart, *his condition of the heart*, a psychic state that must be experienced, must be "lived" to be understood (and accordingly *resists* all fixed definitions and the reduction to absolute positions or dogma),[3] his followers effectively violate the very condition (*A* 32) according to which he communicates at all, and promptly literalize a symbolic message fundamentally resistant to literalization.

In suggesting that "it is precisely on condition that nothing he says is taken literally that this antirealist can speak at all," Nietzsche of course echoes a sentiment expressed by the author of Matthew, who says of Jesus: "he did not say anything to them without using a parable" (13: 34). Unlike the Gospel writers, however, the self-professed "foremost psychologist of Christianity" takes it upon himself to ask *why. Why* would someone not say anything "without using a parable?" In addition to his explicit linkage of what he takes to be Jesus' "instinctive hatred of reality" (*A* 30) to his defensive "flight" to a symbolic world-view "undisturbed by reality of any kind" (*A* 29), Nietzsche also implicitly associates the *second* of two "physiological realities upon which . . . the doctrine of redemption has grown"—the "instinctive exclusion of all aversion"—with Jesus' symbolic manner of communication. For while fixed, literal, dogmatic statements (concerning matters spiritual or otherwise) can and do come into conflict with other views, symbolic communication by its very nature is less determinate, and hence less prone to encounter opposition. Having characterized his Jesus as one whose "glad tidings" are that "there are no more opposites," Nietzsche suggests that accordingly, Jesus defensively "cares nothing for what is fixed . . . everything fixed *killeth*" (*A* 32). Indeed, Nietzsche's Jesus' peace-promoting world-view is so "purely inward" (*WP* 160) that "it simply does not know how to imagine an opinion contrary to its own" (*A* 32). As Jaspers astutely observes: "Where everything is a sign, there are no contradictions" (1962, p. 71).

While Nietzsche is willing to recognize that Jesus' unusual manner of communication can be said to have almost *invited* misunderstanding and errors of "translation," he is also adamant that the very specific direction and character of the particular "misunderstanding" that soon overtook the martyred Jesus' "original, primitive Christianity" (*A* 39) was no accident, but in fact a familiar phenomenon only too intelligible to the psychologist.

TRANSLATING THE SYMBOLIC INTO CRUDITIES

> The milieu in which this strange figure moved must have left its mark upon him.
>
> *Antichrist* 31

> I am ashamed to recall what the Church has made of this symbolism.
>
> *Antichrist* 34

> The history of Christianity—and that from the very death on the Cross—is the history of progressively cruder misunderstanding of an *original* symbolism.
>
> *Antichrist* 37

Nietzsche is unwavering in his conviction that much of the blame for the remarkable transformation of Jesus' simple message of "love and humility" (*WP* 169) into "the one immortal blemish of mankind" (*A* 62) must be laid at the feet of the "dysangelist" Paul (*A* 42). He is also adamant that behind the "ship of Christianity's" *first* significant change of course lay subterranean psychological factors much older and indeed much broader than any one unhappy soul. Christianity's change in trajectory, suggests Nietzsche, in fact commences on the very heels of the death at Calvary itself. Well before Paul's history-altering "transformation" en route to Damascus, Nietzsche posits a disturbing, though perhaps inevitable (given the wholly symbolic character of this "antirealist's" communication) mistranslation and corruption of Jesus' message the very moment those around him were left alone to ponder it. "The fate of the Evangel was determined by the death—it hung on the Cross," writes Nietzsche at *Antichrist* 40: "It was only the death, this unexpected shameful death, only the Cross, which was in general reserved for the *canaille* alone—it was only this terrible paradox which brought the disciples face to face with the real enigma: '*Who was that? What was that?*' "

Much of the *Antichrist*, indeed a great portion of the entire Nietzschean corpus from *Human, All Too Human* onwards, is concerned with the exploration of the still unfolding implications of the (for Nietzsche) unfortunate though all too human response to the simple question raised at Calvary: "*Who was that? What was that?*" In order to properly understand the matter of how this question was (and is still being) answered, Nietzsche insists some questions must be raised concerning the first questioners faced with this enigma. Specifically, Nietzsche implores us to ask: Who are these people? How do they think? How do they view the world?

The Gospels are invaluable as evidence of the already irresistible corruption within the first community. What Paul later carried to its conclusion with the cynical logic of a rabbi was nonetheless merely the process of decay which commenced with the death of the redeemer.—One cannot read these Gospels too warily; there are difficulties behind every word. I hope I shall be pardoned for confessing that they are for that very reason a pleasure of the first rank to a psychologist—as the opposite of all kinds of naïve depravity,[4] as refinement par excellence, as artistry in psychological depravity. The Gospels are in a class by themselves. The Bible in general admits no comparison. One is among Jews: first consideration if one is not to lose the thread completely. This self-pretense of "holiness" . . . is not the chance product of some individual talent, some exceptional nature. Race is required for it (A 44).[5]

Quintessentially "Nietzschean" passages such as this inevitably and deliberately elicit strong reactions and numerous lines of questioning. Most significant to our understanding of this "process of decay" said to begin transforming Jesus' original message upon his death—a process Nietzsche tells us "Paul later carried to its conclusion with the cynical logic of a rabbi" (discussed below)—is the extraordinary claim that "Race is required for it." Why does Nietzsche insist that the "*first* consideration if one is not to lose the thread [from Calvary to post-Jesus Christianity] completely" is that "one is among Jews?" What does the matter of race have to do with the "corruption" of Jesus' "good news?" The answer for Nietzsche is that it is only insofar as one bears in mind that the first all-important answers to the suddenly urgent questions voiced at Calvary— "*Who was that? What was that?*"—were products of Jewish minds and what he takes to be a "Jewish instinct," that one can monitor, expose, and perhaps even move beyond the "irresistible corruption" of Jesus' simple message of "love . . . humility," "peace and happiness" (*WP* 169,195).

As we see below, and as commentators such as Walter Kaufmann and Thomas Mann are ever wont to remind us, Nietzsche is capable of applauding any number of aspects of the Jewish people, Jewish history, and Judaism itself. A firm grip on Nietzsche's attitude toward Jews and Judaism proves elusive, however, chiefly because glowing tributes sometimes sit uneasily alongside sharp accusations vis-à-vis "the Jews" that seemingly serve to offset the philosopher's regular and often ebullient praise. As one might expect, Nietzsche's multivalent attitude toward the Jewish people and the Jewish religion continues to give rise to passionate debate and a growing body of scholarship.[6]

Especially relevant to the trajectory of the present study is Duffy and

Mittleman's (1988) careful delineation of the distinction between early "scribal" Israel and later "priestly" Israel built-in to much of Nietzsche's writing on ancient Jewry. What we see in the following pages is that the mature Nietzsche often celebrates the accomplishments and vitality of early Israel, but is highly ambivalent and sometimes very hostile toward the later, politically hobbled "priestly" "Judea" he compares so unflatteringly with her Roman conquerors and blames for preparing the "soil" from which Christianity would emerge. While this distinction is implied rather than formalized, and Nietzsche often is not as precise in his discussion of "the Jews" as we might like, broadly speaking it is the Judeo-Christian continuum in general, and ancient Jewry's posture in the Roman world order in particular, *not* the Israel of the Old Testament, that comes under such intense fire from Nietzsche.

Nowhere are these decisive distinctions more apparent than his ongoing celebration of the Old Testament at the expense of the New.

In the Jewish "Old Testament", the book of divine Justice, there are men, things and speeches of so grand a style that Greek and Indian literature have nothing to set beside it. One stands in reverence and trembling before these remnants of what man once was. . . . To have glued this New Testament, a species of rococo taste in every respect, on to the Old Testament to form a *single* book, as "bible", as "the book of books": that is perhaps the greatest piece of temerity and "sin against the spirit" that literary Europe has on its conscience (*BGE* 52).

All honor to the Old Testament! I find in it great human beings, a heroic landscape, . . . what is more, I find a people. In the New one on the other hand, I find nothing but petty sectarianism, mere rococo of the soul, mere involutions, nooks, queer things. . . . it is plain that there is no trace of good breeding. How can one make such a fuss about one's little lapses as these pious little men do! Who gives a damn? Certainly not God" (*GM* 3, 22).

Such unabashed celebration of certain aspects periods of Jewish history notwithstanding, as modern philosophy's ardent and notorious champion of "master morality" and "aristocratic" values,[7] Nietzsche nonetheless recognizes in much of the history of Judaism the quintessential embodiment of a dangerous but all too familiar life-devaluing, denaturalizing spirit. "The Jews," writes Nietzsche in the *Genealogy of Morals* (1, 16) "were the priestly nation of *ressentiment* par excellence," and as such, "the best haters there have ever been" (*D* 377).

RESSENTIMENT

Nietzsche's thoroughly psychological emphasis on *ressentiment*[8] as a heretofore neglected but deceptively powerful determinant underlying an astonishing range of human actions, sentiments, relationships, and valuations, has rightly been described as "one of his major contributions to psychology" (*Genealogy*, intro., p. 7). Nietzsche, who in the foreword to his *Twilight of the Idols* quite accurately describes himself "an old psychologist" and "one who has ears behind his ears," ingeniously manages to locate what he takes to be evidence of *ressentiment* in such seemingly diverse matters as socialism, anti-Semitism,[9] Christianity's staunch emphasis on "equality,"[10] and the allied matters of St. Paul's relation to Judaism and Luther's to the priestly-ascetic ideal.[11] But nowhere does the notion of *ressentiment* figure more prominently than Nietzsche's conception of the birth of post-Jesus Christianity from the extraordinary and seething womb of first-century Judaism.

To do full justice to Nietzsche's representation of "the Jews" as a people characterized by hatred and *ressentiment*, and the all-important transmission of this *ressentiment*-fueled *Weltanschauung* not to Jesus, but to *post*-Jesus Christianity, one would have to recapitulate much of Nietzsche's ground-breaking thinking concerning the unexplored psychological origins of history's dominant ethico-religious traditions. In essence, one would have to review the entirety of the *Genealogy of Morals'* famous first essay, "Good and Evil, Good and Bad." Such an exploration is clearly beyond the scope of the present investigation. Accordingly, we are obliged to limit ourselves to simply outline Nietzsche's emphasis on the impact of *ressentiment* on valuation in general insofar as it pertains to his account of those first-century Jews faced with the daunting task of deciphering the meaning and message of the suddenly absent "symbolist *par excellence*" (*A* 32).

Nietzsche's extraordinary and influential investigation of the far-flung implications of the "slave morality—master morality" opposition, introduced in *Beyond Good and Evil* (260) and fully explored in the first essay of the *Genealogy*, is at bottom about the different valuations of those possessing power and those lacking it. According to Nietzsche, the notions "good" and "bad" effortlessly stem from the day-to-day experience of the former. Quite naturally, possessors of power come to view their own actions and experience as good, as things of value. Conversely, those traits most obviously characterizing the powerless, the common, the lowly, come to be regarded as bad. For their part, those without power instinctively *reverse* the meanings of power-based, "noble," or "master" morality. Moreover, due to the envious, resentful instincts of the powerless, the notions good and bad come to be replaced by the more vengeful "good" and "evil."[12] Because of what the *Genealogy of Morals* (1, 11) calls "the venomous eye of *ressentiment*," of the all too human impulse for revenge, the underprivileged and impotent understandably come to regard their masters as "evil," and accordingly define evil by the degree to which something resembles their masters, and good according to what is *not* like their masters. According to the *Genealogy*

(1, 11): "one should ask rather precisely who is "evil" in the sense of the morality of *ressentiment*. The answer, in all strictness, is: precisely the "good man" of the other morality, precisely the noble, the powerful man, the ruler, but dyed in another color, interpreted in another fashion, seen in another way by the venomous eye of *ressentiment*."

Central to Nietzsche's model of the origin of moral valuation is that in contrast to moralities emanating from power, the "slave morality" of the powerless is fundamentally *reactive*, a product of negation, a function of *ressentiment*. To the extent that they are unable to partake of the direct, value-generating world of the powerful—a milieu characterized by such worldly, "natural" (and not coincidentally, decidedly "Nietzschean") values as strength, action, prosperity, pride, beauty, and vitality—these qualities come to be resented by the powerless and accordingly are considered "evil."

But "the slave revolt in morality," insists Nietzsche, *truly* "begins when *ressentiment* itself *becomes creative* and gives birth to values: the *ressentiment* of natures that are denied the true reaction, that of deeds, and compensate themselves with an *imaginary revenge*" (*GM* 1, 10, my italics). Having declared the "natural" values of the powerful to be "evil," the subterranean spirit of *ressentiment* ultimately gives rise to its own compensatory, reactive, decidedly nonworldly, unnatural values (in essence, values emanating from the will to power of the *powerless*). For Nietzsche, nowhere is this vengeful yet *creative* phenomenon more apparent than in what the *Genealogy* (1, 16) characterizes as the "deadly contradiction" of "Rome against Judea, Judea against Rome."

THE BIRTH OF CHRISTIANITY OUT OF THE SPIRIT OF *RESSENTIMENT*[13]

Characterizing the Romans as "strong and noble" and insisting "nobody stronger or more noble has yet existed on earth or even been dreamed of," the *Genealogy* (1, 16) goes on to suggest that "the Jews, on the contrary, were the priestly nation of *ressentiment par excellence*." "It was the Jews," insists Nietzsche,

who with awe-inspiring consistency, dared to invert the aristocratic value-equation (good=noble=powerful=beautiful=happy=beloved of God) and to hang on to this inversion with their teeth, the teeth of the most abysmal hatred (the hatred of impotence), saying 'the wretched alone are the good; the poor, impotent, lowly alone are good . . . are blessed by God' (*GM* 1, 7).

The Jews—a people "born for slavery" as Tacitus and the whole ancient world says, "the chosen people" as they themselves say and believe—the Jews achieved that miracle of inversion of values . . . their prophets fused together "rich," "godless," "evil," "violent," "sensual" into one and were the first to coin the word "world" as a term of infamy. It is in this inversion of values . . . that the significance of the Jewish people resides: with *them* there begins the *slave revolt in morals* (*BGE* 195).

Nietzsche's conception of first-century Jewry as a morally "inverted," politically militarily "castrated" (*WP* 184) people "that had already renounced politics and lived a kind of parasitic existence within the Roman order of things" (*WP* 204), a people compensated *only* by "unnatural, purely *imaginary* presuppositions (as chosen people, as community of saints, as the people of the promise, as 'church')" and "*imaginary* revenge" upon their masters (*WP* 199; *GM* 1, 10—my italics), proves crucial to the birth of post-Jesus Christianity he detects at Calvary. For *this* is the general "*milieu* in which this strange figure moved" (*A* 31), a milieu characterized by the vengeful "*falsification* of all nature, all naturalness, all reality" and populated by a people capable of inverting "morality, history, psychology one after another in an irreparable way into the *contradiction of all natural values*" (*A* 24).[14]

More specifically—and not surprisingly given the Evangel's message of radical equality, that "everyone is a child of God" (*A* 29)—it is the *least* successful, *least* potent, and accordingly *most* resentful underclass of this already *ressentiment*-fueled culture, that are drawn to the "warm" (*HH* 235), "innocent and longing heart" (*BGE* 269) of Jesus. Characterized by "an even *more abstract* form of existence, an even *more unreal* vision of the world than one conditioned by an organized Church," Nietzsche sees in this Jewish "chandala" "the priestly instinct which can no longer endure the priest" (*A* 27).[15] Most significantly for Nietzsche, it is *this* instinct of distilled *ressentiment, this* "movement from below" (*WP* 182), *these minds* above all, that are fated to "translate" and "*coarsen* . . . a being [and a message] immersed entirely in symbols" (*A* 31).

COARSENING THE "TYPE"

> . . . but we had hoped that he was the one who was going to redeem Israel.
>
> Luke 24:21

> Clearly the little community had failed to understand precisely the main thing.
>
> *Antichrist* 40

At *Antichrist* 31 and 40, Nietzsche tightens the focus of this suggestion of serious post-Calvary ramifications from the collision of Jesus' ahistoric, wholly symbolic message, with the limited "intelligence" and very particular, historically determined Jewish "instinct" and "understanding" of "the first Christian community." He invites us to consider the all-important matter of the psycho-spiritual *needs* of this very specific community. As he does so handily at *Daybreak* 68 in the context of the troubled Pharisee Paul's vengeful, history-altering vision of Jesus, so at *Antichrist* 31 and 40 we witness the turning of Nietzsche's exceptional "psychological antennae"[16] to the inseparable matters of the *needs* of this hate-filled first-century Jewish "chandala," and their idiosyncratic "translation" of Jesus' simple message.

Beginning with the suggestion that the "type of the redeemer has been preserved to us only in a very distorted form," *Antichrist* 31 goes on to propose that:

the strange and sick world to which the Gospels introduce us—a world like that of a Russian novel, in which refuse of society, neurosis and "childlike" idiocy seem to make a rendezvous—must have in any case have coarsened the type: the first disciples in particular had to translate a being immersed entirely in symbols and in incomprensibilities into their own crudity in order to understand anything of it at all—for them such a type could not exist until it had been reduced to more familiar forms. . . . The prophet, the Messiah, the judge who is to come, the moral preacher, the miracle-worker, John the Baptist—so many opportunities for misunderstanding the type. . . . One has to regret that no Dostoyevsky lived in the neighborhood of this most interesting *decadent*. . . . When the first community had need of a censuring theologian to oppose the theologians they *created* their "God" according to their requirements: just as they unhesitatingly put into his mouth those totally un-evangelic concepts which they could not do without, "Second Coming", "Last Judgment", every kind of temporal promise and expectation.

Calling this vulnerable and deeply disappointed first community's terrifying "suspicion" that the Evangel's "unexpected" death on the Cross "might be the refutation of their cause . . . only too understandable," and employing language reminiscent of *Daybreak* 68's psychohistorical rendering of Paul's instantaneous need-fulfilling "enlightenment" en route to Damascus (at once a "liberating idea" and the "perfect revenge"), *Antichrist* 40 conjectures that:

Only now did the chasm open up: "*Who* killed him? *Who* was his natural enemy?"—this question came like a flash of lightening. Answer: *ruling* Judaism, its upper class. From this moment one felt oneself in mutiny against the social order, one subsequently understood Jesus as having been *in mutiny against the social order*. Up till then this warlike trait, this negative trait in word and deed, was lacking in his image; more, he was the contradiction of it. Clearly the little community had *failed* to understand precisely the main thing, the exemplary element in his manner of dying, the freedom from, the superiority over every feeling of *ressentiment*:—a sign of how little they understood of him at all! Jesus himself would have desired nothing by his death but publicly to offer the sternest test, the *proof* of his teaching. . . . But his disciples were far from *forgiving* his death—which would have been evangelic in the highest sense . . . Precisely the most unevangelic of feelings, *revengefulness*, again came uppermost. The affair could not possibly end with this death: one required "retribution", "judgment" (—and yet what can be more unevangelic than "retribution", "punishment" "sitting in judgment"!). The popular expectation of a Messiah came once again into the foreground; an historic moment appeared in view: the "kingdom of God" is coming to sit in judgment on its enemies . . . But with this everything is misunderstood: the "kingdom of God" as a last act, as a promise! For the Evangel had been precisely the existence, the fulfillment, the *actuality* of this "kingdom". Such a death was precisely this "kingdom of God". Only now was all that contempt for and bitterness against Pharisee and theologian worked into the type of the Master—one thereby *made* of him a Pharisee and theologian! On the other hand, the enraged reverence of these utterly unhinged souls could no longer endure that evangelic equal right of everyone to be a child of God which Jesus had taught, and their revenge consisted in *exalting* Jesus in an extravagant fashion, in severing him from themselves: just as the Jews, in revenge on their enemies, had previously separated their God from themselves and raised him on high. The *one* God and the one Son of God: both products of *ressentiment* . . . [17]

It is often the case with Nietzsche that only when he endeavors to clarify what his position is *not*, what he emphatically does *not* want to be construed as saying, that he says most clearly what his position actually *is*. This certainly can be said of his controversial image of Jesus of Nazareth. As the above two *Antichrist* excerpts demonstrate, rarely does a more rounded representation of Nietzsche's Jesus emerge than when the philosopher is at pains to demonstrate how and why others have utterly misconstrued "this strange figure" (*A* 31), why the Jesus of others is in fact "unevangelic" in the extreme. The "psychological type of the Galilean is still recognizable—but only in a completely degenerate form (which is at once a mutilation and an overloading with foreign traits)," Nietzsche informs us at *Antichrist* 24. Both explicitly and implicitly, it is in his psychological castigation of such "mutilation," be it at the hands of first-century Jewish "chandala" or "Monsieur Renan, that buffoon *in psychologicis*" (*A* 29) in the nineteenth century, that the sharpest picture of the Nietzschean Jesus may be said to emerge.

The "miracle-worker" posture was a familiar demonstration of one's special status throughout antiquity in general and among Jews in particular.[18] Nietzsche detects in the first Christian community's translation of this unique and *"purely inward"* figure (*WP* 160) into a "miracle-worker" (*A* 31) evidence both of the efforts of this community to ensure that the Evangel's sudden departure from the scene would not mark the end of their cause, and more importantly, one more "sign of how little they understood of him at all" (*A* 40). Because the very essence and embodied message of Nietzsche's Jesus—the radical immediacy of the "kingdom of heaven"—is strictly a matter of an "inward change in the individual" (*WP* 161) and as such has nothing whatsoever to do with outward demonstrations such as miracles, Nietzsche is acutely suspicious of those who would cast this wholly original redeemer in such well-worn imagery. For Nietzsche, the "feeling of the transfiguration of all things (blessedness) . . . the feeling of perfection and eternity" (*A* 34) embodied in Jesus are, qua *feelings*, things to be *experienced*, but never "demonstrated" via the crudity of the "miracle." It bears repeating that not only is Jesus himself *"purely inward"* (*WP* 160), but so of course is his "kingdom." "The kingdom of God is within you."

While Nietzsche formally discusses these famous words of Luke's Jesus (17:20) at *Antichrist* 29, they echo tacitly throughout the entire *Antichrist*. Jesus is "purely inward," and it is in the individual that his "Kingdom of Heaven" (potentially) abides. Gospel accounts that fail to agree with this foundational focus on *individual* "inward change" (*WP* 161), the very "psychological reality of 'redemption' " itself (*A* 33), are summarily dismissed as cases of self-interested "translation." "Such a faith", insists Nietzsche at *Antichrist* 32, "does not prove itself, either by miracles or rewards and promises . . . *his* proofs are inner "lights", inner feelings of pleasure and self-affirmations." For Nietzsche then, the enduring and supposedly special-status-affirming image of Jesus as "miracle-worker" ultimately serves, not as demonstration of the redeemer's potency, but of the essential crudity of the first "translators" and their unwavering tendency to reduce and transform this extraordinary figure to what *Antichrist* 31 calls "more familiar forms." To quote *Will To Power* 198 once again: "The founder of Christianity had to pay for having directed himself to the lowest class of Jewish society and intelligence. They conceived him in the spirit they understood . . . the miracle in place of the psychological symbol."

Since their casting of Jesus as "one in mutiny against the social order" demonstrates to Nietzsche that "the little community had failed to understand precisely the *main thing*" about him, it is only appropriate to examine in detail both *what* this "main thing" about Jesus is, and *why* the philosopher maintains this early (and enduring) conception of Jesus is erroneous. We have already discussed at length the marked emphasis Nietzsche, in work after work, places on Jesus' suffering in general, and extraordinary manner of dying in particular. Above all, recall Nietzsche's singular insistence that: "This 'bringer of glad tidings' died as he lived, as he taught—not to "redeem mankind" but to demonstrate how one ought to live . . . Not to defend oneself, not to grow angry, not to make responsible . . . not to resist even the evil man—to love him" (*A* 35). Nietzsche returns to the crucial theme of Jesus' singularly revealing martyrdom as part of *Antichrist* 40's treatment of the first community's rapid transformation of his message upon his death. Like aphorisms 33 and

35, *Antichrist* 40—in casting Jesus' death in terms of "the sternest test, the proof of his teaching"—stresses the fundamental continuity between the Evangel's message and his martyrdom. It bears repeating that for Nietzsche, Jesus' death is to be understood above all as a telling confirmation, as a *consummation* of his inseparable life and message. There was no resistance, no opposition, no finger pointing, no anger, nothing but unalloyed *love*. What *Antichrist* 40 adds to this continuity is the suggestion of a relationship between Jesus' truly extraordinary posture, and the only too ordinary posture of *ressentiment*. As surely as *ressentiment* is ultimately to be understood in terms of animosity, vengefulness, and contrariety, so Nietzsche's Jesus is ultimately to be understood in terms of the complete and utter *absence* of these traits. In essence, to define Jesus in terms of "the main thing, the exemplary element in his manner of dying, the freedom from, the superiority over every feeling of *ressentiment*" is to deliberately and diametrically oppose his spirit and embodied message to both "the priestly nation of *ressentiment par excellence*" (*GM* 1, 16) that preceded and surrounded him in life, and the "lowly" and "crude" "first Christians" who coarsely seize upon his pliable message upon his death.

One would be hard pressed to over-emphasize the significance of this image of Jesus as one having attained "freedom from . . . [and] superiority over every feeling of *ressentiment*." Such a characterization represents far more than another in a long line of Nietzsche's positive remarks about this extraordinary soul. That Nietzsche maintains that this remarkable "freedom" and "superiority" qualifies as the "main thing" about his Jesus is hardly surprising. For to an even greater degree than his recurring characterization of the Nazarene as explicitly "noble" and "sublime," Nietzsche's notable emphasis on his *ressentiment*-free status puts the Nietzschean Jesus in very rarefied, and once again very autobiographical company. We have already noted Nietzsche's emphasis upon *ressentiment*'s essentially universal character, the diversity of socio-politico-religious phenomena it is said to underlie, and the *degree* to which subterranean *ressentiment* fuels human behavior and thought. Since *ressentiment* is so omnipresent—at times rivaling the will to power as the principal psychological drive identified by Nietzsche—it is telling to consider who, besides Jesus, the philosopher considers *beyond* or *free of* this all too human quality.

In addition to Nietzsche's already noted celebration of the decidedly life-affirming, natural, and direct (i.e., non-reactive) values and spirit of his beloved *Imperium Romanum*,[19] we note that the philosopher's ebullient praise of the Hellenistic spirit is similarly rooted in no small part in his fundamental image of the (pre-Socratic) Greeks as a people acting largely from strength, joy, and nobility (and correspondingly free of the *ressentiment* which inevitably compensates lesser men). Articulating the already discussed master-morality/slave-morality distinction for which his *Genealogy of Morals* is famous, Nietzsche writes of the Greeks (1, 10): the "well-born" *felt* themselves to be the "happy"; they did not have to establish their happiness artificially by examining their enemies, or to persuade themselves, *deceive* themselves, that they were happy (as all men of *ressentiment* are in the habit of doing). . . ."

While on the topic of the Greeks and the matter of *ressentiment*, we may note the following with respect to Nietzsche's overzealous interest in the manner in which Socrates exited the stage of life (see chapter 3). What we have not discussed is Nietzsche's profound sense of disappointment with Socrates' final sentiments insofar as he detects in them the all too human impulse for *revenge*. After confessing "I admire the courage and wisdom of Socrates in everything he did, said—and did not say," aphorism 340 of the *Gay Science*, entitled *The Dying Socrates*, goes on to lament:

I wish he had remained taciturn also at the last moment of his life; in that case he might belong to a still higher order of spirits. Whether it was the poison or piety or malice—something loosened his tongue at that moment and he said: "O Crito, I owe Asclepius a rooster." This ridiculous and terrible "last word" means for those who have ears: "O Crito, *life is a disease*." Is it possible that a man like him, who had lived cheerfully and like a soldier in the sight of everyone, should have been a pessimist? He had merely kept a cheerful mien while concealing all his life long his ultimate judgement, his inmost feeling. Socrates, Socrates *suffered life*! And then he still revenged himself—with this veiled, gruesome, pious, and blasphemous saying. Did a Socrates need such revenge?

While this is not the forum for treating the fertile topic of *why* Nietzsche is so reluctant to draw such an unfortunate conclusion concerning the ultimate 'blasphemous' judgement of Socrates, we may note the following. What Nietzsche is here so strongly reacting to—what is "ridiculous and terrible . . . gruesome, pious, and blasphemous"—is of course not Socrates' actual remark to Crito as reported in the *Phaedo*, but his own *interpretation of* Socrates' words (an interpretation, it bears repeating, Nietzsche went so far as placing in the mouth of the Greek—see chapter 3).

Nietzsche's tendency to put words into the mouths of great men and then draw significant and far-reaching conclusions about those figures on the basis of his own historical ventriloquy has already been noted. What is crucial to our understanding of just *how extraordinary* is the claim that "the main thing" about Jesus' life, dying, and death is the radical absence of any instinct for revenge, his utter freedom from *ressentiment*, is the fact that even Socrates—the sage a young Nietzsche heralded as "the first *Lebensphilosoph*"[20]—even an extraordinary "man like him, who had lived cheerfully and like a soldier in the sight of everyone," was not untainted by the all too human impulse for revenge. Nietzsche's profound disappointment with *his* Socrates' "terrible" last words is at once powerful testimony to the frighteningly pervasive nature of revenge and *ressentiment*, and witness to just how remarkable a figure the Nietzschean Jesus is. As Nietzsche's prophet Zarathustra—seemingly looking to the coming of the superman—solemnly proclaims: "For that man may be freed from the bonds of revenge: that is the bridge to my highest hope and a rainbow after protracted storms" (Z 2, "*Of The Tarantulas*").

But it is Nietzsche's conception of his own posture vis-à-vis *ressentiment* that is most informative in this context. Triumphantly lauding his "Freedom from *ressentiment*" (the very same words he chooses to portray his Jesus), Nietzsche's literary autobiography (*EH* 1,6) goes on to speak ebulliently of his

enlightenment about *ressentiment*—who knows how much I am ultimately indebted, in this respect also, to my protracted sickness! . . . *Ressentiment* is what is forbidden *par excellence* for the sick . . . This was comprehended by that profound physiologist, the Buddha. His "religion" should rather be called a kind of *hygiene* . . . its effectiveness was made conditional on the victory over *ressentiment* . . . [citing *The Dhammapada*]. "Not by enmity is enmity ended; by friendliness enmity is ended": these words stand at the beginning of the doctrine of the Buddha. It is not morality that speaks thus; thus speaks physiology.[21]

Especially interesting about this autobiographical claim regarding *ressentiment* is Nietzsche's paralleling of *his* victory over *ressentiment* with the Buddha's (a figure he consistently compares with both himself and his Jesus, but routinely *contrasts* with Paul and Pauline Christianity—see below). Like his Buddha, it is Nietzsche's much discussed "sickness" that is here said to have afforded him the insight that "*ressentiment* is what is forbidden *par excellence* for the sick." Though Nietzsche nowhere formally attributes the Nazarene's remarkable ressentiment-free status to his "morbid" psychophysiological condition, we have already treated Nietzsche's insistence that Jesus' extraordinary psychospiritual posture and message of love are to be viewed as products of his pathological sensitivity. Clearly the same spirit that informs Nietzsche's representation of the Buddha's "victory" over *ressentiment*[22] as matter of psychophysiological "hygiene"—"It is not morality that speaks thus; thus speaks physiology"—also lies behind the *Antichrist*'s foundational claims (1) that Jesus' very "incapacity for resistance here becomes morality" (29), and (2) that such a morbidly susceptible condition "could not but end in a religion of love" (*A* 30).

Like the noble Greeks and Romans, like the admired Buddha, and like Nietzsche's image of himself, Nietzsche's Jesus has achieved "superiority over every feeling of *ressentiment*" (*A* 40), and with that, truly separated himself from the psychology, the motivation, and the vengeful world-view of the *all too human* in general, but the *ressentiment*-drenched Judeo-Christian continuum in particular. Indeed, in situating Jesus well above the *ressentiment*-driven fray of both Judaism and burgeoning Christianity, Nietzsche at once emphasizes the essential continuity of these movements[23]—a point underlined by *Antichrist* 40's deliberate reference to "the one God and the one Son of God: both products of *ressentiment*"—and his understanding of a Jesus wholly and equally distinct from both Christianity and Judaism. Nietzsche's Jesus is a "free spirit" (*A* 32) in the philosopher's overtly autobiographical sense of the term, one "who thinks differently from . . . the dominant views of the age . . . [and] has liberated himself from tradition (*HH* 225).[24] Put simply, the Jesus of the *Antichrist* is no more a Christian than he is a Jew.[25]

SECOND COMING IN JUDGMENT

> "We shall practice revenge and outrage against all who are not as we are"—thus the tarantula-hearts promise themselves . . . Thus, however, I advise you, my friends: Mistrust all in whom the urge to punish is strong!
>
> *Zarathustra* 2, "Of the Tarantulas"

It is the spirit of this history-altering collision of the symbolic communiqués of this *ressentiment*-free, ahistoric "free spirit" with the utterly foreign religious-historically determined *ressentiment*-based understanding and needs of this first-century underclass that must, for Nietzsche, inform any reading of what is essentially the only account of this jarring clash, the New Testament. It is precisely this collision that allows Nietzsche to trace the "translation" of what he takes to be the original significance of Jesus' death—as exemplary of a new way of life—into the basis of the thoroughly vengeful doctrine of "the Second Coming." For Nietzsche, it is *not* a teaching of Jesus that one encounters in the doctrine of a Second Coming to "sit in judgment" of "enemies," but the pressing *need* of this "little community"—which had erroneously come to conflate "*their* cause" with what they took to be Jesus'—to assuage the suddenly pressing "suspicion that such a death might be the refutation of their cause." Translated through the reactive, *ressentiment*-drenched understanding of this crude and powerless Jewish assemblage, the urgent *needs* of the "shaken and disappointed" chandala rapidly gives rise—much like Paul's pressing pre-Damascus torment—to its own "answer."

"*Who* killed him? *Who* was his natural enemy?"—this question came like a flash of lightning. Answer: ruling Judaism, its upper class . . . far from *forgiving* his death—which would have been evangelic in the highest sense . . . an historic moment appeared in view: the "kingdom of God" is coming to sit in judgment on its enemies (*A* 40).

It is well to point out that Nietzsche's psychological rendering of the first Christians' rancorous and convenient "translation" of Jesus' loving, wholly nonvengeful, exemplary "manner of dying" in fact constitutes a pristine example of the heretofore hidden phenomenon Nietzsche prided himself on exposing two years earlier in the *Genealogy of Morals*. Recall Nietzsche's warning concerning the very real danger when the will to power of the *powerless* rears its head (when "*ressentiment* itself *becomes creative*"). Anticipating the *Antichrist*'s more focused treatment of the psychology underlying the composition of the Gospels, the *Genealogy* (1, 10) uncovers the all too human tendency of "natures that are denied the true reaction, that of deeds, . . . [to] compensate themselves with an imaginary revenge." *Antichrist* 40, then, speaks of the same compensatory phenomenon first outlined in the *Genealogy*. But in place of Judea's *national ressentiment* of the "strong and noble" Romans culminating in John's Apocalypse—"the most wanton of all literary outbursts that vengefulness has on its conscience" (*GM* 1, 16)[26]—it discerns in the early Christians' patently "unevangelic" notion of Jesus' return "in judgment," the *ressentiment* of the Jewish "chandala"—"the priestly instinct which can no longer endure the priest" (*A* 27)[27]—toward "ruling Judaism, its upper class."

It is also noteworthy that the enemies alluded to in this compensatory notion of a "Second Coming in judgment" are clearly the enemies not of Jesus, but of the resentful "chandala" in question (i.e., "ruling Judaism, its upper class"). It is *these* resentful spirits "which can no longer endure the priest," *not* Jesus. It is *their ressentiment* that "becomes creative," that gives rise to the compensatory "imaginary revenge" underlying the utterly "unevangelic" notion of a return in judgment, *not* Jesus'. It is because *they* stood in opposition to "Pharisee and theologian," because *they* "had need of a censuring theologian to oppose the theologians [that] they created their God according to their requirements" (*A* 31).

To demonstrate just how erroneous, how *need*-fulfilling and *requirement*-meeting such "translations" of the first Christians were, one need only remind oneself of the altogether different needs and requirements of Nietzsche's Jesus. As discussed in chapter 3, Nietzsche's Jesus *does not* manifest "bitterness against Pharisee and theologian," *does not* count himself among the enemies of "ruling Judaism," because he *cannot*. If such a hypersensitive soul is to survive, let alone thrive, "the instinct of self-preservation" itself dictates either a life of solitude or one essentially devoid of conflict, anger, enmity, opposition, and resistance. Jesus' thoroughly "morbid" psychophysiological *needs* simply necessitate a path of radical nonresistance. As the *Antichrist* stresses in its extraordi-

nary case history of Jesus, its "psychology of the redeemer," the Nazarene's utter "*inability* for enmity," his very "incapacity for resistance here
becomes morality" (*A* 29). Such a soul has no enemies because he can
endure no enemies. Such a neurasthenic opposes no one and no thing
because he can *withstand* no opposition. Hence we have the psychophy-
siologically dictated "glad tidings" that "there are no more opposites,"
that there need be no more opposition (*A* 32). For such a soul, precisely
because "it feels every contact too deeply" (*A* 30), the path of nonresistance and nonenmity is quite literally the "sole . . . [and] last possibility
of life" (*A* 30).

THE MORAL PREACHER

For essentially the same reasons he is suspicious of the first Christians'
need-based casting of Jesus in the familiar Judaic roles of miracle-worker
and judge-to-come, Nietzsche likewise resists the representation of this
extraordinary soul as one more "moral preacher" as yet another blatant
"misunderstanding [of] the type" (*A* 31). Nietzsche devotes considerable
attention to the notion of the moral preacher in *Human, All Too Human*'s
sometimes neglected second sequel, 1880's *The Wanderer and his Shadow*.
There (*WS* 19 and following), seemingly anticipating the good vs. bad /
good vs. evil distinction masterfully explored in the *Genealogy*'s first essay, Nietzsche is at pains to distinguish between the more mundane,
comparatively effortless valuations of "the moralist," and the
ressentiment-fueled moral judgmentalism of the "preacher of morals" (or
"moral judge").[28] The former is portrayed as one who measures and val-
uates quite naturally, quite innocently, on a case-by-case basis, while the
moral preacher/judge is one advancing a fixed (and typically reactive)[29]
moral *system*. Accordingly, while it is certain that Nietzsche conceives of
himself as a "moralist" (or "immoralist" as the case may be),[30] the matter
of how he would characterize his Jesus in this regard is not perfectly
clear.

Certainly *Antichrist* 31 makes explicit that the Nietzschean Jesus is no
more a "moral preacher" than he is a wrathful "judge to come." Indeed,
insofar as the moral preacher's agenda is typically born of *ressentiment*,
and is one of advancing one fixed system of beliefs in response to another,[31] one could not imagine a less appropriate characterization of Jesus. Most obviously, because his absolute freedom from *ressentiment*—
the all too human disposition underlying the bulk of moral preaching,
of moral *judging*—is said by Nietzsche to be precisely "the main thing"
about his Jesus (*A* 40).

Because the Nietzschean Jesus' message—a symbolic communication
concerning an *inner* condition of the heart, a psychic state that must be
lived to be understood—is indeterminate by its very nature, it accord-

ingly resists reduction to dogma and fixed, absolute positions.[32] While
fixed, absolute positions are the stock and trade of the *moral preacher*—
see chapter 7 of St. Paul's first letter to the Corinthians, for example—
Nietzsche's Jesus, a true "free spirit," cares nothing for what is fixed: the
word *killeth*, everything fixed killeth . . . the *experience* "life" in the only
form he knows it is opposed to any kind of word, formula, law, faith,
dogma" (*A* 32).

And last, with respect to the tendency of one moral preacher's doctrine
to be a response or rebuttal to another, we remind ourselves of just how
blissfully unaware of other positions Nietzsche's "purely inward" redeemer is (*WP* 160). After emphasizing that "*his* proofs are inner 'lights',
inner feelings of pleasure and self-affirmations," *Antichrist* 32 says the
following on the topic of the relation of Jesus' glad tidings to *other* opinions: "it simply does not know how to imagine an opinion contrary to
its own. . . . Where it encounters one it will, with the most heartfelt sym-
pathy, lament the "blindness"—for it sees the "light"—but it will make
no objection."

As one might expect, Nietzsche's ongoing tendency to paint portraits
of those with whom he identifies with patently autobiographical nuance
and color reemerges here, in the philosopher's assessment of the redeemer's relationship to moral judgmentalism in particular, and notions
of morality in general. Given the centrality to his philosophical enterprise
as a whole of Nietzsche's call not only to *question* accepted moral systems, but to *transcend* them, to move *beyond* conventional notions of good
and evil, it is hardly surprising that both his fundamentally indeterminate Jesus, gentle leader of "a Buddhistic peace movement" (*A* 42), and
the Nietzschean Buddha come to be presented as figures having attained
a stance similarly above and beyond traditional notions of morality.
Seemingly heeding his career-defining call to "take a stand beyond good
and evil [and] put beneath one the illusion of moral judgment" (*Twi.* 6,
1), of Buddhism and its founder Nietzsche insists:

It already has—and this distinguishes it profoundly from Christianity—the self-
deception of moral concepts behind it—it stands, in my language, *beyond* good
and evil (*A* 20).

"Good and Evil" says the Buddhist—"both are fetters; the Perfect One became
master over both . . . he has gone beyond both good and evil" (*GM* 3, 17).

Likewise, in an aphorism as isolated as it is brief, *Beyond Good and Evil*
164 insists: "Jesus said to his Jews: 'The law was made for servants—
love God as I love him, as his son!; What have we sons of God to do
with morality!' "

Somewhat ironically, considering *Ecce Homo*'s heroic depiction of its author standing *alone*, high above all notions of morality, all conceptions of good and evil, Nietzsche appears to have forgotten some of his earlier statements vis-à-vis Jesus and the Buddha's not altogether dissimilar positions. In fact, *Ecce Homo* uses very similar language in situating its author's position with respect to moral concepts, to notions of good and evil, as Nietzsche elsewhere does with respect to both Jesus and the Buddha. In Section 6 of *Ecce Homo*'s "Why I am a Destiny" for example, Nietzsche boasts: "I have chosen the word immoralist as a symbol and badge of honor for myself; I am proud of having this word which distinguishes me from the whole of humanity. Nobody yet has felt Christian morality to be beneath him: that requires a height, a view of distances, a hitherto altogether unheard of psychological depth and profundity." Though Nietzsche's Jesus is by no means one in possession of "unheard of psychological depth and profundity"—but rather an "innocent from the country" (*WP* 383)—he, like the Nietzschean Buddha, is nonetheless presented by the philosopher as one operating from a sufficient *height* and *distance* to regard prevailing religious-moralistic systems as thoroughly beneath him. Such a "distance" is implied by the Nietzschean Jesus' declaration that "The law was made for servants. . . . What have we sons of God to do with morality!," and is made *explicit* at *Antichrist* 36. There, Nietzsche marvels: "That mankind should fall on its knees before the opposite of what was the origin, the meaning, the right of the Gospel, that it should have sanctified in the concept 'Church' precisely what the 'bringer of glad tidings' regarded as *beneath* him, *behind* him— one seeks in vain a grander form of *world-historical* irony."

Though the full meaning of this extraordinary assertion that in the concept "Church," Christians come to sanctify "precisely what the 'bringer of glad tidings' regarded as *beneath* him, *behind* him" unfolds below in our analysis of Nietzsche's return to the theme of Paul's refashioning of nascent Christianity according to *his* very specific needs, at this juncture we note the following. For Nietzsche, *inherent* to the Judeo-Christian notion "Church," *underlying* the ecclesiastical focus on sin, guilt, punishment, judgment, and so forth, is *ressentiment* in general, and the *ressentiment* characterizing *slave morality* in particular. It bears emphasizing that for Nietzsche, the entire and massive edifice "Church" is born of and built atop the reactive, resentful phenomenon of *slave morality*, the quintessential manifestation of the will to power of the otherwise powerless. This then, is what Nietzsche's " 'bringer of glad tidings' regarded as *beneath* him, *behind* him." With that in mind, we note that taken together, *Beyond Good and Evil* 164's positioning of a Jesus well removed from all matters of mere "morality," and *Antichrist* 36's passionate insistence that it is everything "sanctified in the concept 'Church' " that Jesus considered "beneath" and "behind" him, suggest a posture, a "height," a "distance," and an *object* notably reminiscent of those boasted of in Nietzsche's literary autobiography.

It bears emphasizing however, that the note-worthly Nietzschean posture of the philosopher's Jesus vis-à-vis the concepts "Church" and "morality," no more makes him Renan's "aggressive fanatic, the mortal enemy of theologian and priest," than the "censuring theologian to oppose the theologians" conceived of by the first Christians (*A* 31). Nietzsche situates his Jesus' *above* and *beyond* such notions as "Church" (*A* 36), wholly *apart* from the concept "morality" (*BGE* 164), and "*outside* of all religion" (*A* 32) *not* because of any theological or moralistic rivalry or animosity. Far from being the "aggressive fanatic, the enemy of theologian and priest" that Renan suggests, Nietzsche is adamant that this very characterisation effectively *annuls* the very "type" of the redeemer altogether.[33]

As we have seen, Nietzsche's Jesus is the enemy of no one, including those inflicting "every kind of calumny and mockery" upon him. On the contrary, "he suffers, he loves *with* those, *in* those who are doing evil to him . . . *not* to grow angry . . . not to resist even the evil man—to *love* him" (*A* 35). For these same reasons he is not, indeed he *cannot be*, the "censuring theologian to oppose the theologians" needed and therefore envisioned by the first Christian community (*A* 31).[34] Indeed, "the 'glad tidings' are precisely that there are no more opposites," that there need not be any opposition at all. "The faith which here finds utterance is not a faith which has been won by struggle—it is there, from the beginning. . . . Such a faith is not angry, does not censure, does not defend itself; it does not bring 'the sword'—it has no idea to what extent it could one day cause dissension" (*A* 32). To repeat, Nietzsche's Jesus is one *above*, *beyond*, *apart* from, and *outside of* these matters, not for religious, moral, or theological reasons. His "distance" in fact, is absolutely unrelated to theoretical contrariety or contention of any kind. Precisely and quite literally the opposite is true. His extraordinary stance, his position well above and beyond such matters is for Nietzsche, a matter of wholly instinctual noncontrariety. "Precisely the opposite of all contending, of all feeling oneself in struggle has here become instinct: the incapacity for resistance here becomes morality" (*A* 29). To borrow a remark from *Ecce Homo* made in the context of Jesus' kindred spirit, the Buddha: "It is not morality that speaks thus; thus speaks physiology" (1, 6). With Jesus' extraordinary relationship to morality and religion understood in these terms, the rationale underlying Nietzsche's charge that to the *psychologist*, all depictions of the Nazarene as simply *one more* "censuring theologian," *one more* "moral preacher," are blatant "misunderstandings [of] the type," is clear indeed.

That the first Christians—crude, needy, impotent and resentful Jews, "the priestly instinct which can no longer endure the priest" (*A* 27)—

"adjust their Master into an apologia of themselves" (*A* 31) and come to see *in him* "bitterness against Pharisee and theologian," an "enemy" of "ruling Judaism," a wrathful "judge to come," and so forth, Nietzsche considers patently obvious and a glaring example of all too human needs. It is precisely for this reason that the study of the Gospels constitutes "a pleasure of the first rank to a psychologist" (*A* 44). That trained philologist Ernest Renan arrives at many of these same (mis)conceptions about Jesus some *nineteen centuries later*, suggests at least two things to Nietzsche. First, that "Monsieur Renan" is a "buffoon in *psychologicis*" (*A* 29), and second, that "only we, we *emancipated* spirits, possess the prerequisite for understanding something nineteen centuries have misunderstood" (*A* 36).

NOTES

1. In a fascinating section of *Training In Christianity* entitled "The Impossibility of Direct Communication," Kierkegaard maintains that "direct communication" requires that the communicator must be "known" to the recipient of the communication. Accordingly, even though Jesus *seems* to communicate directly to those around him, because who he *really was*—literally God made flesh—was unknown even to his closest disciples due to his taking on a human nature (what Kierkegaard terms his "incognito"), *all* of Jesus' communication was necessarily indirect. Even "when one says directly 'I am God; the father and I are one' . . . [because] he who says it is an individual man, quite like other men, then this communication is not just perfectly direct; for it is not just perfectly clear and direct that an individual man should be God" (p. 134).

2. As we saw in the case of the message Nietzsche's Jesus offers the thief on the Cross, the good news has to do with a "feeling," a subjective *experience* of blessedness. Indeed, such a feeling *is* the "psychological reality of redemption" (*A* 33) lived by and embodied in Jesus of Nazareth.

3. "Neither does this faith formulate itself—it *lives*, it resists formulas" (*A* 32).

4. Also on this topic of the Jew's apparent lack of naiveté and innocence, and speaking of their "instinctive ability to create an advantage, a means of seduction out of every superstitious supposition," *Will To Power* 199 insists:

Nothing is less innocent than the *New Testament*. One knows from what soil it sprang. This people of an inflexible self-will which knew how to prevail after it had lost every natural support and had long since forfeited its right to existence, and to that end had to raise itself up by unnatural, purely imaginary presuppositions (as chosen people, as community of saints, as the people of the promise, as "church") . . . When Jews step forward as innocence itself the danger is great.

5. *Antichrist* 44 continues: "In Christianity, as the art of holy lying, the whole of Judaism, a schooling and technique pursued with the utmost seriousness for hundreds of years, attains its ultimate perfection. The Christian, that *ultima ratio* of the lie, is the Jew once more—even thrice more."

6. See Kaufmann (1974), Duffy and Mittleman (1988), Santaniello (1994), Golomb (1997), and Mandel (1998).

7. See especially part nine of *Beyond Good and Evil*, "What is noble?", and the praise of Rome in Essay One of *The Genealogy of Morals*, "Good and Evil, Good and Bad."

8. In the absence of a suitable German equivalent Nietzsche consistently employs the French *"ressentiment."* While it would not be wholly incorrect to substitute the usual English translation of *ressentiment*—"resentment"—I have opted to join the philosopher in his use of the French form both in the name of consistency, and because in places Nietzsche's *"ressentiment"* seems to denote bitterness and hatred to a degree not normally associated with "resentment."

9. *Will To Power* 864: *Why the weak conquer*: "The anti-Semites do not forgive the Jews for possessing 'spirit'—and money. Anti-Semites—another name for the 'underprivileged'."

10. "The doctrine 'equal rights for all'—this has been more thoroughly sowed by Christianity than by anything else . . . it has forged out of the *ressentiment* of the masses its chief weapon against us, against everything noble, joyful, high-spirited on earth . . . Christianity is a revolt of everything that crawls along the ground directed against everything that which is elevated"(*A* 43).

11. *Daybreak* 68 relates Paul's frustration toward "the torture of the unfulfilled law" to Luther's frustrated desire to "become the perfect man of the spiritual ideal" and ensuing "deadly" hatred of that "spiritual ideal and the Pope and the saints." Likewise the *Antichrist* characterizes St. Paul as a "genius of hatred" (42) and sees in Luther "the vindictive instincts of a failed priest" (61).

12. In Book Two, Chapter One, of his *Nietzsche*, Jaspers characterizes the weak man's "evil" as specifically, and deliberately *condemning*. The strong man's "bad," on the other hand, is likened to a challenge—a challenge to others to raise and transcend themselves.

13. Extolling the virtues of his *Genealogy* two years later, Nietzsche (with obvious indebtedness to the title of his inaugural work) declares: "The truth of the *first* inquiry [essay] is the birth of Christianity: the birth of Christianity out of the spirit of *ressentiment*, not, as many people may believe, out of the "spirit"— a counter-movement by its very nature, the great rebellion against the dominion of *noble* values (*EH* on *GM*).

14. The *Genealogy* (1, 16) further articulates the essential continuity from pre-Jesus Judaism to post-Jesus Christianity:

Rome felt the Jew to be something like anti-nature itself, its antipodal monstrosity as it were. . . . How, on the other hand, did the Jews feel about Rome? A thousand signs tell us; but it suffices to recall the Apocalypse of John, the most wanton of all literary outbursts that vengefulness has on its conscience . . .

15. Insisting that the Jewish nation "had lost two of their castes, that of the warrior and that of the peasant," *Will To Power* 184 suggests that the Jews were left with only "the priests—and then immediately the chandala—As is only fair, a break develops among them, a revolt of the chandala: the origin of Christianity. . . . The Christian is the chandala who repudiates the priest."

16. *Ecce Homo*, "Why I am So Wise," Section 8.

17. The "world-historic irony" of what Christianity makes of the Nietzschean Jesus' simple message is again evident. *Antichrist* 33 observes that through Jesus "every kind of distancing relationship between God and man is abolished—*pre-*

cisely this is the 'glad tidings.' " But what do Nietzsche's "first Christians" do? In "severing him from themselves," they push away precisely the radical immediacy of Jesus' message, the "good news" itself.

18. The Roman historian Tacitus for example, offers a colorful account of the many miracles of Vespasian. That the arrival of Israel's Messiah would be marked by miracles—the blind seeing, the deaf hearing, the lame walking—was of course a familiar theme among Israel's prophets (cf. Robertson, pp. 82, 144).

19. In addition to the *Genealogy's* first essay, see *Antichrist* 59 and 60.

20. A characterization found in the young Prof. Nietzsche's lectures on Greek philosophy (in Kaufmann, p. 396).

21. At once picking up on this fascinating theme of Buddhism as a form of *hygiene*, and demonstrating Nietzsche's pervasive and all too human tendency to celebrate, accentuate, and when necessary *generate* those qualities in others (Jesus, Buddha, Socrates, etc.), most in accord with his own life and self-image, we note *Antichrist* 20's suggestion that—"against . . . depression Buddha takes hygienic measures. He opposes it with life in the open air, the wandering life; with moderation and fastidiousness as regards food; with caution towards all alcoholic spirits."

Nietzsche's *own*, difficult experience is even more apparent in a very similar remark from the *Twilight*:

The means by which Julius Caesar defended himself against sickliness and headache: tremendous marches, the simplest form of living, uninterrupted sojourn in the open air, continuous toil—these, broadly speaking, are the universal preservatives and protective measures against the extreme vulnerability of that subtle machine working at the highest pressure which is called genius (31).

22. "The fight against *ressentiment*," writes Nietzsche at *Will To Power* 204, "seems to be almost the first duty of the Buddhist: only thus is peace of soul assured. To disengage oneself, but without rancor: that presupposes, to be sure, an astonishingly mild and sweet humility—saints." Revealingly, we note that the Nietzschean Jesus embodies each and every one of the qualities—astonishingly mild, sweet, humble, disengaged, and free of rancor—here celebrated in the context of Buddhism's "saints."

23. "The Christian, that *ultima ratio* of the lie, is the Jew once more—even thrice more" (*A* 44). "Christianity can be understood only by referring to the soil out of which it grew—it is *not* a counter-movement against the Jewish instinct, it is actually its logical consequence, one further conclusion of its fear-inspiring logic" (*A* 24).

24. While Nietzsche explicitly calls Jesus a "free spirit" at *Antichrist* 32, the corresponding image is of course writ large on every page of that volume. This easily missed characterization is significant both because it captures the radical differentiation of the Nietzschean Jesus from Judaism and Christianity alike, and is one of Nietzsche's favorite terms to describe both *himself* (*HH* preface; *GS* 343; *A* 13,36) and the potential audience for whom his philosophy is targeted (again, see the Preface to *Human, All Too Human*—tellingly subtitled *A Book For Free Spirits*.

25. Nietzsche similarly bids to extricate his beloved Goethe from the distaste-

ful ranks of the Germans. "*Goethe*," declares Nietzsche in the *Twilight of the Idols* (9, 49), "not a German event but a European one."

26. The Old Testament is awash in warnings and prophesies of God smiting the enemies of his people, and John's Revelation seems firmly rooted in the tradition of the judgment stories found in Joel, Malachi, and Zechariah. Considering what is now known about John's Apocalypse, Nietzsche's charge of compensatory imagined Jewish revenge seems reasonable indeed. As Fredriksen (p. 82) dryly remarks: "Happy people do not write apocalypses."

Characterized as "the most Jewish book that ever found its way into the New Testament" (Robertson, p. 153), scholars tend to date his book of Revelation—which tellingly alludes to the reign of both Nero and Domitian—to approximately 95 A.D., the very time Roman authorities began enforcing the cult of Emperor worship and Jews and Christians faced growing persecution. Interestingly, like Paul's letters, John's Apocalypse has little interest in the Jesus of history and contains next to no references to the redeemer's career or message. Like Paul's Damascus vision, the risen Christ is said to have appeared to John (then exiled to the island of Patmos, likely the site of a Roman penal colony). John reports receiving visions of coming earthquakes (Revelation 6:12); hail and fire mixed with blood (8:6); locusts (9:1-12); seas, rivers and springs turning to blood (16:3-7); the fall of Babylon [Rome?]; the return of Christ for a thousand year reign on earth; Satan being "thrown into the lake of burning sulfur"; the dead being marshaled before "a great white throne" of judgment; a sword-wielding blood-marked Jesus serving "the flesh of kings, generals, and mighty men" to vultures, and a "new heaven and a new earth" replacing "the first earth [that] had passed away" (Rev. 18—Rev. 21).

Writing of the Jewish apocalyptic tradition in general, and in full accord with Nietzsche's *ressentiment* model, Fredriksen observes: "The apocalyptic description of the joyful future that awaits them . . . is the mirror image of present times, which are seen as uniquely, indeed terminally, terrible . . . The final enemy was always the apocalyptic 'Babylon', be it incarnated as the Seleucid Empire or Rome" (p. 82).

Woe! Woe, O great city, dressed in fine linen, purple and scarlet, and glittering with gold, precious stones and pearls! In one hour such great wealth has been brought to ruin! (18: 16, 17)

27. *Antichrist* 27 continues: "I fail to see against what the revolt was directed whose originator Jesus is understood or *misunderstood* to be if it was not a revolt against the Jewish Church—'Church' taken in precisely the sense in which we take the word today. It was a revolt against the 'good and the just', against 'the saints of Israel', against the social hierarchy."

28. Jaspers (1965), pp. 139–45.

29. "That which an age feels to be evil is usually an untimely after-echo of that which was formerly felt to be good—the atavism of an older ideal" (*BGE* 149).

30. For Nietzsche of course, among life's experiences to be evaluated are specific moralities themselves. To the critical eye of the true moralist, the very notion of "immoralism" is meaningless and something imposed from without (there being no reason why the valuating of the moralist should exclude particular

moral values, constructs, or systems). Says Nietzsche (*HH-WS* 19): "Moralists must now accept the fact that they are regarded as immoral because they dissect morals."

31. Again, while this work predates 1887's *Genealogy*, it is that work's chronicling of what Nietzsche characterizes as the "deadly contradiction" and *collision* of "Judea against Rome" that best captures the philosopher's understanding of moral preaching as an essentially *reactive* phenomenon (*GM* 1, 16).

32. "Neither does this faith formulate itself—it *lives*, it resists formulas" (*A* 32).

33. "I resist, to repeat it, the incorporation of the fanatic into the type of the redeemer: the word *imperieux* alone which Renan employs already *annuls* the type" (*A* 32).

34. "When the first community had need of a censuring theologian to oppose the theologians they *created* their 'God' according to their requirements: just as they had unhesitatingly put into his mouth those totally unevangelic concepts they could not now do without, 'Second Coming', 'Last Judgment', every kind of temporal promise and expectation" (*A* 31).

6

The Genius of Paul

To the Jews I became like a Jew, to win the Jews. To those under the law I became one under the law . . . so as to win those under the law. To those not having the law I became like one not having the law . . . so as to win those not having the law. To the weak I became weak, to win the weak. I have become all things to all men so that by all possible means I might save some.

Paul's first letter to the Corinthians 9:19

He understood what the pagan world had the greatest need of . . .

Will To Power 167

While Nietzsche makes it very clear that the birth of post-Jesus Christianity is to be considered a "process of decay" and "not the chance product of some individual talent, some exceptional nature," he is also adamant that it is Paul who takes this process "to its conclusion" (*A* 44) and that "without this remarkable history, without the storms and confusions of such a mind, of such a soul, there would be no Christianity; we would hardly have heard of a little Jewish sect whose master died on the cross" (*D* 68). That in mind, the question then becomes just what it is about his Paul that allows Nietzsche, qua first "psychologist of Christianity," to conclude that without him, without his exceptional nature, "there would be no Christianity?" Surely Paul, as our treatment of Nietzsche's psychological reading of his famed Damascus-road experience makes clear, is not *that* different than the Jewish "chandala" that become the first Christians? Both come to resent, due to their own insufficiencies, dominant Jewish orthodoxy, and both self-interestedly interpret or "translate" the necessarily pliable figure of Jesus of Nazareth—as "destroyer of the Law" and "judge to come" respectively—according to their own needs. But that, according to Nietzsche, is largely the extent of commonality between those he calls the "first Christians" and Paul of Tarsus. Indeed, it is fruitful to contrast the language Nietzsche employs in his portrayal of these "first Christians"—those disappointed figures first left wondering, *"What was that*?" upon Jesus' sudden departure—with his very different rendering of the Apostle Paul (a figure uniquely equipped and extraordinarily motivated to provide an answer to their pressing question).

As discussed, Nietzsche sees in the Jewish "chandala" that will become the first Christians, the impotent underclass of a thoroughly "priestly" culture.[1] Not surprisingly, every aspect of their existence—their intellect, their character, their abilities, their world-view and its consequences—is uniformly slandered by our self-professed "antichrist" (*EH* 3, 2). Among other epithets, this "movement from below" (*WP* 182) of "utterly unhinged souls" (*A* 40) is said to consist of "the lowest class of Jewish society and intelligence" (*WP* 198), and the "refuse of society" (*A* 31). For these "vulgar" (*WP* 206), "lowly and little people" (*WP* 213), these "little bigots and three-quarters mad-men" (*A* 43), "one should have built madhouses . . . and nothing more" (*WP* 202). In sum: "People of the basest origin, in part rabble, outcasts not only from good but also from respectable society, raised away from even the *smell* of culture, without discipline, without knowledge . . . ignorance itself" (*WP* 199).

How different then is the scope of the philosopher's ongoing characterization of Paul. The very opposite of "rabble . . . raised away from even the *smell* of culture," "Paul's home," Nietzsche pointedly observes at *Antichrist* 42, "was the principal center of Stoic enlightenment": Tarsus. This culturally diverse, cosmopolitan Hellenistic seaport city was exposed to wide-ranging ideas and was home to celebrated schools of Greek philosophy and flourishing mystery religions (particularly the cult of Mithras, as Nietzsche was only too aware).[2] A well-educated Roman citizen[3] who rose to early eminence as Pharisee, Paul, in letters full of references to urban Hellenistic life,[4] boasts of his understanding of his Jewish heritage while demonstrating considerable acquaintance with the Stoic teachings of the day.[5] Clearly, when dealing with Paul of Tarsus, one is encountering a figure very different from the unsophisticated "rabble" and "refuse" Nietzsche sees in the "first Christians."

Nor is one dealing with another "unhinged" candidate for the "madhouse." Quite the contrary is true. Speaking of Paul's extraordinary promise at 1 Corinthians 6:3—"Know ye not that we shall judge angels?"—Nietzsche tellingly laments, "Unfortunately *not* merely the ravings of a lunatic" (*A* 45). In a marked and deliberate contrasting of the

Apostle with his Dostoyevskyesque "redeemer," the philosopher is adamant that Paul "was definitely no idiot."[6] Nietzsche's Paul is someone
to be reckoned with, taken seriously, and accordingly is far more dangerous than any naïf, idiot, lunatic or "unhinged soul." Paul, Nietzsche
tells us again and again, is a "genius" (*A* 58; *WP 175*), an intuitive and
extraordinarily "cunning" figure (*D* 68) who "recognized" (*WP* 175), who
"understood" (*A* 47), who "divined . . . [how] one could ignite a 'world
conflagration' " (*A* 58) of such enormity and significance, that two millennia later it remains without parallel. Though described by Nietzsche
as a "moral cretin" (*WP* 171), a "frightful impostor" (*A* 45), and "this
epileptic" (*D* 68),[7] conspicuous in its absence is any impugning of the
Apostle's *intellect*.[8]

It is something other than his upbringing or intellect that separates
him from the "chandala" first faced with the task of continuing Christianity after Jesus' death, and allows Nietzsche to conclude that without
him "there would be no Christianity" (*D* 68). For Nietzsche, all other
attributes Paul brings to the table of history pale in significance next to
his extraordinary thirst for power. While the specific implications for the
history of Christianity, and indeed the history of the world, of Paul's
"intractable lust for power" (*D* 68) are examined below, we note that it
is this singularly defining characteristic that ultimately may be said to
inform each and every one of Nietzsche's increasingly numerous reflections on the figure of Paul.

From *Daybreak's* skillful tracking of the psychohistorical metamorphosis of the troubled Pharisee into the celebrated Apostle to the
Gentiles, to the *Antichrist's* less restrained but no less insightful accusations concerning Paul's role in the utter metamorphosis of Christianity
itself, power is a term associated with Paul on line after line, page after
page. *Daybreak* 68 alone speaks of Paul's "intractable lust for power," his
"extravagant lust for power," his "intoxication" with power, and asks,
"who, apart from a few scholars," discerns in Paul's letters, the "history
of one of the most ambitious and importunate souls."[9] By the time of
the writings of 1888, not only is Nietzsche reflecting on the topic of Paul
with growing frequency and vitriol, but the philosopher seems to have
essentially reduced the matter of Paul *to* the desire for power.

Also noteworthy about these later reflections, and fundamental to his
portrayal of not merely a power-hungry, but a power-*attaining* Paul, is
the regularity with which the words *"lie"* and *"priest"* come to be associated with the theme of Paul and power. "With Paul" observes Nietzsche, "the priest again sought power" (*A* 42),[10] "power in opposition
to ruling Judaism" (*WP* 173). To attain that power, Nietzsche's Paul is
said to employ "the same well-pondered baseness with which the Jewish
priesthood established its power and the Jewish church was created' (*WP*
172): The lie, the "holy lie."[11]

"Paul understood the need for the lie" (*A* 47). *Antichrist* 42 for example, divines in Paul's "lie of the 'resurrected' Jesus" (discussed below) one more instance of "the radical falsification" (*A* 24) of reality mastered long ago by ruling Judaism.[12] Indeed, the same rationale that underlies so many of Nietzsche's striking associations of Paul with so-called "rabbinical insolence,"[13] also lies behind his repeated claims that the spirit behind post-Jesus Christianity is but a modified Judaism.[14] As far as Nietzsche is concerned, the power-hungry Paul—who in his letter to the Galatians retrospectively describes himself as one "advancing in Judaism beyond many Jews of my own age" and "extremely zealous for the traditions of my fathers" (1:14)—simply *repeats* the power-amassing procedure of falsification masterfully implemented with such success by those fathers. "The origin of the holy lie is the will to power," insists Nietzsche at *Will To Power* 142. What differs is the *particular* lie in question. "The 'Law', the 'will of God', the 'sacred book', 'inspiration'—all merely words for the conditions *under* which the priest comes to power, *by* which he maintains his power" (*A* 55).

As the quest for power of the Jewish priesthood resulted in the "great literary forgery" (*A* 26) of Judaic history and morality,[15] so Nietzsche's globe-trotting Apostle devotes the same "resolute determination" (*A* 47) once devoted to mastering Judaism (Gal. 1:14) and savagely persecuting the early Christians (Gal. 1:13; Phil. 3:6), to the pliable movement and figure of Jesus of Nazareth. The objective however, is exactly the same: "Preserving the power of the priest" (*A* 26).

Nietzsche is clear that the transformation of the "relative rationality" (*WP* 196) of Jesus' "Buddhistic peace movement, . . . an actual and not merely promised happiness on earth," into a superstitious, other-worldly religion built atop false promises and "priestly tyranny" (*A* 42) is a massive and convoluted "process" (*A* 44). *Within* that process however, Nietzsche detects two functionally inseparable subtexts, both rooted in Paul's intractable will to power in opposition to ruling Judaism, and both highly injurious to the delicate, indeterminate, and fundamentally original message of Jesus of Nazareth.

1. The ingenious modification of nascent Christianity so that it might not only find, but actively attract and indeed *solicit* the interest, allegiance, and worship of not just *Jewry's* underprivileged, but "the outcast and underprivileged of *all kinds*" (*WP* 172 my italics).
2. The recasting of the redeemer's "genuine, primitive Christianity" (*A* 39)[16] in such a manner that utterly "unevangelic" concepts such as guilt, punishment, sin, and reward become increasingly important.

The astonishing success of Nietzsche's Paul, indeed his indisputable history-altering "genius," may be said to lie in his awareness that by adapting a number of ideas circulating within "this little sectarian move-ment on the edge of Judaism" (*A* 58) to the needs of an audience (and potential priestly power-base) far larger than Judaism itself, that this minor movement could indeed serve as a means to procure significant "power in opposition to ruling Judaism." So it is that *Antichrist* 58 pro-poses that "the genius of Paul consists" in his realization that by placing "the ideas by which" the Roman Empire's many subterranean "Chandala religions exercised their fascination . . . in the mouth of the 'Savior' *he* had invented . . . on the road to Damascus," "one could sum up every-thing down-trodden, everything in secret revolt." It is this acute under-standing not only of the needs of this broad constituency, but of the ideas and images capable of exploiting these powerful needs, hopes, and de-sires that distinguishes the Apostle's "translation" of primitive Christi-anity from that of the so-called first Christians.

Recall that *Antichrist* 31 suggests that the first Christian community similarly "put into his mouth those totally unevangelic concepts which *they* could not do without" and adjusted the figure of Jesus "according to *their* requirements" (my italics). Their very particular "translation" is largely attributed to the convergence of Jesus' fundamentally indefinite message with the pressing "needs" and essential "crudity" of the Jewish chandala in question. In "order to understand anything of it at all," Nie-tzsche observes at *Antichrist* 31: "the first disciples in particular had to translate a being immersed entirely in symbols and incomprehensibilities into their own crudity . . . for them such a type could not *exist* until it had been reduced to more familiar forms." That the "familiar forms" to which these simple, downtrodden souls quickly reduce the suddenly ab-sent Jesus—"Messiah, the judge who is to come," the "enemy . . . [of] ruling Judaism," and so forth (*A* 31,40)—are so familiar, so obviously in their *own* best interest and validating of *their* cause, is all too human, and for Nietzsche as "understandable" as their pressing fear that Jesus' death "might be the *refutation* of their cause" (*A* 40). While certainly no accident, the reduction and mistranslation of Jesus' symbolic message at the hands of the *ressentiment*-fueled first Christians is presented, not as the product of careful deliberation or systematic planning, but arising *spontaneously* from very human needs and fears.

Paul's manipulation of Jesus' meaning and message on the other hand, while also stemming (as *Daybreak* 68 makes abundantly clear) from the pressing needs of the interpreter, is consistently presented by Nietzsche as a calculated bid to understand and deliberately *cater to* these very human religious needs, fears, and desires. As the powerful *ressentiment* of the "first Christians" is said to ultimately determine their image of Jesus, in the case of Paul's movement we are told rather that it is pre-cisely the "*ressentiment* which these lowly-placed persons feel toward everything held in honor [that] is constantly gambled upon" (*WP* 172).

As the limited "understanding" of the Jewish chandala is said to have determined their conception of Jesus, it is Paul's extraordinary understanding of the religious needs of the pagan masses that is said to determine the Jesus he self-interestedly advances.

Christianity: a naïve beginning to a Buddhistic peace movement in the very seat of *ressentiment*—but reversed by Paul into a pagan mystery doctrine. . . . Paul starts from the need for a mystery felt by the broad, religiously excited masses: he seeks a sacrifice, a bloody phantasmagoria which will stand up in competition with the images of the mystery cults. . . . He understood what the pagan world had the greatest need of, and from the facts of Christ's life and death made a quite arbitrary selection, giving everything a new accentuation, shifting the emphasis everywhere—he *annulled* primitive Christianity as a matter of principle (*WP* 167).

To better appreciate the trajectory of Nietzsche's charge, a word or two on the topic of Paul and the "pagan mystery doctrine[s]" in question is warranted. The term "mystery religion" is generally used with reference to innumerable secretive and highly ritualized cults found throughout the Mediterranean from approximately the seventh century B.C. to the fifth century A.D. While the Dionysian cult was Greek in origin, and other mysteries, such as those of Isis, Mithras, and Attis came from the East, a number of themes were common to most of the cults as practiced in the Mediterranean at this time: A more intensified form of worship than that characterizing official Greek or Roman religion; highly secretive rites of initiation; an emphasis on ritual purification; initiates seeking connection with the honored deity via the reenacting of events associated with that deity in general, and that deity's suffering in particular; ritualized means of securing salvation, rebirth and immortality. According to Kennedy, "the element prized above all others" by initiates was the possibility of "escape" from death (pp. 199–200).

It is also well to note that the question of precisely how far the flourishing Greco-Roman mystery religions of the day influenced nascent Christianity has become the subject of considerable scholarship.[17] Though the terminological influence of these subterranean movements on early Christian writing, Paul's letters especially, is today rarely disputed, the degree to which they exerted influence on the actual *content* of the Christian canon is a hotly debated topic. Such striking similarities exist between Paul's writings on (for example) the Lord's supper, or expiation, rebirth and immortality, and the teachings of the contemporary mystery religions, that early apologists such as Justin Martyr (ca.150 A.D.) came to attribute these commonalties to acts of demonic counterfeiting.[18] While more than willing to agree with Justin that something *diabolical* lay behind such curious cases of correspondence, Nietzsche, both skilled classicist and self-professed "foremost psychologist of Christianity," points to an altogether more mundane series of events.

While the *Antichrist* alludes to Paul's calculated paganization of "the 'Savior' *he* had invented . . . so as to *make* of him something even a priest of Mithras could understand" (58), it is to several notebook entries from the time of its composition that one looks for the most detailed unpacking of the Apostle's "new accentuation" according to the *needs* of "the broad, religiously excited masses." *Will To Power* 196, for example, also begins with the supposition that the "entire transformation is an adaptation to the needs and the level of understanding of the religious masses of that time," but takes a closer look at the specific "needs" in question when it suggests that "those masses which believed in Isis, Mithras, Dionysus, the 'Great Mother' ":

desired of a religion: (1) hope of a beyond, (2) the bloody phantasmagoria of the sacrificial animal (the mystery), (3) the redemptive deed, the holy legend, (4) asceticism, world-denial, superstitious "purification", (5) a hierarchy, a form of community. In short: Christianity accommodated itself to already existing and established anti-paganism, to the cults that had been combated by Epicurus[19]— more precisely, to the religions of the lower masses, the women, the slaves, the non-noble classes.[20]

We therefore have the following misunderstandings:

1. the immortality of the person;
2. the presumed other world;
3. the absurdity of the concept of punishment and the concept of sin at the heart of existence;
4. instead of the deification of man his un-deification, the digging of the deepest chasm, which only a miracle, only prostration in deepest self-contempt can bridge;
5. the whole world of corrupt imagination and morbid affects instead of a kindly and simple way of life, instead of a Buddhistic happiness attainable on earth;
6. an ecclesiastical order with priesthood, theology, cult, sacrament; in short everything that Jesus of Nazareth had combated;
7. miracles all over, superstition: while the distinguishing mark of Judaism and earliest Christianity is its repugnance to miracles, its relative rationality.

Once again, Nietzsche's tendency to reveal most clearly just *who* his Jesus is when refuting the interpretation of others is evident. This passage contains one of many references to what he clearly takes to be one of the more egregious and ultimately "ironic" (*A* 36) examples of Paul's "shifting" of emphasis (*WP* 167) and "ruthless violence to the truth" of Jesus' message (*A* 58). For in reorienting the hope and "good news" of Christianity from a "Buddhistic happiness attainable on earth" to the "presumed other world" of the pagan mystery religions, Paul renders that good news *unattainable*, and effectively removes the very essence of Jesus' message from "Christianity."

BUDDHA AGAINST THE CRUCIFIED[21]

> Nothing is further from Buddhism than the Jewish fanaticism of a Paul.
>
> *Will To Power* 155

Since Paul's otherworldly "beyond" simply does not exist for Nietzsche—nor, as we see below, likely even for Nietzsche's Paul himself—with his shifting of post-Jesus Christianity's "emphasis" *away* from "earthly things" and *toward* that "other world," "all at once the Evangel became the most contemptible of all unfulfillable promises" (*A* 41). Indeed, the essential *unfulfillablity* of post-Jesus Christianity's "promises"—"redemption through faith; resurrection after death," and so forth. (*WP* 169)[22]—ranks both as one of the principal reasons for Nietzsche's unmitigated contempt toward all things "Christian," and one of the sharpest points of contrast between it and Jesus' own "Buddhistic peace movement" (*A* 41; *WP* 167).

Though Buddhism ultimately elicits the frequently-levied Nietzschean charges of "nihilism" and *"decadence,"* compared to his assessment of Pauline Christianity, the philosopher's esteem for aspects of the eastern religion is high indeed.[23] *Antichrist* 42, on the topic of "the basic distinction between the two decadence religions" remarks: "Buddhism makes no promises but keeps them, Christianity makes a thousand promises but keeps none." As was the case in our treatment of the matter of Jesus, Buddhism, and the transcendence of morality, it is well to point out that on the basis of this telling contrast of religious "promises," Jesus' "peace movement" plainly has nothing in common with Pauline Christianity, but rather is praised by the philosopher for precisely the same reason he applauds Buddhism. Like Buddhism, it has nothing whatsoever to do with the "unfulfillable promises" of a "presumed other world," and everything to do with the actuality of an *attainable* earthly happiness. "Buddhism" suggests Nietzsche at *Antichrist* 21 "is not a religion in which one merely aspires after perfection: perfection is the normal case." As it is with Buddhism, so it is with Jesus' "Buddhistic peace movement." "Blessedness," insists Nietzsche at *Antichrist* 33, "is not promised, it is not tied to any conditions: it is the *only* reality." To the question, "What are the 'glad tidings'?," the Nietzschean Jesus, loosely reflecting Luke 17:21 answers: "True life, eternal life has been found, it is not being promised, it is here, it is *within you*" (*A* 29).

Accordingly, when Nietzsche nonchalantly maintains—"The Christian way of life is no more a fantasy than the Buddhist way of life: it is a means to being happy" (*WP* 159)—there can be no doubt as to which (or *whose*) variety of Christianity he is referring. In each of the above cases, the "true life," the "blessedness," the "Christian way of life" Nietzsche compares so favorably with Buddhism, is not the "Christianity" of Paul's promises, but that *realized* in the person of Jesus of Nazareth. What was realized in the person of Jesus was a comparatively "rational" (*WP* 196), wholly realizable path to blessedness, an entirely *earthly* "means to being happy" (*WP* 159) as far removed from the unfulfillable otherworldly promises of Mithras, Isis, and St. Paul, as is Buddhism.

THE MOST CONTEMPTIBLE OF ALL UNFULFILLABLE PROMISES

> If only for this life we have hope in Christ, we are to be pitied more than all men.
>
> 1 Corinthians, 15:19

We have already devoted considerable attention to Nietzsche's repeated and cardinal claims concerning what he considers the *real* significance of Jesus' death.

Jesus himself would have desired nothing by his death but publicly to offer the sternest test, the proof of his teaching . . . Such a death *was* precisely this "kingdom of God" (*A* 40).

This "bringer of glad tidings" died as he lived, as he *taught*—not to "redeem mankind" but to demonstrate how one ought to live (*A* 35).

He died for *his* guilt—all ground is lacking for the assertion, however often it is made, that he died for the guilt of others (*A* 27).

Yet Nietzsche accuses his power-hungry Apostle, one in search of "a sacrifice, a bloody phantasmagoria which will stand up in competition with the images of the mystery cults" (*WP* 167) not only of recasting Jesus' inherently individualized and exemplary death as the supreme "guilt sacrifice"—in the "most repulsive, barbaric" "symbol [of] 'God on the Cross' " (*A* 41,58)—but of calculatingly linking this "sacrifice" to the resurrection and immortality of the individual Christian. But with the central, recurring, and fundamentally Pauline notion that "God gave his Son for the forgiveness of sins, as a *sacrifice*":[24]

All at once it was over for the Gospel! The *guilt sacrifice*, and that in its most repulsive, barbaric form, the sacrifice of the *innocent man* for the sins of the guilty! What atrocious paganism! . . . Paul, with that rabbinical insolence which characterizes him in every respect, rationalized this interpretation, this indecency of an interpretation, thus: "If Christ is not resurrected from the dead our faith is vain."—All at once the Evangel became the most contemptible of all unfulfillable promises, the impudent doctrine of personal immortality . . . Paul himself even taught it as a reward! (*A* 41).

Just what is it about the notion of "the sacrifice of the *innocent man* for the sins of the guilty" that causes Nietzsche to declare: "All at once it was over for the Gospel!"? Why does he call Paul's variation on the sin-sacrifice-reconciliation motif (as familiar to Judaism as the mystery religions) "contemptible?" Because it is precisely these notions, upon which the Pauline doctrine of a necessary atoning "guilt sacrifice" is built—sin, guilt, punishment, the need of retribution, distance between man and God, blessedness tied to conditions—that Jesus, *through the very practice of his life*, wholly transcended. Indeed, as unfailingly as his Paul is associated with power, Nietzsche's Jesus is consistently tied to the embodied transcendence of and radical freedom from all feelings and conceptions of sin. As discussed in chapter 1, in Nietzsche's earliest scattered musings on the figure of Jesus, what separates the bringer of glad tidings from the surrounding Jewish milieu (the very people "who had invented sin" *GS* 138), what makes him a single ray of sunshine capable of piercing the dark, tear-filled, sin-obsessed Jewish landscape, is "the feeling of complete freedom from sin" (*HH* 144).

As was the case in our treatment of *Antichrist* 35's remarkable insertion of the matter of *feeling* into Jesus' conversation with the thief on the Cross—"If thou *feelest* this . . . thou art in Paradise"—Nietzsche's easily missed phraseology at *Human, All Too Human* 144 (his "*feeling* of complete freedom from sin") is of tremendous importance. Once again, "feeling," *psychological reality*, is the locus of Nietzsche's interest. Though perhaps based on illusion, it bears emphasizing that for Nietzsche, there is nothing less than real about Jesus' "*feeling* of complete freedom from sin" (*HH* 144). In fact, as the *Antichrist* articulates some ten years later, this *feeling* of utter sinlessness, of there being no distance between man and God, *is* Jesus' psychological redemption, the inner condition of "blessedness" he embodies and has to offer others. "This alone is the psychological reality of redemption" (*A* 33).

"Sin" of course for Nietzsche, is not objectively *real* but a matter of life-negating *belief*. The mighty Greeks, insists Nietzsche, had no notion of sin, for they had no need of such a concept. Like the good versus evil distinction, "sin" (as *Gay Science* 135 and 138 suggest and the *Genealogy* examines), is a vengeful idea brought into the world via Judaism, a compensatory and reactive concept born of the will to power of the *powerless*. But it is precisely because sin for Nietzsche is strictly a matter of belief, of *psychological reality*, that the *belief*, the *feeling* that one is free of sin, may be said to constitute a genuine redemption (what *Antichrist* 42 calls "an actual and *not* merely promised *happiness on earth*"). On the topic of these altogether *real* "glad tidings," Nietzsche says the following:

In the entire psychology of the "Gospel" the concept guilt and punishment is lacking; likewise the concept reward. "Sin", every kind of distancing relationship between God and man *is abolished—precisely this is the "glad tidings"* . . . He has settled his accounts with the whole Jewish penance-and-reconciliation doctrine; he knows that it is through the *practice* of one's life that one feels "divine", "blessed", "evangelic", at all times a "child of God" (*A* 33).

Jesus starts directly with the condition the "Kingdom of Heaven" in the heart, and he does not find the means to it in the observances of the Jewish church; . . . He likewise ignores the entire system of crude formalities governing intercourse with God: he opposes the whole teaching of repentance and atonement; he demonstrates how one must live in order to feel "deified"—and how one will not achieve it through repentance and contrition for one's sins: "Sin is of no account" is his central judgment. Sin, repentance, forgiveness—none of this belongs here— It is acquired from Judaism, or it is pagan (*WP* 160).

Though Paul is not mentioned in these parallel passages, they are of considerable relevance to the philosopher's career-long effort to distinguish the Nazarene's "genuine, primitive Christianity" from Paul's remarkable melange of pagan and Jewish teachings. Nietzsche's nonchalant claims that Jesus "has settled *his* accounts with the whole Jewish penance-and-reconciliation doctrine" (my italics), and understood "that it is through the practice of one's life that one feels 'divine' " (*A* 33) warrants our attention for two reasons.

First, we note this so-called "settling of accounts" is emphatically *singular*. Jesus is said to have "settled *his* accounts" with the Jewish tradition, not mine, not yours, and certainly not Paul's (my italics). As *Antichrist* 35 and 27 insist, Jesus died "not to 'redeem mankind' but to demonstrate how one ought to live . . . all ground is lacking for the assertion, however often it is made, that he died for the guilt of others." Second, because this account settling is inextricably bound up with the day-to-day "practice of one's *life*" (my italics), *not* to a mystical, and bloody atoning *death*.[25] Life, not death, it bears repeating, is the key to the "Kingdom of Heaven" embodied and practiced by Nietzsche's Jesus.

Of course on both these points, the message and significance of Paul's Jesus is another matter altogether. Most obviously, because inherent to the notion of the guilt sacrifice, "the sacrifice of the innocent man for the sins of the guilty," is a Jesus mysteriously capable of settling the "accounts" for *all* believers (including the unhappy Paul, who *Daybreak* 68 suggests was incapable of living up to the spiritual ideal of his people). Also significant is that Paul's Jesus settles this *collective* account, not through the practice of his life, but through his sin- and guilt-erasing death. Only too aware of the notable lack of interest in Jesus' life evidenced in Paul's letters, *Antichrist* 42 cynically concludes: "In fact he could make no use at all of the redeemer's life—he needed the death on the Cross." As Paul himself makes clear in his first letter to the Corinthians: "we preach Christ crucified" (1:22).

Revealingly, on this matter of the inapplicability of Pauline Christianity's linkage of Jesus with notions of sin, guilt, penance, and punishment, we note once again that the Nietzschean Jesus' transcendent posture has much in common not only with the philosopher's image of Buddhism,[26] but with his image of *himself*. Indeed, extrication from notions of sin and guilt is fundamental to Nietzsche's understanding of his *own* calling, and in a real sense, the very essence of his own "glad tidings."[27] On the topic of the all too human *"desire to counterbalance guilt with punishment" Daybreak* 202, for example, asks:

but can we not get beyond this? What a relief it would be for the general feeling of life if, together with the belief in guilt, one also got rid of the old instinct for revenge, and even regard it as a piece of prudence for the promotion of happiness to join Christianity in blessing one's enemies and *to do good* to those who have offended us. Let us do away with the concept *sin*—and let us send after it the concept *punishment*! May these banished monsters henceforth live somewhere other than among men. . . .

Nietzsche here speaks of "joining Christianity" in the interest of happiness and "do[ing] away with the concept *sin*." We may note that whereas the Christianity he associates with Paul is precisely about the reemergence of the Jewish "priestly instinct," and with it, the focus on sin, guilt, revenge, and punishment, the only brand of "Christianity" at all interested in either the "promotion of happiness," "the feeling of *freedom* from sin," or "in blessing one's enemies and . . . do[ing] good to those who have offended us," is what Nietzsche calls the "genuine, primitive Christianity" embodied in Jesus of Nazareth (*A* 39): "an actual and not merely promised happiness on earth" (*A* 42).[28] "That mankind should fall on its knees before the opposite of what was the origin, the meaning, the right of the Gospel, that it should have sanctified in the concept 'Church' precisely what the 'bringer of glad tidings' regarded as *beneath* him, *behind* him—one seeks in vain a grander form of *world-historical irony*" (*A* 36). The question, then, is *why*? Why this extraordinary notion of the *"guilt sacrifice . . .* the sacrifice of the *innocent man* for the sins of the guilty . . . [when] Jesus had done away with the concept "guilt" itself" (*A* 41)? Why this version of Christianity so utterly at odds with what Nietzsche here calls "the origin, the meaning, the right of the Gospel?"

On the one hand, the incomparably attractive promise of Jesus' "sacrifice" affording personal immortality to believers, to would-be Christians, is one more example of what Nietzsche takes to be Paul's competition for the allegiance of "the broad, religiously excited masses" (*WP* 167). *Antichrist* 43, for example, attributes the "victory" of rapidly expanding Christianity over other religious movements of antiquity precisely to its shrewd employment of "flattery" and appeal to "every sort of egoism" in "the great lie of personal immortality": "it is to *this* pitiable flattery of personal vanity that Christianity owes its *victory*—it is with this that it has persuaded over to its side everything ill-constituted, rebellious-minded, under-privileged, all the dross and refuse of mankind. 'Salvation of the soul'—in plain words: 'The world revolves around me'." The reason *Will To Power* 196 resolutely cites the notion of "the immortality of the person" as the first of numerous "misunderstandings" resulting from the "adaptation" of genuine Christianity "to the needs and the level of understanding of the religious masses" is clear. It has nothing to with the "eternal life" embodied in Nietzsche's Jesus. For Nietzsche, all facets of Jesus' "Kingdom of Heaven" (including the *feeling* of "eternity") are "condition[s] of the heart—not something that comes 'upon the earth' or 'after death' " (*A* 34). The "eternal life" in question when Nietzsche: (1) celebrates Jesus' "profound instinct for how one would have to live in order to feel oneself 'in Heaven', to feel oneself 'eternal', while in every other condition one by no means feels oneself 'in Heaven' " (*A* 33), and (2) insists (with Luke 17:21) that the "glad tidings" are precisely that "True life, eternal life has been found, it is not being promised, it is here, it is in you" (*A* 29), has nothing to do with what *Antichrist* 41 calls "the impudent doctrine of personal immortality."[29] As was made clear in chapter 3's treatment of Jesus' bearing before his persecutors and message to the dying thief, Jesus' "Kingdom of Heaven" is about attaining the *feeling*, the inner condition of "blessedness here on earth, in spite of distress, opposition and death" (*WP* 169). For Nietzsche, the difference between the "immortality of the person" offered by Paul (and numerous mystery cults of the day) and the *feelings* of "heaven" and "eternity" embodied in and advanced by Jesus, is once again that of an obviously seductive but ultimately unfulfillable *promised* post-death condition, and a wholly realizable "condition of the heart" available in *this* life, in *this* world, *despite* suffering.

On the other hand, the notion that the immortality of the person is causally linked to the "sacrificial" death of Jesus is much more than merely another attractive promise in what Nietzsche takes to be Paul's tireless bid for "priestly power." As Epicurus was well aware, the concept of personal immortality might well be described as a double-edged sword. Far more than just a masterful appeal to "personal vanity" (*A* 43), the belief in a personal immortality (together with the allied themes of eternal reward or punishment)—ideas which historically distinguished Paul's Pharisaic Judaism from other branches of that religion[30]—also carries with it a potent means of control. If one *attracts* believers to a movement with the promise of eternal life, one *keeps* and controls those believers by persuading them that the rewards and punishments meted out in *this* life are but a foretaste of the eternal rewards and punishments awaiting in an "afterlife." "Sin" (as defined, emphasized, and absolved by the priests of that movement), despite earthly evidence to the contrary, will not go unpunished, while "virtue" (likewise defined and also despite earthly evidence) is capable of garnering eternal reward. What is the result of such a belief system? "From now on all things of life are so ordered that the priest is *everywhere indispensable*" (*A* 26).

With stakes so frighteningly high, the priest's expertise in such matters as what behavior and ideas may result in eternal punishment, and what in eternal reward, is paramount (as is the *power* of the priest in such situations). Neither fact is lost on Nietzsche's power-hungry Pharisee, who as early as 1881's *Daybreak* is accused of creating "sin and sinners and eternal damnation" in the name of the "voluptuousness of power" (113), and in the *Antichrist* is said to have coldly realized "that the concept 'Hell' will master even Rome" (58). Characterizing the concepts "Beyond" and "immortality of the soul" as "forms of systematic cruelty by virtue of which the priest has become master, stays master" (*A* 38), Nietzsche accusingly asks: "*What* was the only thing Mohammed later borrowed from Christianity? The invention of Paul, his means for establishing a priestly tyranny, for forming herds: the belief in immortality—*that is to say the doctrine of 'judgment'* " (*A* 42).

As we have seen, Nietzsche's Jesus is simply not interested in such matters as "judgment," "priestly tyranny," and a literal "immortality." On the contrary, he lived a life and offered a message quite the *opposite* of such notions (a nontemporal *feeling* of eternity, non-judgementalism, a direct means of attaining a heaven-like "condition of the heart" for which no priestly involvement is required). This incongruity proved little more than an inconvenience for Paul. The actual "person of Jesus" after all, is characterized by Nietzsche as "a mere 'motif' " to which Paul "wrote the music" (*WP* 177).[31] Given the extraordinary needs and outright *genius* of its composer, that this 'music' both wooed and helped establish priestly tyranny over the "underprivileged of all kinds" (*WP* 172) is hardly surprising. That this self-serving refrain *still* reverberates throughout the world two thousand years later is nothing short of "*world-historical-irony*" (*A* 36).

It is highly doubtful that Nietzsche's Paul believes in the resurrection- and immortality-securing "sacrificial" death of Jesus for the sins and guilt of others. Indeed, given the *Antichrist*'s ongoing portrayal of a shrewd and tireless Apostle whose "Christianity" emerges not from religious conviction but an extraordinary thirst for power, it seems reasonable to conclude that Nietzsche's Paul does not even believe in the existence of the "other world" which to this day remains so bound up with Christianity. Speaking—once again as "a psychologist"—of Paul's famed vision on the road to Damascus, for example, *Antichrist* 42 says *explicitly* what was simply implied in *Daybreak* seven years earlier. The Apostle has not fooled himself, nor like the "first Christians" actually embraced a convenient version of "Christianity," but deliberately trades in lies.

To regard as honest Paul whose home was the principal center of Stoic enlightenment when he makes of a hallucination the *proof* that the redeemer is *still* living, or even to believe his story *that* he had this hallucination, would be a real *niaiserie* on the part of a psychologist: Paul willed the end, *consequently* he willed the means. . . . What he himself did not believe was believed by the idiots among whom he cast *his* teaching.

What *is* certain for Nietzsche is that by bringing the notion of a "blissful, atoned afterlife of the individual soul . . . into a causal relationship *with* that sacrifice (after the type of Dionysus, Mithras, Osiris)" the power-hungry Apostle discovers at least two things: A "bloody phantasmagoria which will stand up in competition with the images of the mystery cults" (*WP* 167, my italics), and a means of inserting the familiar Judaic themes of sin,[32] guilt, punishment, and reward into a "Buddhistic peace movement" originally characterized not merely by the absence of such notions, but indeed their embodied *abolition*. The "central judgment[s]" of Nietzsche's Jesus—that "sin is of no account," that blessedness "is not tied to any conditions" but a directly attainable reality available *now*, indeed "the *only* reality" (*WP* 160, *A* 33)—while "glad tidings" for those living under the dark clouds of guilt, sin, and other *"ecclesiastical* teaching," are *bad* tidings for those responsible for such clouds, for those *benefiting* from them.

"From a psychological point of view," observes Nietzsche in a point not lost on his astute and power-seeking Paul, " 'sins' are indispensable in any society organized by priests: they are the actual levers of power, the priest *lives* on sins" (*A* 26). Failing to discover the "indispensable" ecclesiastical themes of sin, guilt, and punishment in Jesus' "Kingdom of Heaven," Paul puts them there. With "the absurdity of the concept of punishment and the concept of sin [replaced] at the heart of existence," Jesus' "relatively rational" Christianity (*WP* 196), "a Christianity intended above all to soothe diseased nerves" (*WP* 240) and "to lighten the heart" (*HH* 119) has successfully *and deliberately* been transformed into precisely its oppressive opposite. "This is the humor of the situation, a tragic humor: Paul re-erected on a grand scale precisely that which Christ had annulled through his way of living" (*WP* 167).

In his influential first letter to the church at Corinth, Paul declares: "Christ, our Passover lamb, has been sacrificed" (5:7). On this matter above all, Nietzsche is in agreement with Paul. But for the philosopher, "the *real* history of Christianity" (*A* 39) is not that Jesus became *God's* sacrificial lamb in the name of guilt and sin, but *Paul's*. Paul sacrifices the redeemer's "glad tidings" so that the priestly "levers of power" could move freely once more. From *Daybreak's* bold rendering of his Damascus-road "vision" in 1881, to the *Antichrist's* unflinching focus on the far-reaching implications of the Apostle's history-altering "genius" seven years later, Nietzsche exhibits no doubt concerning the principal bene-ficiary of this still misunderstood "sacrifice." "On the heels of the "glad tidings" came the *worst of all*: those of Paul. In Paul was embodied the antithetical type to the "bringer of glad tidings", the genius of hatred, of the vision of hatred, of the inexorable logic of hatred. *What* did this dysangelist not sacrifice to his hatred! The redeemer above all: he nailed him to *his* Cross" (*A* 42).

THE *NEW* COVENANT

> The whole fatality was possible only because there was already in the world a related, racially-related megalomania, the *Jewish*.
>
> *Antichrist* 44

Not surprising for such a fateful combination of "genius" (*A* 42,58; *WP* 175) and an "intractable lust for power" (*D* 68), Nietzsche detects in Paul's reworking and shifting of emphasis within nascent Christianity, the bid of one endeavoring not only to "sum up" and "stand up in competition with the images of the mystery cults" (*A* 58, *WP* 167), but one intent on "*outbidding* all the subterranean cults" (*A* 58, my italics). Allusions to this one-upmanship are frequent. Whereas Jesus' "true Christianity" is characterized in the *Will To Power* by "not wanting to be rewarded" (169), Pauline Christianity "promises blessedness, advantage, privilege . . . [and] fills poor little foolish heads with insane conceit" (172). While Paul's already mentioned claim at 1 Corinthians 6:3— "Know ye not that we shall judge angels?"[33]—is perhaps the most *egregious* reward or conceit promised the Christian believer, surely the most *masterful* is what *Will To Power* 173 calls Paul's "revaluation of the con-cept 'Jew' " (a maneuver rooted both in the Apostle's deep understand-ing of the Jewish experience and his extraordinary sense of what is necessary to "outbid" rivals for the belief and allegiance of the Empire's underprivileged masses).

Once again taking Paul far more seriously than he does "the first Christians," *Will To Power* 175 gives credit to the Apostle for recognizing something fundamental to the Jewish experience, to *his* experience, something "perhaps not understood in the whole Roman Empire." What Paul understood, suggests Nietzsche, is that a subtle yet tremendous power, a "concealed pride . . . disguised as humility," lay behind the Jewish self-conception as "chosen people," in the notions of being "God's people" and having a special "covenant" with God Himself.[34] And further, that heretofore untapped power was available to him capable of *freeing* that pride, that "racially-related megalomania" (*A* 44), from what *Daybreak* 68 calls its "Jewish ballast" and offering this attractive, inherently potent and history-altering self-conception to a broader constituency than ever before.

To do this, says Nietzsche, " 'race' is set aside" (*WP* 173). Through bold notions such as a *new* covenant[35] and a "circumcision of the heart"[36] Paul "outbids" rival cults with nothing less than the idea of Gentile membership in God's "household" and "chosen people."[37] By effectively reducing these puissant notions to matters of (Christian) *belief* rather than race,[38] Nietzsche's Paul makes the "blissful condition" and "pride" (*WP* 175) heretofore known only to Jews seemingly available to *all* the Empire's "chandala," and with each addition to "God's household" (Eph. 2:19) assuages his "intractable lust for power" (*D* 68). Describing the notion of "the chosen people" as a "means by which a particular species of man preserves and enhances himself," and once again giving credit to the Apostle's formidable psycho-political handiwork, Nietzsche insists:

To have recognized in this a form of power, to have recognized that this blissful condition was communicable, seductive, infectious to pagans also—that was Paul's genius: to employ this store of latent energy, of prudent happiness for a "Jewish church of freer confession"—the entire Jewish experience and mastery of communal self-preservation under foreign rule, also Jewish propaganda—he divined that as his task (*WP* 175).

That such a radical "revaluation of the concept 'Jew' " functionally "negated . . . the Jewish reality itself" (*A* 27; *WP* 173), was apparently of little concern to Nietzsche's power-hungry Apostle,[39] one capable of "ruthless violence to the truth" of the Evangel (*A* 58). Again, in a note entitled *"Toward a psychology of Paul"* Nietzsche concludes: "That an explanation may be true or false has never entered the minds of such . . . holy epileptics and seers of visions. . . . Here, the sudden feeling of power that an idea arouses in its originator is everywhere accounted proof of its value" (*WP* 171).

For Nietzsche, Paul's astounding and masterful "revaluation of the concept 'Jew' "—like his employment of the "flattery" of personal immortality, his offering of such "rewards" as an after-death "beyond" and Christians being in a position to judge angels, and his calculated reintroduction of the Jewish notions of sin and guilt—is ultimately about one thing. Such Pauline notions are all about expanding the "Christianity" not of Jesus, but one of his own invention, according to his own needs: An attractive and history-altering combination of pagan mysteries and Jewish "ecclesiastical teachings" infinitely and deliberately more amenable to the operation of priestly "levers of power"). "On the heels of the 'glad tidings' " laments Nietzsche at *Antichrist* 42, "came the *worst of all*: those of Paul."

NOTES

1. Recall *Will To Power* 184's suggestion that the Jewish nation of the day consisted of "the priests—and then immediately the chandala."

2. "The heathen religions," observes Pfleiderer (157) "scarcely could be learned better anywhere than in Tarsus . . . As early as Pompeii's time, Tarsus was a seat of the Mithra religion." Nietzsche's keen suggestion of a linkage between the Mithra cult and the version of Christianity promulgated by the Apostle is discussed below.

3. The final stage of Paul's education is said (at Acts 22:3) to have been undertaken in Jerusalem under Rabbi Gamaliel.

4. See 1 Cor. 3:10–15, 4:9, 9:25–27.

5. Even more important than the fact that Athenodorus, famed Stoic teacher of Cicero and Augustus, hailed from Tarsus, is that a version of *popular* Stoicism (such as that found in the writings of Seneca and Epictetus), was widely circulated among Tarsus' educated populous. This public philosophy, says Pfleiderer (157), was "enunciated daily on the streets and in the market-places [of Tarsus] by public speakers, who called themselves philosophers." Paul's awareness and employment of popular Stoicism is especially apparent at Acts 17:22–31 (see also Rm. 1:18–32, 1 Cor. 6:9–10, 2 Cor. 6:4–10, Gal. 5:19–23, Eph. 5:22 to 6:9, and Col. 3:18 to 4:1). Paul's knowledge of Stoic ideas is not only *evident* in his epistles, but "they contain such remarkable coincidences of thought and speech with the Stoic writer Seneca, that some have held that Seneca was the teacher of Paul while others maintain that Seneca was Paul's pupil" (Pfleiderer, 157).

6. Nachlass, cited by O'Flaherty pp. 107–8.

7. As discussed in chapter 4, "epilepsy" for Nietzsche has more to do with feelings of inadequacy and self-contempt (*D* 68,549) or the need for absolute, fanatical convictions (*A* 54) than intellectual ability. Indeed, far from any suggestion of intellectual deficiency, Nietzsche's roster of "epileptics"—Alexander, Caesar, Luther, Rousseau, Napoleon, and so forth, speaks quite to the contrary.

8. Likewise, on the topic of "Christian agitators" like St. Augustine, *Antichrist* 59 observes: "One would be deceiving oneself utterly if one presumed a lack of intelligence of any sort on the part of the leaders of the Christian movement—oh they are shrewd, shrewd to the point of holiness, these Church Fathers! What they lack is something quite different."

9. *Daybreak* goes on to advance a key psychological distinction with respect to power that is both relevant to the philosopher's fundamental vision of a power-hungry Paul, and seemingly anticipates the difficult notion of the "will to

power" (which does not formally emerge until Book One of *Zarathustra*, written two years later). Entitled *Feeling of Power*, *Daybreak* 348 goes on to warn: "Be sure you mark the difference: he who wants to acquire the feeling of power resorts to any means and disdains nothing that will nourish it. He who has it, however, has become very fastidious and noble in his tastes . . ." Of course, the unifying theme in Nietzsche's scattered reflections on Paul, is not merely his thirst for power, but the tremendous lengths he is willing to go to in the service of this extraordinary thirst. From the comparatively narrow focus of *Daybreak* 68, to *Antichrist* 58–60's sweeping castigation of the Apostle for the very ruination of the Roman Empire, Nietzsche's Paul is consistently and without exception a deeply troubled soul willing to "resort to any means," who "disdains nothing that will nourish" this insufficiency-driven lust for power.

When considering the actual doctrine of the "will to power" in the particular context of the life, psyche, and career of Nietzsche's Paul, we may note the following: While Nietzsche in places makes remarkably broad pronouncements with respect to the absolute ubiquity of the "will to power" (cf. *WP* 1067), he also suggests that the "will to power" is less about the living being's desire to *accumulate* power (the very charge consistently levied at Paul) than the "discharge" of one's surplus "strength" (*BGE* 13). Building upon *Daybreak* 348's distinction between the ruthless desire to *amass* power and the more "noble" posture of the man in true possession of power, *Gay Science* 370 differentiates between those capable of luxuriating in the "over-fullness of life" and "those who suffer from the *impoverishment of life*" and go to desperate lengths in search of "redemption from themselves." The difference here (as with the *pre*-"will to power" *D* 348) is apparently that between the repose of abundance and the frenzy borne of spiritual impoverishment. While he does not discuss Paul in terms of his notion of the "will to power" per se, such passages suggest that the drive at work in the case of the power-hungry and insufficiency-driven Apostle is far from the "purer" manifestations of the "will to power" Nietzsche sometimes celebrates.

10. Recall Nietzsche's characterization of the earliest Jewish-Christians as "the priestly instinct which can no longer endure the priest" (*A* 27).

11. *Antichrist* 36 insists that insofar as the priestly lie, the holy lie, is reducible to the "shameless self-seeking" of "*one's* own advantage," and culminates in the construction "*Church* out of the antithesis to the Gospel," that "we *emancipated* spirits" declare "war on the 'holy lie' even more than any other lie." The philosopher's "war" on the "holy lie" however, turns out to be waged with considerable subtlety. "Ultimately the point is to what *end* a lie is told," adds Nietzsche at *A* 56. "That "holy" ends are lacking in Christianity is *my* objection to its means." Insisting that it "does indeed make a difference for what purpose one lies: whether one preserves with a lie or *destroys* with it," *Antichrist* 58 proceeds to passionately chart the corrosive consequences of Paul's self serving "Christianity" on nothing less than the Roman Empire itself.

12. While Nietzsche is adamant that the Jewish priesthood *perfected* the art of the holy lie, he by no means limits the phenomenon to Judaism, or even religion per se. *Twilight of the Idols*, "Improvers of Mankind," 5, for example, paints a distinctive and psychologically informed picture of what is for Nietzsche an unfortunately pervasive tendency.

This is the great, the *uncanny* problem which I have pursued farthest: the psychology of the "improvers" of mankind. A small and really rather modest fact, that of so-called *pia fraus*, gave me my first access to this problem: *pia fraus*, the heritage of all philosophers and priests who have "improved mankind". Neither Manu, nor Plato, neither Confucius nor the Jewish and Christian teachers, ever doubted their *right* to tell lies.

13. *Antichrist* 44 for example, sees in Paul, "the cynical logic of a rabbi," while *Antichrist* 41 speaks of the "rabbinical insolence which characterizes him in every respect."

14. "The Christian . . . is the Jew once more—even thrice more" (*A* 44). "Christianity can be understood only by referring to the soil out of which it grew—it is *not* a counter-movement against the Jewish instinct, it is actually its logical consequence, one further conclusion of its fear-inspiring logic" (*A* 24).

15. "The Jews are the most remarkable nation of world history because, faced with the question of being or not being, they preferred, with a perfectly uncanny conviction, being *at any price*: the price they had to pay was the radical *falsification* of all nature, all naturalness, all reality, the entire inner world as well as the outer . . . they inverted religion, religious worship, morality, history, psychology one after another in an irreparable way into the *contradiction of all natural values*" (*A* 24). Interestingly, Shapiro (1981, p. 125) suggests that Nietzsche's account of Judaism's thoroughgoing de-naturalization of history at *Antichrist* 24–27 is likely a "radicalization" of ideas that emerged ten years earlier with the publication of Julius Wellhausen's *Prolegomena to the History of Ancient Israel*. While the *Antichrist* does not mention Wellhausen by name, Shapiro points out that according to Janz's *Nietzsche Biographie* (II, 578, 627), Nietzsche had been reading Wellhausen just prior to its composition.

16. It is noteworthy that Nietzsche uses the expression "Genuine, primitive Christianity" (*A* 39), or simply "primitive Christianity" (*WP* 167, 169) to describe what we—following Nietzsche at *Will to Power* 169—might call "true Christianity," Christianity as Christ *lived*. For Nietzsche, "Only Christian *practice*, a life such as he who died on the Cross *lived*, is Christian" (*A* 39).

17. In addition to Kennedy's *St. Paul and the Mystery-Religions*, see for example, Pfleiderer's *Christian Origins*, and Robertson's *Origins of Christianity*.

18. Paul's use of terminology employed by the mystery cults is well documented. Robertson (p. 66) points to the fact that in the Greek original, Paul (1 Cor. 2:6–8) refers to his teaching as a "mystery" and his converts as "initiates" (now generally rendered as a "secret" or "hidden wisdom," and "the mature" or "full grown" respectively). New Testament scholars have also noted that Paul's pronounced disdain for "earthly things," for the material world and "worldly" values, at once differentiates his letters from the synoptic gospel tradition, and is highly reminiscent of many mystery cults of the day.

Since Nietzsche repeatedly links Paul's teachings to those of the Mithras cult in particular, we note the following: On the topic of the Apostle's employment of imagery highly reminiscent of the symbolic *initiation* into the Mithras cult— the centerpiece of which involved a "mystical dying and rebirth, by which the guilt of the old life is cleansed and extirpated and a new, immortal life is created through the spirit . . . [after which] the initiated spoke of themselves as 'reborn for eternity' "—Pfleiderer, for example, concludes the following: "So striking is the connection of these ideas with Paul's teaching of Christian baptism as a community of death and resurrection with Christ"—as articulated at Romans 6:3–5—"that the thought of historical relation between the two cannot be evaded" (p. 158).

Vivid parallels have also been noted between Paul's teaching of the Lord's supper at 1 Cor. 10:16 and the sacred meal of the Mithras cult, "where sanctified bread and wine served as mystic means of distributing divine life to the Mithra believer. . . . When it is remembered that the mystical teaching of both sacraments, the baptism and the Lord's Supper, is peculiar to the Apostle Paul and finds no explanation in the older tradition of the congregation, the suspicion is natural, that it is based on a combination of Christian ideas and rites of the Mithra religion, as Paul might have known them from his home in Tarsus" (Pfleiderer pp. 158–59).

19. Nietzsche's quiet but regular mention of Epicureanism within his treatment of Christianity is interesting indeed. We have already cited *Antichrist* 30's favorable comparison of Jesus' message to that of Epicurus. Calling Jesus' gentle way of living "a sublime further evolution of hedonism on a thoroughly morbid basis," Nietzsche suggests: "Closest related to it, even if with a considerable addition of Greek vitality and nervous energy, is Epicureanism, the redemption doctrine of the pagan world . . . The fear of pain, even of the infinitely small in pain—*cannot* end otherwise than in a *religion of love* (*A* 30). Like Epicurus, Nietzsche's Jesus embodies and offers a means of genuine, attainable redemption. And not insignificantly, *both* of these ancient "redemption doctrune[s]," like Nietzsche's conception of his own "good news," are presented as being born of great suffering. Like the Nazarene's lauded ability to extract a state of "blessedness," a "sublime" condition of the heart, from overtly hellish circumstances, so Epicurus' path of redemption "could be invented only by a man who was suffering continually" (*GS* 45). But while Epicurus and Epicureanism are regularly *compared* with Jesus and his gentle way of living, *post-Jesus* Christianity is something Nietzsche sharply and unfavorably *contrasts* with Epicureanism. Going even further than *Will To Power* 196's lumping of Pauline Christianity in with "the cults that had been combated by Epicurus" (above), *Antichrist* 58 insists: "One must read Lucretius to understand *what* it was Epicurus opposed: *not* paganism but 'Christianity', which is to say the corruption of souls through the concept of guilt, punishment and immortality.—He opposed the subterranean cults, the whole of latent Christianity—to deny immortality was already in those days a real *redemption*.—And Epicurus would have won, every mind of any account in the Roman Empire was an Epicurean: *then Paul appeared*."

20. Nietzsche is alone neither in his vision of, nor his choice of words to describe, the figures in whom expanding Christianity found its first Gentile converts. Friedlander, in his influential *Roman Life and Manners under the Early Empire* (III, pp. 206–7) observes: "It was a joke amongst the heathen that the Christians could only convert the simple-minded, only slaves, women and children; that they were rude, uneducated, and boorish." Friedlander (p. 207) goes on to cite the words of no less an authority than Jerome: "The community of Christ is recruited, not from the Lyceum and the Academy, but from the lowest rabble" (*de vila plebecula*).

21. The telling title "Buddha against the 'Crucified,' " appearing above a notebook entry from spring 1888 (*WP* 154), strangely parallels the famous final sen-

tence of Nietzsche's literary autobiography, *Ecce Homo* (4, 9): "Have I been understood?—*Dionysus versus the Crucified.*"

22. "A God who died for our sins: redemption through faith; resurrection after death—all these are counterfeits of true Christianity for which that disastrous wrong-headed fellow [Paul] must be held responsible" (*WP* 169).

23. Typically, Nietzsche's reflections on the Buddha and Buddhism, like his thoughts on Jesus, Paul and Christianity, are multifaceted and by no means free of ambivalence. While Nietzsche regularly applauds Buddhism's relative rationality, worldliness, and emphasis on practice, impassioned polemics *against* aspects of Buddhism also abound in the Nietzschean corpus. Two noteworthy efforts to clarify and understand Nietzsche's complicated attitude toward Buddhism are Mistry (1981), and Morrison (1997). Mistry's psychohistorical leitmotif, that the polymorphous character of Nietzsche's thoughts on Buddhism is partly the result of his ever-changing feelings about Schopenhauer and Wagner, is particularly interesting. The importance of these two figures (both serious students of Buddhism, and both repeatedly associated with the religion by Nietzsche) in the life and thought of the philosopher can hardly be overstated.

24. See 1 Cor. 12:19 for Paul's general linkage of Jesus' death and resurrection to that of believers. On the topic of Jesus' "sacrificial" death, Paul variously declares that Jesus "was handed over to death for our trespasses" (Rom. 4:25); that "God made him who had no sin to be sin for us" (2 Cor. 5:21); that God "presented" Jesus "as a sacrifice of atonement through faith in his blood" (Rom. 3:25); that "Christ, our Passover lamb, has been sacrificed" (1 Cor. 5:7); and that "we have now been justified by his blood" (Rom. 5:9). Pfleiderer (p. 221) for example, insists that the notion of Jesus' death constituting "a vicarious atonement" for the sins of others is certainly "a thought entirely strange to Jesus himself." According to Pfleiderer, allusions to this theme of "vicarious atonement" in the Gospels themselves (cf. Mk. 10:45, 14:24) likely stem, not from any teachings of Jesus, but Paul's influence as the teacher of Mark (cf. Philem. 24, Col. 4:10, Acts 12:12, 2 Tim. 4:11) *prior to* the composition of his Gospel.

25. For Nietzsche, the Christian notion of "atonement" (literally, *at one-ment*, the reconciliation of God with sinful man through the suffering and death of Jesus) flies in the face of Jesus' embodied message not only insofar as it is built atop the utterly un-Jesus like notions of sin, guilt, and punishment, but because *through* Jesus, *in* Jesus, "every kind of distancing relationship between God and man is abolished—*precisely this is the 'glad tidings'* " (*A* 33). *Antichrist* 41 likewise announces that "he had denied any chasm between God and man, he *lived* this unity of God and man as *his* 'glad tidings.' " Where no distance exists, when no chasm separates, there simply is neither room for nor a genuine need of atonement or reconciliation (which is not to say that there is neither room for nor need of *the doctrine* of a necessary reconciliation).

26. Calling it "a hundred times more realistic than Christianity," *Antichrist* 20 insists that Buddhism "no longer speaks of 'the struggle against *sin*' but, quite in accord actuality, 'the struggle against *suffering*'. It already has—and this distinguishes it profoundly from Christianity—the self-deception of moral concepts behind it—it stands, in my language, *beyond* good and evil."

27. In a remark immodest even by Nietzsche's standards, the philosopher announces: "I am a bringer of glad tidings like no one before me; I know tasks of

such elevation that any notion of them has been lacking so far; only beginning with me are there hopes again" (*EH* 4,1).

28. On the matter of Nietzsche's passionate celebration of "blessing one's enemies and . . . [doing] good to those who have offended us," recall *Antichrist* 35's unambiguous picture of Jesus' ultimate gift to mankind: "What he bequeathed to mankind was his *practice*: his bearing before the judges, before the guards, before the accusers and every kind of calumny and mockery—his bearing on the Cross . . . not to resist even the evil man—to *love him*. . . ."

29. *Will To Power* 166 is even less diplomatic on this topic: "Jesus opposed the commonplace life with a real life, a life in truth: nothing was further from him than the stupid nonsense of an 'eternalized Peter', an eternal personal survival."

30. In marked contrast to other parties within Judaism at the time of Paul, the Pharisees believed in "angels, resurrection, judgment and retribution in the world to come" (Pfleiderer, p. 73).

31. "Consider with what degree of freedom Paul treats, indeed almost juggles with, the problem of the person of Jesus . . . A mere "motif": *he* then wrote the music to it—a zero in the beginning."

32. Recall *Gay Science* 138's far-reaching characterization of the Hebrews as a people "who had invented sin."

33. Marveled at by an incredulous Nietzsche at *Antichrist* 45 and 46.

34. As discussed, Nietzsche sees in the Jew's self-conception "as chosen people, as community of saints, as the people of the promise," merely the compensatory "imaginary presuppositions" of an otherwise powerless people (*WP* 199). Significantly, this fascinating psychohistorical notion of the impotent deriving psychological succor and recourse from the appearance or idea of a special status as "chosen people" appears years previous, in section 136 of 1882's *Gay Science*. There, in an insightful aphorism plainly anticipating the celebrated psychoanalytic notion of *verleugnung*—the defensive "denial" or "disavowal" of distressing reality (first formalized by Freud in 1924, p. 184)—Nietzsche writes:

The chosen people.—The Jews, who feel that they are the chosen people among all the nations because they are a moral genius among the nations (because they had a *more profound contempt* for the human being in themselves than any other people)—the Jews' enjoyment of their divine monarch and saint is similar to that which the French nobility derived from Louis XIV. This nobility had surrendered all of its power and sovereignty and had become contemptible. In order not to feel this, in order to be able to forget this, one required royal splendor . . . By virtue of this privilege, one rose to the height of the court, and from that vantage point one saw everything beneath oneself and found it contemptible—and thus got over an irritable conscience.

35. 2 Corinthians 3:6.

36. In his letter to the church at Rome Paul declares that; "A man is not a Jew if he is only one outwardly . . . a man is a Jew if he is one inwardly; and circumcision is circumcision of the heart, by the Spirit" (2:28–29).

37. "I ask then: Did God reject his people? By no means! I am an Israelite myself. A descendent of Abraham, from the tribe of Benjamin . . . Again I ask: Did they stumble so as to fall beyond recovery? Not at all! Rather, because of their transgression, salvation has come to the Gentiles to make Israel envious . . . I am talking to you Gentiles. Inasmuch as I am the apostle to the Gentiles . . . If

some of the branches have been broken off, and you, though a wild olive shoot, have been grafted in among the others and now share the nourishing sap from the olive root, do not boast over those branches. If you do, consider this: You do not support the root, but the root supports you. You will say then, 'Branches were broken off so that I could be grafted in.' Granted. But they were broken off because of unbelief, and you stand by faith." (Rom. 11:1–20)

38. Because of the resurrected Jesus, Paul tells the Ephesians (2:19): "you are no longer foreigners and aliens, but fellow citizens with God's people and members of God's household." Likewise at Galations 3:7 Paul writes: "Understand, then, that those who believe are children of Abraham." Since Abraham was considered both the spiritual and physical father of the Jewish people, Paul's reduction of the matter of the "children of Abraham" to a question of *belief*, while indeed an egregious and self-interested "revaluation of the concept 'Jew,' " also anticipates his ultimate, radical reduction of "Christianity" from a peaceful *way of life*, to a matter of belief. "It is false to the point of absurdity," writes Nietzsche in yet another Kierkegaardian passage, "to see in a 'belief', perchance the belief in redemption through Christ, the distinguishing characteristic of the Christian: only Christian practice, a life such as he who died on the Cross lived, is Christian." The reduction of "Christianness, to a holding something to be true . . . means to negate Christianness" (*A* 39).

39. While Nietzsche emphasizes that Paul's "revaluation" is chiefly about deriving power for himself, insofar as such a notion negates "the Jewish reality itself," it can also be considered one more example of a failed Pharisee's revenge. Paul's eventual negation of the "Jewish reality" itself needs to be understood in the context of *Daybreak* 68's suggestion of a seething unconscious (though no less potent) "hatred" of "the spiritual ideal" Paul (like Luther) had originally hoped to attain.

Conclusion

In our introduction it was pointed out that one of the cardinal characteristics of a psychoanalytic case history is that it rarely reads linearly in
the manner of conventional biography or history. Instead, such research-
ers tend to focus their analysis on only one or two events, statements,
or experiences of particular *psychological* significance. As we have seen,
if there is such an event in Nietzsche's investigation of Jesus of Nazareth,
it is unquestionably his martyrdom and death. From his early characterization of Jesus' cry on the Cross as "the bitterest of all exclamations"
and the somber presentation of the "too early" death of the "still immature" Jesus in the *Daybreak* and *Thus Spoke Zarathustra* respectively, to
the mature philosopher's recognition of a "good news"-embodying, life-
consummating death at Calvary, the event at the very center of the philosopher's extraordinary "psychology of the redeemer" is the Nazarene's
martyrdom. Most significantly, because it is at Calvary that the Nietzschean Jesus' instinct-dictated posture of radical nonenmity, non-
ressentiment and nonresistance is put to the sternest test. As Nietzsche
remarks at *Will To Power* 162: "When even the criminal undergoing a
painful death declares: 'the way this Jesus suffers and dies, without rebelling, without enmity, graciously, resignedly, is the only right way,'
he has affirmed the gospel."

Of course Jesus' martyrdom and death are also of singular interest to
Nietzsche because it is at this very point in the history of Christianity
that the "ship of Christianity" itself takes what is for Nietzsche an unfortunate but all too human turn. It is at Calvary, at the very moment

when the early Christians find themselves faced with the all important question—"*Who* was that? *What* was that?"—that "misunderstandings" and "mistranslations" rooted equally in these unsophisticated figures' ignorance and what Nietzsche calls their "Jewishness" begin to steadily overwhelm Jesus' "good news": To transform, to *reduce* the truly extraordinary embodied symbolic message of an ahistoric "free spirit" to a series of all too ordinary, all too literal, all too familiar and obviously need-based and historically determined clichés (the Messiah, the vengeful Judge to come, the moral preacher, the miracle-worker, etc.). To have "translated" a gentle soul capable of going to an agonizing death without a trace of *ressentiment* or anger—indeed who *loves* those doing evil to him—to someone who curses and causes to wither a fig tree for not bearing fruit (Mt. 21:18; *WP* 164); one who tells of a rich man going to hell and a poor man to the bosom of Abraham *not* because of sinfulness, but simply on the basis of riches (Lk. 16:19); as one set to return as a wrathful judge, a sword-wielding warrior to smite the Church's enemies and feed the flesh of kings and other "mighty men" to vultures (Rev. 19:18; *GM* 1, 16), tells Nietzsche, one who "never read[s] a word without seeing an attitude" (*A* 44), all he needs to know about the "translators" in question. "One cannot read these Gospels too warily," cautions Nietzsche, "there are difficulties behind every word. I hope I shall be pardoned for confessing that they are for that very reason a pleasure of the first rank to the psychologist" (*A* 44).

But of course the martyrdom and death of Jesus are of paramount importance to Nietzsche for a *third* reason: Because they are of paramount importance *to Paul*. As we have seen, it is precisely upon consideration of what Paul comes to make of Jesus' martyrdom and death that Nietzsche concludes that: "All at once it was over for the Gospel!" (*A* 41). The early *Daybreak* concerns itself with Paul's *first* "interpretation" of Jesus' death, as signaling the "end" and "abolition" (Rm. 10:4; Eph. 2:15) of the very Law that had apparently been a source of great distress for the fanatical Pharisee. But it is what the later Paul, the powerful globe-trotting Apostle to the Gentiles, makes of Jesus' martyrdom and death, that was of singular, and singularly choleric concern to the philosopher in the last months of his career. As we have seen, the *Antichrist* and notes from the period are especially suspicious of two aspects of the Apostle's notable focus on the Nazarene's martyrdom and death. His masterful linkage of that martyrdom and death with (1) the familiar Judaic concepts of atonement, sin, guilt, and punishment, and (2) the promise of a mysteriously procured personal, *literal* immortality for the individual believer.

Nietzsche returns again and again to the scene of the Nazarene's martyrdom because it is here, at the very place where the extraordinary message of his Jesus is so painfully embodied, his extraordinary life so utterly consummated, that Paul effectively reduces this message, *this life*, to what Nietzsche calls "the most contemptible of all unfulfillable promises": Pauline Christianity. "This is the humor of the situation, a tragic humor: Paul re-erected on a grand scale precisely that which Christ had annulled through his way of living" (*WP* 167). Calvary then is the site, the battlefield on which Nietzsche wages the most personal, most passionate and hardest fought struggle of his notoriously confrontational career: An ideological struggle with the principal architect of Christianity over the true meaning of Jesus' martyrdom and death. Though Paul is the subject of personal vilification without equal in the Nietzschean corpus, the ferocity with which the philosopher carries out this career-culminating struggle clearly owes to the (essentially unrecognized) enormity of what he considers at stake. Stated simply, Nietzsche's objective is nothing less than the reclamation, the *rescue* of Jesus from (Pauline) Christianity.

Confessing that "I am warlike by nature," and that "Attacking is one of my instincts," *Ecce Homo*'s account of how, why, and *with whom* its author opts to engage in intellectual battle, helps us to better situate Nietzsche's own understanding of his passionate struggle with Paul over the meaning of Jesus' life and death.

The strength of those who attack can be measured in a way by the opposition they require: every growth is indicated by the search for a mighty opponent. . . . Equality before the enemy: the first presupposition of an *honest* duel. Where one feels contempt, one *cannot* wage war . . . where one sees something beneath oneself, one has no business waging war.

My practice of war can be summed up in four propositions. First: I only attack causes that are victorious. . . .

Second: I only attack causes against which I would not find allies, so that I stand alone. . . .

Third: I never attack persons; I merely avail myself of the person as of a strong magnifying glass that allows one to make visible a general but creeping and elusive calamity.

Fourth: I only attack things when every personal quarrel is excluded, when any background of bad experiences is lacking. On the contrary, attack is in my case a proof of good will, sometimes even of gratitude. I honor, I distinguish by associating my name with that of a cause or a person: pro or con—that makes no difference to me at this point. When I wage war against Christianity I am entitled to this because I have never experienced misfortunes and frustrations from that quarter—the most serious Christians have always been well disposed toward me. I myself, an opponent of Christianity *de riguer*, am far from blaming individuals for the calamity of millennia (1, 7).

We have seen that while Nietzsche is quick to disparage both what he considers the patently transparent "misunderstandings" of the Jewish "rabble" first faced with the daunting task of making sense of the figure and message of Jesus, and modern scholarly treatments of Jesus that fail to bring psychology to bear in their examination of the obvious handiwork of these "lowly" figures, his estimate of Paul is another matter altogether. Paul, Nietzsche informs us again and again, is a tireless "genius" characterized by a truly incredible, perhaps unprecedented, hunger for power. Here then, alone in the New Testament, is a "mighty opponent," a worthy "enemy" with which Nietzsche can have an "honest duel."

If the "strength of those who attack can be measured . . . by the opposition they require," upon consideration of the task Nietzsche sets for himself in the *Antichrist* vis-à-vis extricating Jesus of Nazareth from Pauline Christianity, we may conclude with its self-satisfied author that he is indeed one in possession of considerable strength. Given the name-calling and vitriol with which his struggle with Paul is often waged, it is difficult not to regard Nietzsche's insistence that "I never attack persons," "I only attack things when every personal quarrel is excluded," and that "attack is in my case a proof of good will," as examples of Nietzsche's oft-inflated sense of his own character. What we have seen to be *not* a boast is *Ecce Homo*'s recognition of Nietzsche's tendency to "avail myself of the person as of a strong magnifying glass that allows one to make visible" more general phenomena. As we have seen, the psychological magnifying glass with which he examines the figure of Paul is such that Nietzsche regularly sees *through* the Apostle, to underlying and far broader matters such as the will to power in general and priestly power in particular, the "holy lie," fanaticism and the need for absolute convictions, the tendency of inner psychic conditions to manifest themselves as outward behavior, the fundamental religious-moral continuum of Judaism and post-Jesus Christianity, and so forth. Of course, Nietzsche's tendency to avail himself of "the person as of a strong magnifying glass" is not limited to those individuals he considers his "enemy," those against whom he "wages war." For as we have seen, his unusual investigation of the figure of Jesus of Nazareth often serves as a graphic entrée for the philosopher's ruminations on any number of fascinating topics: love, pity, and suffering; the potential psychophysiological origins of morality; the problematic character of communication, and so forth.

Albert Schweitzer's famous overview of the modern *Life of Jesus* genre, *The Quest of the Historical Jesus*, climaxes with a disappointing but perhaps inevitable conclusion: "The most consistent feature of historical-Jesus research" writes Schweitzer, "is that Jesus ends up looking like the investigators." As we have seen, and as is so often the case with Nietzsche and twentieth-century thought, the self-professed "foremost psychologist of Christianity" had come to a similar conclusion a half-century earlier. Not about scholarly *investigators* of Jesus however, but Jesus' immediate *followers*. For its part, Nietzsche's psychohistorical research into the birth of Christianity concludes that the most consistent feature of the New Testament Jesus is that he ends up *looking like* and reflecting the *needs of* the earliest Christians. Speaking of the "plentiful measure of gall (and even *esprit)* [that] has overflowed on to the type of the Master out of the excited condition of Christian propaganda," Nietzsche notes: "for one knows very well how resolutely all sectarians adjust their Master into an apologia of themselves" (*A* 31).

But as we have seen, and as Schweitzer understood, the first Christians and St. Paul are not alone in their tendency to "adjust" their image of Jesus "into an apologia of themselves." Nietzsche of course does precisely this as well. Perhaps as a result of his vigorous effort to wrench Jesus well away from the grip of Paul, perhaps because of the frustrating dearth of followers in his own lifetime, the redeemer Nietzsche eventually extricates from Christianity ends up resembling the philosopher's self-image to a remarkable degree. Both of course are paradigmatic "free spirits," and both belong to that rarefied group of individuals that have altogether transcended the all too human proclivity for *ressentiment*. Both Nietzsche and his Jesus seem to undergo profound change as a result of tremendous pain and suffering. Both occupy a space well above all notions of morality, all traditional conceptions of good and evil. Both Nietzsche and his "redeemer" stand completely apart from "religion" in general and the Judeo-Christian continuum in particular. "Let us do away with the concept *sin*," Nietzsche cries in *Daybreak* (202). "Sin is of no account," answers his redeemer seven years later (*WP* 160). Similarly in the *Twilight of the Idols* one finds the confession: "we immoralists especially are trying with all our might to remove the concept of guilt and the concept of punishment from the world" (6, 7). In the *Antichrist*, written immediately afterward, Nietzsche discovers the heretofore-ignored means by which these destructive concepts might be eliminated. "In the entire psychology of the 'Gospel' the concept guilt and punishment is lacking; likewise the concept reward. 'Sin', every kind of distancing relationship between God and man *is abolished—precisely this is the 'glad tidings'* (*A*" 33).

In a notebook entry written toward the close of his career Nietzsche declares that "a Christianity is possible but without the absurd dogmas (the most repellent abortions of antique hybridism)" (*WP* 239). As our examination of his extraordinary account of the birth of Christianity makes clear, Nietzsche has little doubt concerning not only *what* Christianity's "absurd dogmas" are and *who* we have to thank for their introduction, but precisely *when, how*, and most importantly (psychologically speaking) *why* such "dogmas" became a part of Christianity. Nietzsche is just as confident as to what "a Christianity" free of such "absurd dog-mas" would look like. For this is precisely what he detects, *who* he de-tects, *behind* at least two distinct and firmly entrenched layers of New Testament "mutilation": The "genuine, primitive Christianity" (*A* 39) of Jesus of Nazareth. Behold the men.

Bibliography

Barker, Kenneth, ed. *The NIV Study Bible: New International Version*. Grand Rapids, Mich.: Zondervan Publishing, 1985.

Barth, Karl. *Protestant Theology in the Nineteenth Century: Its Background and History*. London: S.C.M. Press, 1972.

Biser, Eugen. "Nietzsche's Relation to Jesus: A Literary and Psychological Comparison." In *Nietzsche and Christianity*, edited by Claude Geffre and J.P. Jossua. New York: Seabury Press, 1981.

Bonifazi, Conrad. *Christendom Attacked: A Comparison of Kierkegaard and Nietzsche*. London: Rockliff, 1953.

Clark, Maudemarie. *Nietzsche on Truth and Philosophy*. Cambridge: Cambridge University Press, 1990.

Copleston, Frederick Charles. *Friedrich Nietzsche, Philosopher of Culture*. London: Burns, Oates & Washbourne, 1942.

Dannhauser, Werner J. *Nietzsche's View of Socrates*. Ithaca, N.Y.: Cornell University Press, 1974.

Dougall, Lily, and Cyril W. Emmet. *The Lord of Thought: A Study of the Problems Which Confronted Jesus Christ and the Solutions He Offered*. New York: George Doran Co., 1922.

Duffy, Michael, and Willard Mittleman. "Nietzsche's Attitude toward the Jews." *Journal of the History of Ideas* 49 (1988).

Ellenberger, Henri F. *The Discovery of the Unconscious: The History and Evolution of Dynamic Psychiatry*. New York: Basic Books, 1970.

Erikson, Erik. *The Young Man Luther: A Study in Psychoanalysis and History*. New York: W. W. Norton, 1969.

Fredriksen, Paula. *From Jesus to Christ: The Origins of the New Testament Images of Jesus*. New Haven: Yale University Press, 1988.

Freud, Sigmund. *Standard Edition of the Complete Psychological Works of Sigmund Freud*. 24 vols. Translated and edited by James Strachey. London: Hogarth Press, 1953–74.

———. *Further Remarks on the Neuro-Psychosis of Defense*. Standard Edition, 3. 1896.

———. *The Loss of Reality in Neurosis and Psychosis*. Standard Edition, 19. 1924.

———. *An Autobiographical Study*. Standard Edition, 20. 1925.

———. *The Question of Lay Analysis*. Standard Edition, 20. 1926.

———. *The Future of an Illusion*. Standard Edition, 21. 1927.

———. *Moses and Monotheism*. Standard Edition, 23. 1939.

Freud, S., and W. C. Bullitt. *Thomas Woodrow Wilson: A Psychoanalytic Psychological Study*. Boston: Houghton Mifflin, 1966.

Friedlander, Ludwig. *Roman Life and Manners under the Early Empire*. 3 vols., 7th ed. London: Routledge and Sons, 1908.

Gay, P. *A Godless Jew*. New Haven,: Yale University Press, 1987.

Geffre, Claude, and J. P. Jossua, eds. *Nietzsche and Christianity*. New York: Seabury Press, 1981.

Golomb, Jacob, ed. *Nietzsche and Jewish Culture*. New York: Routledge, 1997.

Golomb, Jacob, Weaver Santaniello, and Ronald Lehrer, eds. *Nietzsche and Depth Psychology*. New York: SUNY Press, 1999.

Grant, Michael. *Jesus: An Historian's Review of The Gospels*. New York: Scribner, 1977.

Hall, Sidney. *Christian Anti-Semitism and Paul's Theology*. Minneapolis: Fortress Press, 1993.

Hamilton, Edith, and Huntington Cairns, eds. *The Collected Dialogues of Plato, Including The Letters*. New York: Pantheon Books, 1961.

Harpur, Tom. *For Christ's Sake*. Toronto: Oxford University Press, 1986.

Heidegger, Martin. *Nietzsche*. 4 vols. Translated with notes and an analysis by David Farrell Krell. San Francisco: Harper & Row, 1979–87.

Howard, J. Keir. "Epilepsy." In *The Oxford Companion to the Bible*, edited by Bruce M. Metzger and Michael D. Coogan. New York: Oxford University Press, 1993.

Jaspers, Karl. *Nietzsche and Christianity*. Translated from the German by E.B. Ashton. Chicago: H. Regnery Co., 1961.

———. *Socrates, Buddha, Confucius, Jesus: The Paradigmatic Individuals*. New York: Harcourt, Brace & World, 1962.

———. *Nietzsche: An Introduction to his Philosophical Activity*. Chicago: H. Regnery Co., 1965.

Kaufmann, Walter. *Nietzsche: Philosopher, Psychologist, Antichrist*. 4th ed. Princeton, N.J.: Princeton University Press, 1974.

Kautsky, Karl. *Foundations of Christianity*. New York: Monthly Review Press, 1972.

Kennedy, H. A. *St. Paul and the Mystery-Religions*. London: Hodder and Stoughton, 1913.

Kierkegaard, Søren. *Training in Christianity*. Translated by Walter Lowrie. Princeton, N.J.: Princeton University Press, 1964.

Lavrin, Janko. *Nietzsche and Modern Consciousness: A Psycho-Critical Study*. New York: Haskell House, 1973.

Löwith, Karl. *From Hegel to Nietzsche: The Revolution in Nineteenth-Century Thought*. New York: Holt, Rinehart and Winston, 1964.

Mack, Burton L. *Who Wrote the New Testament?* New York: HarperCollins, 1995.

Mandel, Siegfried. *Nietzsche and the Jews*. Amherst, Mass.: Prometheus, 1998.

Mann, Thomas. *Nietzsche's Philosophy in the Light of Contemporary Events*. Washington, D.C.: Library of Congress, 1948.

McKenna, David. *The Psychology of Jesus*. Waco, Tex.: Word Books, 1977.

Metzger, Bruce M., and Michael D. Coogan, eds. *The Oxford Companion to the Bible*. New York: Oxford University Press, 1993.

Miller, C.A. "Nietzsche's Discovery of Dostoyevsky." *Nietzsche-Studien* 2 (1973).

———. "The Nihilist as Tempter-Redeemer: Dostoyevsky's Man-God in Nietzsche's Notebooks." *Nietzsche-Studien* 4, (1975).

Mistry, Freny. *Nietzsche and Buddhism*. Berlin: Walter de Gruyter, 1981.

Morrison, Robert G. *Nietzsche and Buddhism: A Study in Nihilism and Ironic Affirmation*. New York: Oxford University Press, 1997.

Nietzsche, Friedrich Wilhelm. *Thus Spoke Zarathustra: A Book for Everyone and No One*. Translated, with an Introduction by R. J. Hollingdale. Harmondsworth, England Penguin Books, 1961.

———. *The Birth of Tragedy, and The Case of Wagner*. Translated, with commentary, by Walter Kaufmann. New York: Vintage Books, 1967.

———. *The Will To Power*. Translation by Walter Kaufmann and R.J. Hollingdale. Edited, with commentary, by Walter Kaufmann. New York: Random House, 1967.

———. *On the Genealogy of Morals: A Polemic*. Translated by Walter Kaufmann and R.J. Hollingdale. *Ecce Homo*. Translated by Walter Kaufmann. Both works edited, with commentary, by Walter Kaufmann. New York: Vintage Books, 1969.

———. *Twilight of the Idols*, and *The Antichrist*. Translated, with an Introduction and commentary by R.J. Hollingdale. Harmondsworth: Penguin Books, 1971.

———. *Beyond Good and Evil: Prelude to a Philosophy of the Future*. Translated, with an Introduction and commentary by R.J. Hollingdale. Harmondsworth: Penguin Books, 1973.

———. *The Gay Science: With a Prelude in Rhymes and an Appendix of Songs*. Translated, with commentary, by Walter Kaufmann. New York: Random House, 1974.

———. *Daybreak: Thoughts on the Prejudices of Morality*. Translated by R.J. Hollingdale; with an Introduction by Michael Tanner. Cambridge: Cambridge University Press, 1982.

———. *Untimely Meditations*. Translated by R.J. Hollingdale; with an Introduction by J.P. Stern. Cambridge: Cambridge University Press, 1983.

———. *Human, All Too Human: A Book for Free Spirits*. Translated by R.J. Hollingdale; with an Introduction by Erich Heller. Cambridge: Cambridge University Press, 1986.

———. *Human, All Too Human*. Vol. II, Part 1, *Assorted Opinions and Maxims*. Translated by R.J. Hollingdale; with an Introduction by Erich Heller. Cambridge: Cambridge University Press, 1986.

———. *Human, All Too Human*. Vol. II, Part 2, *The Wanderer and His Shadow*.

Translated by R.J. Hollingdale; with an Introduction by Erich Heller. Cambridge: Cambridge University Press, 1986.

O'Flaherty, J.C., ed. *Studies in Nietzsche and the Judaeo-Christian Tradition*. Chapel Hill: University of North Carolina Press, 1985.

O'Hara, Daniel, ed. *Why Nietzsche Now?* Bloomington: Indiana University Press, 1981.

Pfeiffer, Ernst, ed. *Friedrich Nietzsche, Paul Ree, Lou von Salome: Die Dokumente ihrer Begegnung*. Frankfurt am Main, Insel Verlag, 1970.

Pfleiderer, Otto. *Christian Origins*. New York: B.W. Huebsch, 1906.

Renan, Ernest. *The Life of Jesus*. New York: The Modern Library, 1927.

Robertson, Archibald. *The Origins of Christianity*. New York: International Publishers, 1954.

Roth, Robin. "Verily, Nietzsche's Judgment of Jesus." *Philosophy Today* (winter 1990).

Sanders, E. P. *The Historical Figure of Jesus*. London: Penguin Books, 1993.

Santaniello, Weaver. *Nietzsche, God, and the Jews*. Albany: SUNY Press, 1994.

Schweitzer, Albert. *The Quest of the Historical Jesus*. New York: Macmillan, 1961.

Shapiro, Gary. "Nietzsche's Graffito: A Reading of the *Antichrist*." In *Why Nietzsche Now?*, edited by Daniel O'Hara. Bloomington: Indiana University Press, 1981.

———. "Nietzsche Contra Renan." *History and Theory* (May 1982).

Shepherd, Robert H.W. *The Humanism of Jesus*. London: James Clarke and Co., 1926.

Stendahl, Krister. *Paul Among Jews and Gentiles (and Other Essays)*. Philadelphia: Fortress Press, 1976.

Strauss, David Friedrich. *The Life of Jesus, Critically Examined*. Edited and with an Introduction by Peter C. Hodgson; translated from the 4th German ed. by George Eliot. Philadelphia: Fortress Press, 1973.

Wellhausen, Julius. *Prolegomena to the History of Ancient Israel*. Preface by W. Robertson Smith; Foreword by Douglas A. Knight. Atlanta, Ga.: Scholar's Press, 1994.

Index

About the Author

MORGAN REMPEL is an assistant professor in the Philosophy Department at Calvin College, Grand Rapids, Michigan. He has published scholarly articles on Freud, Nietzsche, and the philosophy of religion.